TENURED RADICALS

TENURED RADICALS

HOW POLITICS HAS CORRUPTED OUR HIGHER EDUCATION

ROGER KIMBALL

HarperPerennial
A Division of HarperCollinsPublishers

A hardcover edition of this book was published in 1990 by Harper & Row, Publishers.

First HarperPerennial edition published 1991.

Designed by Cassandra J. Pappas

The Library of Congress has catalogued the hardcover edition as follows:
Kimball, Roger, 1953–
Tenured radicals : how politics has corrupted our higher education / Roger Kimball.—1st ed.
p. cm.
Includes bibliographical references.
ISBN 0-06-016190-6
1. Education, Higher—United States. 2. Education, Humanistic—United States. I. Title.
LA227.3.K56 1990 89-45049
378'.012'0973—dc20

ISBN 0-06-092049-1 (pbk.)
92 93 94 95 AG/M 10 9 8 7 6 5 4 3

To Hilton Kramer

CONTENTS

ACKNOWLEDGMENTS

This book is dedicated to Hilton Kramer, my friend and the editor of *The New Criterion.* Without his editorial guidance and unstinting intellectual generosity, I could not have written *Tenured Radicals.*

I am also happy to take this opportunity to acknowledge my great debt to Erich Eichman, editor extraordinaire, who saved me from innumerable wrong turns and blind alleys. I owe much to many others, but would like to mention in particular my gratitude to Alexandra Mullen, who helped me in multitudinous ways, and to Glen Hartley, who first suggested that I write a book on the academy. I must also thank Cynthia Barrett, my editor at Harper & Row, for her uncommon patience. Finally, it is a pleasure to acknowledge the John M. Olin Foundation and the Institute for Educational Affairs for their generous help in the early stages of this project.

I am grateful to all these people and institutions. It goes without saying that none of them is responsible for the opinions expressed in this book or the imperfections that mar it.

PREFACE

I

It is no secret that the academic study of the humanities in this country is in a state of crisis. Proponents of deconstruction, feminist studies, and other politically motivated challenges to the traditional tenets of humanistic study have by now become the dominant voice in the humanities departments of many of our best colleges and universities. And while there are differences and even struggles among these various groups, when seen from the perspective of the tradition they are seeking to subvert—the tradition of high culture embodied in the classics of Western art and thought—they exhibit a remarkable unity of purpose. Their object is nothing less than the destruction of the values, methods, and goals of traditional humanistic study. This book is a chronicle of the progress of that destruction.

Whether one turns to Princeton University's Elaine Showalter, who has called for a complete revolution in the teaching of literature to enfranchise "gender as a fundamental category of literary analysis," or to University of Pennsylvania's Houston Baker, who touts the black power movement of the 1960s as a desirable alternative to the white Western culture he sees enshrined in the established literary canon, or to Duke University's Fredric Jameson, who propounds a Marxist vision of criticism that takes the "extreme position"[1] that "the political perspective" is "the absolute horizon of all reading and all interpretation,"[2] one finds a thoroughgoing animus to the traditional values of Western thought and culture.

[1]Fredric Jameson, *The Political Unconscious: Narrative as a Socially Symbolic Act* (Ithaca: Cornell University Press, 1981), 17.

[2]Ibid.

The same is true—albeit in a more rarefied way—of the legions of deconstructionists, poststructuralists, and other forbiddingly named academics who congregate in departments of English, French, and comparative literature. With their criticism of the "logocentric" and "phallocentric" Western tradition, their insistence that language always refers only to itself, and their suspicion of logic and rationality, they exhibit a species of skepticism that is essentially nihilistic and deeply at odds with the ideals of a liberal arts education—ideals, it must be added, that also underlie the democratic institutions and social life of the West. The conviction uniting these disparate groups received dramatic expression recently at Stanford University when Jesse Jackson and some 500 students marched chanting, "Hey hey, ho ho, Western culture's got to go." The influential philosopher Richard Rorty, a professor at the University of Virginia and himself an influential champion of many recent trends in the humanities, accurately summed up the situation when he noted that "a new American cultural Left has come into being made of deconstructionists, new historicists, people in gender studies, ethnic studies, media studies, a few left-over Marxists, and so on. This Left would like to use the English, French, and Comparative Literature Departments of the universities as staging areas for political action."[3]

In this war against Western culture, one chief object of attack within the academy is the traditional literary canon and the pedagogical values it embodies. The notion that some works are better and more important than others, that some works exert a special claim on our attention, that "being educated" requires a thoughtful acquaintance with these works and an ability to discriminate between greater and lesser—all this is anathema to the forces arrayed against the traditional understanding of the humanities. The very idea that the works of Shakespeare might be indisputably greater than the collected cartoons of Bugs Bunny is often rejected as antidemocratic and an imposition on the freedom and political interests of various groups.

At many colleges and universities, students are now treated to courses in which the products of popular culture—Hollywood movies, rock and roll, comic strips, and the like—are granted parity with

[3]Quoted in Sidney Hook, "Civilization and Its Malcontents," *National Review,* 13 Oct. 1989, 33.

(or even precedence over) the most important cultural achievements of our civilization. Typical is the philosopher Stanley Cavell's seminar at Harvard University on the movies of Katharine Hepburn and Spencer Tracy or a recent graduate course at Columbia University on Victorian and modern British literature that repeatedly took time to ponder the relevance of the pop singer Bruce Springsteen and the television series *Star Trek* to the issues at hand. Instead of aspiring to gain a thoughtful acquaintance with (as the Victorian poet and critic Matthew Arnold famously put it) "the best that has been thought and said," these new forces in the academy deliberately blur the distinction between high culture and popular culture. They pretend, to quote Houston Baker again, that choosing between Pearl Buck and Virginia Woolf, say, is "no different from choosing between a hoagy and a pizza." Professor Baker added, "I am one whose career is dedicated to the day when we have a disappearance of those standards."[4]

Even the most cursory glance at what passes for humanities offerings at colleges and universities across the country will serve to corroborate these impressions. With a few notable exceptions, our most prestigious liberal arts colleges and universities have installed the entire radical menu at the center of their humanities curriculum at both the undergraduate and the graduate level. Every special interest—women's studies, black studies, gay studies, and the like—and every modish interpretative gambit—deconstruction, poststructuralism, new historicism, and other varieties of what the literary critic Frederick Crews has aptly dubbed "Left Eclecticism"—has found a welcome roost in the academy, while the traditional curriculum and modes of intellectual inquiry are excoriated as sexist, racist, or just plain reactionary.

Thus what began as an intoxicating intellectual spree at a few elite institutions—places such as Yale, Johns Hopkins, Brown, and certain campuses of the University of California—has quickly spread to many other institutions. This metastasis is indeed one of the most troubling developments in the story of the crisis of the humanities.

Increasingly, second- and third-tier schools are rushing to embrace all manner of fashionable intellectual ideologies as so many

[4]Joseph Berger, "U.S. Literature: Canon Under Siege," *The New York Times*, 6 Jan. 1988.

formulas for garnering prestige, publicity, and "name" professors (and hoping thereby to attract more students and other sources of income) without having to distinguish themselves through the less-glamorous and more time-consuming methods of good teaching and lasting scholarship. One case in point is Duke University, which has recently conducted a tireless—and successful—campaign to arm its humanities departments with the likes of the Marxist literary critic Fredric Jameson, Barbara Herrnstein Smith, Frank Lentricchia, Stanley Fish (and his pedagogically like-minded wife, Jane Tompkins), and other less well known souls of kindred intellectual orientation.

II

It has often been observed that yesterday's student radical is today's tenured professor or academic dean. The point of this observation is not to suggest that our campuses are littered with political agitators. In comparison to the situation that prevailed in 1968, when colleges and universities across the country were scenes of violent demonstrations, the academy today seems positively sedate. Yet if the undergraduate population has moved quietly to the Right in recent years, the men and women who are paid to introduce students to the great works and ideas of our civilization have by and large remained true to the emancipationist ideology of the sixties. Indeed, it is important to appreciate the extent to which the radical vision of the sixties has not so much been abandoned as internalized by many who came of age then and who now teach at and administer our institutions of higher education. True, there is no longer the imminent prospect of universities being shut down or physically destroyed by angry radicals. But when one considers that the university is now supplying many of those erstwhile radicals with handsome paychecks, a pleasant working environment, and lifetime job security, then their quiescence is perhaps not so very extraordinary.

Besides, why shouldn't they act contentedly? To an extent unimaginable just a few years ago, their dreams of radical transformation have been realized. Even if we leave aside the enormous changes that have occurred in social life at our institutions of higher learning, it is patent that the transformation of the substance and even the goals of the typical liberal arts program has been staggering. Who could have guessed that the women's movement would have succeeded in getting gender accepted as a "fundamental category of literary analysis" by departments of literature in nearly every major university? Who could have guessed that administrators would one day be falling over themselves in their rush to replace the "white Western" curriculum of traditional humanistic studies with a smorgasbord of courses designed to appeal to various ethnic and racial sensitivities? Who could have predicted that the ideals of objectivity and the disinterested pursuit of knowledge would not only be abandoned but pilloried as products of a repressive bourgeois society? No, the radical ethos of the sixties has been all too successful, achieving indirectly in the classroom, faculty meeting, and by administrative decree what it was unable to accomplish on the barricades.

The political dimension of this assault on the humanities shows itself nowhere more clearly than in the attempt to restructure the curriculum on the principle of equal time. More and more, one sees the traditional literary canon ignored as various interest groups demand that there be more women's literature for feminists, black literature for blacks, gay literature for homosexuals, and so on. The idea of literary quality that transcends the contingencies of race, gender, and the like or that transcends the ephemeral attractions of popular entertainment is excoriated as naïve, deliberately deceptive, or worse.

At the same time, traditional precepts about the methods and goals of humanistic study are rejected as hopelessly *retardataire.* Basic questions such as What does it mean to be an educated person? are not even entertained as worthy of serious attention. *Reading* is no longer seen as an activity that seeks to construe the meaning of books and ideas, but as an elaborate interpretative game that aims to show the impossibility of meaning. And—as anyone with even a passing acquaintance with the products of the new academic scholarship knows—*writing* no longer means attempting to express oneself as clearly and precisely as possible, but is rather a deliberately "subversive" activity meant to challenge the "bourgeois" and "logocentric" faith in clarity, intelligibility, and communication.

Even more disturbing is the way in which demands for ideological conformity have begun to encroach on basic intellectual freedoms. At an increasing number of campuses across the country, university administrations have enacted antiharassment rules that provide severe penalities for speech or action deemed offensive to any of a wide range of officially designated victims. Ostensibly designed to prevent sexual, ethnic, and racial harassment, these rules actually represent an effort to enforce politically correct attitudes by curtailing free speech. To take just one example: At the University of Pennsylvania recently, a student on a panel for "diversity education" wrote a memorandum to her colleagues in which she expressed her "deep regard for the individual and . . . desire to protect the freedoms of all members of society." A university administrator responded by circling the passage just quoted, underlining the word *individual,* and commenting "This is a 'RED FLAG' phrase today, which is considered by many to be RACIST. Arguments that champion the individual over the group ultimately privileges [*sic*] the 'individuals' belonging to the largest or dominant group."[5] What this alarming development portends is nothing less than a new form of thought control based on a variety of pious new-Left slogans and attitudes.

Nor is the effort to enforce politically correct attitudes and behavior on our campuses confined to new forms of university legislation. At the beginning of 1990, a front-page article in *The New York Times* reported that the Supreme Court had ruled that the confidentiality of independent evaluations and other material collected to assess an individual's qualifications for academic tenure is no longer inviolate. The article notes that henceforth "universities accused of discriminating in tenure decisions must make the relevant personnel files available to Federal investigators."[6] As it happens, the Court's decision was based on a complaint filed against the University of Pennsylvania in 1985 by a Chinese-American woman who was denied tenure at the University's Wharton School of Business. The *Times* gleefully described the decision as "a decisive victory for the Equal Employment Opportunity Commission and for many civil rights groups" that have complained that the confidentiality of the tenure process has functioned as "a shield for discrimination that has kept women and minority candidates out of tenured ranks."

The Court's decision is thus being hailed as a triumph for what Associate Justice Harry A. Blackmun, who wrote the majority opin-

[5]Alan Charles Kors, "It's Speech, Not Sex, the Dean Bans Now," *The Wall Street Journal,* 12 Oct. 1989.

[6]Linda Greenhouse, "Universities Lose Shield of Secrecy in Tenure Disputes," *The New York Times,* 10 Jan. 1990.

ion, called the "compelling government interest" in "ferreting out" racial and sexual discrimination. But as with the virtuous-sounding antiharassment legislation, one wonders. The *Times* reported that some university officials have expressed concern that the new policy will make it "harder to get the candid scholarly assessments needed to make the best decisions." And indeed, one cannot but suspect that the net result of this attack on confidentiality will be to politicize the appointment and promotion process even further. Now that any academic who is denied tenure—and who happens to be female or a member of a racial or ethnic minority—has a legal basis upon which to contest the denial, can we really expect that scholarly accomplishment and effective teaching will be the main criteria for promotion? On the contrary, not only can we look forward to a greater reluctance on the part of scholars to provide honest assessments of their colleagues' work; we can also confidently predict a further erosion of intellectual standards—what once upon a time could be referred to without irony as academic standards—as tenure decisions increasingly become exercises in affirmative action and virtue-mongering.

Already, the institutionalization of the radical ethos in the academy has resulted not only in an increasing politicization of the humanities, but also an increasing ignorance of the humanistic legacy. Instead of reading the great works of the past, students watch movies, pronounce on the depredations of patriarchal society, or peruse second- or third-rate works dear to their ideological cohort; instead of reading widely among primary texts, they absorb abstruse commentaries on commentaries, resorting to primary texts only to furnish illustrations for their pet critical theory. Because many professors have been the beneficiaries of the kind of traditional education they have rejected and are denying their students, it is the students themselves who are the real losers in this fiasco. Presumably, they enrolled in a liberal arts curriculum in the first place because they wished to be educated; alas, after four years they will find that they are ignorant of the tradition and that their college education was largely a form of ideological indoctrination. It may well be the case that the much-publicized decline in humanities enrollments recently is due at least in part to students' refusal to devote their college education to a program of study that has nothing to offer them but ideological posturing, pop culture, and hermetic word games.

The issues raised by the politicization of the humanities have application far beyond the ivy-covered walls of the academy. The denunciations of the "hegemony" of Western culture and liberal institutions that are sounded so insistently within our colleges and universities these days are not idle chatter, but represent a concerted effort to attack the very foundations of the society that guarantees the independence of cultural and artistic life—including the independence of our institutions of higher education. Behind the transformations contemplated by the proponents of feminism, deconstruction, and the rest is a blueprint for a radical social transformation that would revolutionize every aspect of social and political life, from the independent place we grant high culture within society to the way we relate to one another as men and women. It is precisely for this reason that the traditional notion of the humanities and the established literary canon have been so violently attacked by *bien pensants* academics: as the cultural guardians of the ideals and values that Western democratic society has struggled to establish and perpetuate, the humanities also form a staunch impediment to the radical vision of their new academic enemies.

It is my aim in *Tenured Radicals* to expose these recent developments in the academic study of humanities for what they are: ideologically motivated assaults on the intellectual and moral substance of our culture. To that end, I have attempted to present a "report from the front" on some of the most important and representative radical campaigns currently being waged in the academy. To give as concrete and specific a picture as possible, I have not scrupled to spare the reader many examples of academic absurdity. Because simply describing what goes on in the academy today often produces blank incredulity in those not acquainted with its workings, I have drawn on conferences and symposia as well as books, journal articles, and various academic movements in an effort to convey a vivid and immediate sense of both the arguments and the often rebarbative rhetoric that fill the lecture halls and publications of our most prestigious colleges and universities.

To those of my readers who may have heard of the developments I discuss but have not had occasion to become acquainted with them firsthand, I regret to report that the situation is far worse than they are ever likely to have imagined.

Chapter 1

THE ASSAULT ON THE CANON

I • CULTURAL LITERACY?

Of the many issues that have lately commanded the public's attention regarding the state of the humanities in this country, perhaps none has been more hotly contended than the issue of the academic canon. Over the last few years, the battle over the fate of the canon has been waged in myriad academic books, journal articles, and conferences; it has been bruited about in the popular and highbrow cultural press; and it has been settled and resettled concretely in curricular changes that have taken place on campuses from Yale to Stanford.

The term *canon* comes to us from the Roman Catholic Church, where it refers to an official rule or decree, a particular section of the Mass, or the list of canonized saints. Today, as applied to the academy, *canon* refers to the unofficial, shifting, yet generally recognized body of great works that have stood the test of time and are acknowledged to be central to a complete liberal arts education. That this ideal of education can never be fully realized has also been generally acknowledged, as this passage from the *Bulletin of Yale University* for the academic year 1958–1959 suggests:

> The purpose of the program . . . is to provide the student with a broad view of the world he lives in and to equip him with the means of understanding it. This entails a knowledge of inanimate and animate nature through the appropriate sciences, a large view of man in the perspective of time, an acquaintance with the great ideas which have influenced the actions of men in the past, and con-

> tinue to do so in the present, and a knowledge of the significant institutions of modern society. It also entails a comprehension of the art, the ideas, and the aspirations of men. To obtain so large a view in all its fullness is properly the occupation of a lifetime.[1]

Many things that are presupposed by this sober bit of academic prose have now been called into question. Especially with respect to the humanities, the idea that college students should acquaint themselves with the "great ideas which have influenced the actions of men in the past, and continue to do so in the present" would instantly elicit a whole range of objections, from the feminist complaint about the use of *man* and *men* to the more general complaint that there is no agreed on set of "great ideas" that speaks equally to every ethnic and racial group.

In fact, the current debate over the canon—its origins, its composition, the desirability of preserving the values and traditions it represents—really poses two interrelated questions: (1) What should our colleges and universities be teaching? and (2) How should they be teaching the material they present? For the assault on the canon is not simply a matter of debasing the curriculum—of replacing, say, Plato with Navaho folktales or Shakespeare with Jacqueline Susann. It also shows itself in the aggressively opaque jargons favored by many contemporary academics as well as in the widespread insinuation of patently political criteria into teaching. Together, these developments have helped transform liberal studies into an ideological battleground that is also, all too often, an intellectual wasteland.

The enormous public controversy generated by Stanford University's recent decision to drop its required yearlong course in Western culture in favor of a new requirement called "Culture, Ideas, and Values" shows that both questions have the capacity to arouse considerable passion in and out of the academy. And this is as it should be. For what is at stake in these difficult questions is more than an academic squabble over book lists and pedagogy; what is at stake is nothing less than the traditional liberal understanding of democratic society and the place of education and high culture within it. The ruling by the Stanford Faculty Senate that every course in the univer-

[1] "Undergraduate Courses of Study, Fall and Spring Terms," *Bulletin of Yale University*, ser. 54, no. 6 (15 March 1958): 2.

sity's new program must include "works by women, minorities and persons of color," and that at least one work each quarter must address issues of race, sex, or class may be seen by the supporters of the "Culture, Ideas, and Values" program as a triumph for intellectual diversity, social relevance, and ethnic sensitivity. For some of us, however, this self-righteous emphasis on "diversity," "relevance," and "sensitivity" provides a graphic example of the way in which the teaching of the humanities in our colleges and universities has been appropriated by special interests and corrupted by politics.

The situation at Stanford, to be examined in more detail later, is hardly unique. All across the country, colleges and universities are busy revamping their educational programs according to criteria that only a decade or two ago would have been considered blatantly political and, therefore, inappropriate for determining the educational program of a respectable institution of higher learning. It is a measure of how drastically things have changed that although the ubiquitous triumvirate of race, gender, and class is still considered to be blatantly political, it is now for that very reason increasingly held to furnish the *only* appropriate criteria for determining the content of the curriculum and the focus of pedagogical interest.

As it happens, the most widely noticed contributions to the debate over the canon in recent years have also been among the most reviled in the academy: E. D. Hirsch's *Cultural Literacy: What Every American Needs to Know*[2] and Allan Bloom's *The Closing of the American Mind: How Higher Education Has Failed Democracy and Impoverished the Souls of Today's Students.*[3] Indeed, Professor Bloom's book, after an extraordinarily positive reception in the nonacademic press, has been subjected to an unremitting barrage of criticism and abuse from the academic Left, including the charge that it is "Hitleresque."[4] Nonetheless, although they boast many common enemies, these are very

[2]E. D. Hirsch, Jr., *Cultural Literacy: What Every American Needs to Know* (Boston: Houghton Mifflin, 1987).

[3]Allan Bloom, *The Closing of the American Mind: How Higher Education Has Failed Democracy and Impoverished the Souls of Today's Students* (New York: Simon & Schuster, 1987).

[4]The term was used at a university seminar on "Innovations in Education" at Columbia University by Frank Moretti, assistant headmaster at the Dalton School, one of the most prestigious primary and secondary schools in New York City. See my account of the seminar in "Guns and Other 'Hermeneutical Acts' at Columbia," *The New Criterion,* vol. 6, no. 9 (May 1988): 77–79.

different sorts of books. Professor Hirsch's study is a cross between a research report and a primer, while Professor Bloom's book is more in the way of a philosophical meditation on the fate of liberal education in contemporary American society. But both books are highly critical of the current situation in academy. And both garnered extraordinary public attention. *The Closing of the American Mind* was number one on *The New York Times* best-seller list for the better part of a year, while *Cultural Literacy* followed close behind at number two. Whether all or even most of those who bought the books also took the trouble to read them—especially Professor Bloom's book, which is not exactly light reading—is, of course, another question. Yet there can be no question that both books touched a nerve and continue to be much discussed and cited. Their commercial success is one of many suggestions in contemporary cultural life of how widespread is the concern about the state of American higher education.

Much of this concern originally crystallized around former Secretary of Education William J. Bennett's monograph *To Reclaim a Legacy: A Report on the Humanities in Higher Education.* This report was published by the National Endowment for the Humanities in November 1984, when Secretary Bennett was chairman of the endowment.[5] Retailing the recent tribulations of the humanities in the academy—ignorance and apathy on the one hand, overt politicization on the other—the report insisted that "the nation's colleges and universities must reshape their curricula based on a clear vision of what constitutes an educated person." The goal was "a common culture rooted in civilization's lasting vision, its highest shared ideals and aspirations, and its heritage," and Secretary Bennett did not hesitate to name Western civilization as the repository of these "ideals and aspirations" or to provide a list of books that help define the "lasting vision" of that common culture.

Secretary Bennett's report occasioned paroxysms of rage within the academy's expensively cloistered walls. The vision of a common culture, the notion that the West's cultural, intellectual, and political achievements have a special claim on our attention and allegiance, the criticism of importing politics into the humanities, the effrontery of

[5]William J. Bennett, *To Reclaim a Legacy: A Report on the Humanities in Higher Education* (Washington, D.C.: National Endowment for the Humanities, 1984). All quotations from William Bennett are from this monograph.

suggesting that some books are fundamental to any sound education in the humanities: all this drew—and continues to draw—sharp denunciations from like-minded academics across the country. Let us begin, then, by examining some representative responses.

II • GOOD-BYE TO ALL THAT

In a recent issue of *Salmagundi,* an influential quarterly of the humanities published by Skidmore College, we find a lengthy exchange titled "On Cultural Literacy: Canon, Class, Curriculum."[6] Professor Robert Scholes of Brown University set the tone and agenda of the exchange with an essay coyly titled "Aiming a Canon at the Curriculum." Several academics, including Professor Hirsch, Marjorie Perloff of Stanford University, Elizabeth Fox-Genovese of Emory University, and John P. Sisk of Gonzaga University in Spokane, Washington, responded.

Professor Scholes began with some portentous etymological speculations on the relation between the terms *canon* and *cannon,* concluding ominously that "where the Empire went, the cannon and the Canon went too." But the real focus of his essay was Secretary Bennett's report, especially its advocacy of a literary canon, and Professor Hirsch's miscellaneous writings on "cultural literacy" (the book had not yet appeared). About *To Reclaim a Legacy,* Professor Scholes wrote, "I am opposed to the establishment of a canon in humanistic studies because I believe such a move to be fundamentally undemocratic: a usurpation of curricular power by the federal government." He then proceeded to invoke Adolf Hitler, writing that

> the leader who will reclaim a legacy is a potent image, ranging in Western cultural history from the Once and Future King drawing Excalibur from its stone scabbard to Adolf Hitler reviving the spirit of a fallen people by finding suitable scapegoats upon whom to blame their fall. William Bennett's cry for strong leadership from those on top, combined with the charge that the loss of our legacy is the fault of a "failure of nerve and faith" strongly suggests that

[6]E. D. Hirsch, Jr., "On Cultural Literacy: Canon, Class, Curriculum." *Salmagundi* 72 (Fall 1986): 118–124. Quotations from this exchange in the following paragraphs are all taken from these pages of this issue of *Salmagundi.*

the first move of an educational leader should be a purge of those lacking in nerve and faith.

What does it mean, one might ask, that an eminent scholar and a U.S. secretary of education should be blithely compared to one of the greatest monsters of all history simply because they dared advance some criticisms of the academy? Is this an example of the tolerance for diversity that one hears so much about? Even more troubling—because more likely to be taken seriously—is the suggestion that "the establishment of a canon in humanistic studies" is "fundamentally undemocratic." This idea is as pernicious as it is common, implying as it does that political democracy is essentially inimical to authority, tradition, and rigor in its cultural institutions. At bottom, it is another way of suggesting that being democratic means abandoning any claim to permanent intellectual or cultural achievement.

It should also be noted that the substance of *To Reclaim a Legacy* is not the result of Secretary Bennett's private whims but a reflection of the deliberations of a distinguished panel of twenty professors and university administrators whose members included figures as diverse as William Arrowsmith, the well-known translator and professor of classics who is now at Boston University; William M. Banks, professor of Afro-American Studies at the University of California, Berkeley; Hannah H. Gray, the president of the University of Chicago; and Paul Oskar Kristeller, the eminent philosopher and longtime professor of philosophy at Columbia University. Are these figures also to be understood as upholding a Hitlerite position on humanistic education?

Then, too, Professor Scholes acts as if Secretary Bennett had wanted the list of books included in the report to be dogmatically imposed on the nation's colleges and universities. The truth is precisely the opposite. "In providing a list of these works and authors," we read in *To Reclaim a Legacy,* "it is not my intention (nor is it my right) to dictate anyone's curriculum. My purpose is not to prescribe a course of studies but to answer, as candidly as I can, an oft-asked question."

The responses to Professor Scholes's essay covered a fair range of opinion but may be described as generally supporting his position. No one, at any rate, did much to defend *To Reclaim a Legacy.* Marjorie Perloff, for one, praised Professor Scholes's "eloquent, humane" critique of the report's defense of the canon, agreeing that "educational philosophy always masks political ideology." To her credit, however, she did point out that there is an unacknowledged, yet nonetheless rigidly adhered to, alternative canon already in place in the academy. This is the canon whose founders are Freud, Marx, and Nietzsche, and whose contemporary representatives champion a motley variety of avant-garde criticism based on a combination of liberal political pieties and the half-digested tenets of the latest intellectual fads. As if in illustration of Professor Perloff's claim, Elizabeth Fox-Genovese began her response, titled "Gender, Class, Race, Canon," with an admiring reference to the black revolutionary Frantz Fanon. She seemed especially taken by Fanon's ideal of a "purging violence," observing that the notions of "imperialism and colonialization . . . nicely capture the relations between many students and the official culture that is taken to constitute a liberal education." "The canon," she concluded, "can best be taught if it is recognized at least in part as a kind of political spoil." In other words, for Professor Fox-Genovese, today's college students stand in the same relation to their culture as the do the victims of colonial exploitation.

Professor Hirsch's response took the form of an *apologia* explaining why Professor Scholes's attacks on his work had been misplaced. Of course, the chief reason Professor Scholes troubled to criticize Professor Hirsch in the first place is that Professor Hirsch's work on cultural literacy has been widely described as conservative—a tag earned in part because Secretary Bennett endorsed it early on (Professor Hirsch was even cited in *To Reclaim a Legacy*) and in part because it scrupled to point out what a shambles our country's educational system is in. Professor Hirsch's efforts have helped to make the litany of horrors familiar: one-half of our high-school seniors do not recognize the names of Winston Churchill or Joseph Stalin, are not able to locate the half-century in which World War I occurred, and so on.[7] Professor Hirsch is to be commended for bringing the shocking state of our educational system to public notice. But it must be said that his defense against Professor Scholes's attack was really a capitulation. The truth is that although Professor Hirsch's writing on cultural literacy has been generally associated with the spirit of *To Reclaim a Legacy,* his responses, in the pages of *Salmagundi* and elsewhere, have been little more than a series of attempts to distance himself from Secretary Bennett, the report, and everything they stand for. In retrospect, we

[7]Hirsch, *Cultural Literacy,* 218.

can now see that Professor Hirsch's capitulation in *Salmagundi* was only the beginning of a long career of repudiating his earlier positions. But already in the *Salmagundi* exchange, we find him replying to one of Professor Scholes's principal charges by insisting that, in his view, *"The common background knowledge required for literacy does not depend upon specific texts. . . . To be culturally literate, one does not need to know any specific texts."* (Emphasis in the original.) It follows naturally, he continued, that "it's acceptable to take one's entire knowledge of *Romeo and Juliet* from *Cliff Notes*," that is, from a crib.

Now think about that for a moment: "it's acceptable to take one's entire knowledge of *Romeo and Juliet* from *Cliff Notes*." Acceptable to whom? Acceptable to Professor Hirsch, yes, but is it acceptable to the students who wish to be educated—not merely to appear to be educated? Is it acceptable to the students' parents, who are paying for their children to be educated—not merely to acquire a superficial patina of knowledge?

Professor Hirsch's disregard for the substance of humanistic knowledge points to the crippling weakness of *Cultural Literacy:* its thoroughgoing philistinism and superficiality. In some ways, the most questionable part of Professor Hirsch's book is also the most controversial—I mean "The List": the sixty-odd-page, alphabetically ordered confection appended to the main text. Titled "What Literate Americans Know," it is a startling hodgepodge of dates (1066, 1492, 1776, etc.), names, phrases, acronyms, titles, and technical terms. Liberal critics complained that Professor Hirsch was acting in an authoritarian fashion there, attempting to lay down the law, to dictate what should count as knowledge indispensable for cultural literacy in our society. But really they should have been heartened by his efforts. Far from laying down the law about cultural literacy, what his infamous list confirms is that he has abandoned any desire for establishing anything of the kind. Consider the sorts of things that make it onto the list. Toward the end of the *B*s, for example, we encounter

Bryan, William Jennings

bubble (economic)

Bucharest

buck stops here, The

Budapest

Buddha

Buddhism

Buenos Aires

Buffalo, New York

Buffalo Bill

buffer (chemistry)

build castles in the air

And on and on, from "abbreviation (written English)," "abolitionism," and "abominable snowman" to "Zola, Emile," "zoning," and "Zurich." What does this random inventory of cultural trivia have to do with genuine education or cultural literacy? Well, about as much as *Cliff Notes* has to do with Shakespeare. It is, to use a phrase that Professor Hirsch favors, simply a promiscuous blend of general "background knowledge," mastery of which might help one excel in crossword puzzles, quiz games, or faculty cocktail parties but that is totally alien to the spirit of serious humanistic education. Consider only the entry "Am I my brother's keeper?" How many eager but ill-informed students will absorb the phrase but neglect the context—and thereby utterly misconstrue the meaning, taking it for an expression of bold if sour self-absorption rather than a fratricide's evasion?

It should be noted that Professor Hirsch has been quite frank about the rudimentary nature of his enterprise. In the preface to his book, he tells us that "to be culturally literate is to possess the basic information needed to thrive in the modern world," which is to say that in his terms being culturally literate is more or less like having a plumber's license. Recently, he has endeavored to be even more specific about the nature of that basic information, following up on the success of *Cultural Literacy* with *The Dictionary of Cultural Literacy: What Every American Needs to Know,*[8] which is essentially a hypertrophied version of the list that appears at the end of his earlier book. It is unfortunate indeed that many people have continued to assume

[8]E. D. Hirsch, Jr., Joseph F. Kett, and James Trefil, *The Dictionary of Cultural Literacy: What Every American Needs to Know* (Boston: Houghton Mifflin, 1989).

that books featuring the term *cultural literacy* in their title must have something to do with high culture and genuine learning.

III • THE CULT OF THEORY

While many academics continue to keep their distance from Professor Hirsch, the attitudes expressed by Professor Scholes and most of his respondents about the canon are so deeply ingrained in elite opinion in the academy these days as to be taken for granted. Yet among the countless publications, symposia, and administrative declarations informing us that the traditional literary canon is an instrument of repression and so on, there are some few that stand out as exemplary summaries of contemporary academic opinion on the subject. One particularly illustrative event took place in New Haven one Saturday early in May 1987, when Yale's Whitney Humanities Center sponsored a day-long public symposium to examine the subject of literary theory and the curriculum.* That the topic was of more than casual interest was clear from the enthusiastic audience of about 300 students, teachers (from Yale and elsewhere), and curious outsiders who crowded the center's modest lecture hall to overflowing. In a notice announcing the symposium, Sheila Murnaghan, assistant director of the center and associate professor of classics at Yale, explained that "after two decades of intense debate sparked by structuralism, post-structuralism, feminism, Afro-American and Third World Studies, and a resurgence of Marxism, teachers of literature find themselves in a bewildering situation." The symposium, Professor Murnaghan promised, "will bring together some of the most thoughtful members of the profession to compare notes on the current state of literary study and to assess the possibility of finding a common ground from which to respond to these challenges."

It is difficult to quarrel with the accuracy of Professor Murnaghan's list of challenges or her diagnosis of bewilderment. Yet whether what we have witnessed in literary studies in the past two decades is properly termed an *intense debate* is itself highly debatable; a more plausible term might be *usurpation,* motivated partly by intellectual

*Unless otherwise noted, quotations in this section are taken from the presentations and responses delivered at this symposium.

fashion (structuralism, poststructuralism), partly by politics (feminism and the rest). And looking back on the event, one would also have to quibble with Professor Murnaghan's description of what the majority of those "most thoughtful" members of the profession had to contribute to the discussion: compare? assess? respond? As it happened, proselytize was much closer to the truth.

Peter Brooks, who in addition to being the director of the Whitney Humanities Center is the Chester D. Tripp Professor of the Humanities and chairman of the Department of French at Yale, opened the festivities with a few words about the ways in which recent literary theory has called into question traditional approaches to literature and "what we do as teachers of literature." Do we, he asked, still have any fixed point of reference or any common ground in the teaching of English? Has anything like a new consensus emerged from challenges of the sort that Professor Murnaghan rehearsed? Or have literary studies become caught up in the logic of the "post-, post-, post-, poststructuralist, postmodernist, postdisciplinary"? Without attempting to answer these questions, Professor Brooks did suggest something of a common project when he observed at the end of his remarks that the task he and his colleagues now faced was that of "rewriting" tradition "in a more suspicious manner." What one witnessed as the event proceeded, however, were sundry attempts to rewrite the tradition in a manner that, far from being simply suspicious, was blatantly tendentious and ideological.

Although they lamented the loss of consensus in the humanities, the participants that day nonetheless shared a number of important assumptions about what was and wasn't wrong with the academy, the ends of education, and the tasks currently facing literary criticism. A superficial diversity masked a considerable unity of purpose. Taken together, the contributions more or less summarized the range and style of mainstream opinion in the academy on these issues, and so it is worth reviewing the proceedings in some detail.

The symposium was divided into three sessions. The morning session was titled "The State of the Curriculum in the Wake of Two Decades of Literary Theory." J. Hillis Miller, for many years professor of English at Yale but recently lured to the University of California at Irvine, and Michael Riffaterre, professor of French at Columbia University, each presented papers that purported to deal with the announced subject. They were followed by Professors Paul Fry of Yale and Barbara Johnson, lately of Yale but now installed at Harvard, who responded to the papers. As it happened, the participants dealt with the subject of the curriculum only obliquely; but, as is often the case these days, their critical methods and assumptions told us a good deal about how the assault on the canon may proceed as much by trivializing or obscuring great works of literature as by ignoring or replacing them with inferior works.

Professor Miller's contribution was titled "From the Theory of Reading to the Example Read." He began by describing the "spectacular proliferation of powerful and incompatible theories" that have swept contemporary literary criticism and have fundamentally changed the way the subject is taught. In his view, perhaps the most important change wrought by these spectacular theories is in the relationship between theory and example. Where in traditional literary criticism the *example*—that is, particular works of literature—clearly took precedence over *theory,* today the relationship is reversed; now, as Professor Miller cheerfully explained, the example is "arbitrarily chosen." That is to say, it is chosen not for its historical importance, not for its literary value, not for any truth or moral clarity it might be supposed to communicate, but solely for its aptness in illustrating the current pet theory of the critic.

Professor Miller went on to point out that this reversal in the relationship between example and theory has had profound implications for the way in which we read. The reader of this book might respond that Professor Miller's "we" is fortunately still far from universal. But the reversal between theory and example he heralds certainly has had profound implications for the way in which books—or, to use the preferred term, *texts*—are read in the academy. There, as Professor Miller noted, it is widely held that a "resistance to theory is in fact a resistance to reading." This slogan, which Professor Miller took care to repeat two or three times in the course of his presentation, may be said to summarize the burden of his paper. The idea comes from the late Paul de Man, who, along with the celebrated French philosopher Jacques Derrida, was among those chiefly responsible for institutionalizing the tenets of deconstruction in literary studies. At the time of his death in 1983, de Man's reputation as a literary theorist was stratospheric. His death catapulted it into orbit, although the recent discovery that this connoisseur of deconstruction had written scores of articles for newspapers that openly supported the Nazi cause in World War II has had a noticeably diminishing effect on his stature. Nevertheless, even today, in many academic circles, to invoke the authority of Paul de Man is to confer an unimpeachable aura of critical sophistication on one's words, so naturally he is alluded to continuously in the books and articles and symposia of his acolytes.

"The resistance to theory is in fact a resistance to reading"—a prize de Manian specimen, that. And whatever *theory* might mean in this context—it is bad form to indulge in anything so pedestrian as a definition in these intellectual precincts—the rest of Professor Miller's presentation clearly showed that his own resistance to theory is approximately nil. He proceeded to exemplify the triumph of theory over literature with a prolix and convoluted meditation on Nathaniel Hawthorne's short story, "The Minister's Black Veil." Among much else, his presentation featured a turgid discussion of the notion of personification, a good deal of solemn talk about "the act of reading," and the enlightening revelation that "the story is the unveiling of the possibility of the impossibility of the unveiling." So much for Hawthorne.

While Professor Miller's meditations really had little to do with the question of the state of the curriculum in the wake of two decades of literary theory, his approach, which grants explicit priority to theory over literature, represents one of the chief ways by which the assault on the canon is carried out in the academy today. Unlike many of the participants in the symposium, however, Professor Miller did at least make some gesture toward addressing the announced topic. In outlining what he described as the "practical implications" of his paper, he warned that the rejection of theory is "reactionary or stupid or both" and suggested that universities ought to arrange their curricula in such a way as "to make possible the teaching of reading in its uneasy relation to theory."

Professor Miller didn't specify exactly what he meant by this uneasy relation; but he was clearly concerned that his colleagues were backsliding on their commitment to the priority of theory. Indulging in a gloomy pun, he wondered if we weren't witnessing the "wake of literary theory" in a sense quite different from that intended by the title of the session. His concern seemed misplaced, it must be said, because, as he also noted, deconstruction—the *ne plus ultra* of theoretical approaches to literature—has by now firmly established itself not only in literary studies but throughout the humanities and even in certain social sciences. It has even gained a noticeable foothold in legal studies with the critical legal studies movement, which—ensconced as it is at Harvard and elsewhere—is busy applying the teachings of deconstruction to legal texts and theories.

Nevertheless, Professor Miller lamented that Yale no longer deserved its reputation as a bastion of advanced theoretical criticism. Anyone who is at all familiar with the faculties of the departments of English, French, and comparative literature there would find the notion that Yale suffers from a dearth of deconstructionists simply laughable. But who knows; perhaps Professor Miller felt that his own departure deprived the university of its place on the frontiers of advanced thought? In any case, it was his view that if Yale were to recapture its former glory it must not only appoint more senior professors who are sympathetic to the cause of theory—he mentioned several possible candidates—but it must also give tenure to more of their younger disciples—again, he favored us with several names. As things stand, Professor Miller concluded darkly, it might already be too late to stop what he called the Harvardization of Yale.

The next two installments of this session continued in the same vein. Michael Riffaterre performed a kind of set piece titled "Relevance of Theory/Theory of Relevance." "What we must be after is the *je ne sais quoi* that makes literature literary," he told us. But literature got quite lost as he proceeded, employing an extraordinary congeries of categories and distinctions, to deduce the six "necessary properties" of "literariness" and apply them to a reading of *Madame Bovary.* For his part, Paul Fry concentrated on elaborating the theme of the "undecidability of language" that he found expressed in different ways in both Professors Miller and Riffaterre's papers. His delivery was very rapid and often hard to follow; but one caught various fragments, such as his call for an "onto-poetic" theory that would "revise Miller and impose a little specificity on Heidegger" by viewing personification as a "relay station" between being and language. His response was full of many instances of such pretentious nonsense. But my favorite moments were when he dropped phrases such as "from Aristotle to [Jonathan] Culler" and "from Schleiermacher to de Man" as if it were only natural that such illustrious names should be so linked. If nothing else, Professor Fry's response ought to have reassured Professor Miller about the state of the Yale English department.

IV • THE FEMINIST ASSAULT

And indeed, Professor Johnson, the next respondent, also made one wonder what Professor Miller had to fear from the Harvardization of Yale. For if her views are at all typical of her colleagues', he needn't worry that books are being read primarily as literary documents or that theory is getting short shrift in Cambridge, Massachusetts. In fact, Professor Johnson provides us with our first example of what has emerged as the single biggest challenge to the canon as traditionally conceived: radical feminism. As with the cult of theory, with which it is often in collusion, radical feminism does not undermine the canon only or even primarily by proposing an alternative canon—one, for example, in which female authors are read in place of male ones. Instead, it seeks to subordinate literature to ideology by instituting a fundamental change in the way literary works are read and taught. As Brigitte Berger pointed out in a perceptive article, academic feminism is "a revolutionary intellectual movement. Encouraged by initial successes and unfettered by any serious intellectual resistance, professional feminists are driven by their presuppositions toward ever more radical conceptualizations. At the end of their road stands the formulation of a distinctive *feminist standpoint,* which in essence is nothing less than an imperialism of feminist sentiments."[9]

Professor Johnson offered a preliminary illustration of Professor Berger's thesis. Taking as her epigraph "Theory is quicker," she began her presentation with a few theoretical curlicues and then turned to examine Professor Riffaterre's discussion of *Madame Bovary.* That Flaubert's book deals with adultery was a great boon to her presentation, of course, because that opened up an unlimited field for pronouncements about the baleful condition of women. Nor was Professor Johnson lax in capitalizing on this wonderful opportunity.

[9]Brigitte Berger, "Academic Feminism and the 'Left,' " *Academic Questions* vol. 1, no. 2 (Spring 1988): 13. (Emphasis in the original.)

Blending a deconstructionist's obsession with language and a feminist's obsession with male dominance, she summed up Professor Riffaterre's paper as a "masterful demonstration" of "the fact" that "gynophobia [i.e., the fear of women] is structured like a language" and, conversely, that "language is structured like gynophobia." In other words, *language itself* is held to be a repository of sexist attitudes. (All languages? Professor Johnson didn't say.)

Women themselves conspire in perpetuating this unhappy situation, she told us, for "the collective linguistic psyche exists in symbiotic relation to the fallen woman." We also learned, by a similarly elusive logic, that the "literary canon is a defense against its own femininity," a defense "against the woman within." What any of this could possibly mean was never revealed, but no one seemed to mind: it all sounded so exquisitely chic. The assertion that "gynophobia is structured like a language," for example, echoes the French psychoanalyst Jacques Lacan's equally absurd statement that the unconscious is structured like a language, and in this company, such a pedigree was warrant enough to present even patent drivel as fact.

The agenda of the radical feminist assault on the canon showed itself even more clearly at the second session of the Yale conference on literary theory and the curriculum, which was devoted to the literary canon and anticanonical criticism. Elaine Showalter, chairman (or rather, chairwoman) of the English department at Princeton University, and Houston Baker of the University of Pennsylvania each presented papers—Professor Baker's presentation was largely extempore—and Professors Geoffrey Hartman and J. Michael Holquist of Yale responded.

Professor Showalter, who has achieved a position of great power and influence in the academy, read a paper titled "The Other Bostonians: Gender and Literary Study." It was, quite simply, a call for "a transformation of the curriculum" that would accept "gender as a fundamental category of literary analysis." Professor Showalter is obviously nothing if not ambitious. By pursuing the notion of "gender as a fundamental category of literary analysis," she hopes for nothing less than the triumph of feminist ideology over literature. That is to say, she hopes "literary knowledge itself will be redefined" by the feminist crusade. What she wants is not merely mainstreaming, not merely the inclusion of many more women authors in the standard college curriculum—although that, certainly, is a prerequisite for the kinds of change she has in mind. She also wants to enshrine the recognition of "sexual difference" as a "crucial element in the way we all read and write." Only thus could she realize the dream of a "female vernacular" out of which "women can name their own experience." And despite multifarious setbacks, which Professor Showalter was careful to enumerate, progress was being made.

Among the indications of progress she alluded to, we must include the institution of women's studies programs at colleges and universities across the country. Many of these programs offer majors in women's studies, and all take Professor Showalter's insistence that gender is "a fundamental category of literary analysis" as their basis. Consider, for example, the description of the women's studies program in the official bulletin of Yale University for 1988–1989.

> Recent scholarship makes it clear that a full understanding of human behavior, culture, and society cannot be attained without investigating women's experiences. The critical perspective of women's studies establishes gender as a fundamental category of social and cultural analysis, linking gender with class, race, ethnicity, and sexual identity to analyze the diversity of women's experience.[10]

The tone and diction ("Recent scholarship makes it clear") of this passage may be typical of traditional academic officialese—even if it relies on notions ("establishing" "fundamental categories," etc.) that many versions of feminism attack as patriarchal. But despite its relatively sedate tone, the message of this description—that sexual, racial, and ethnic politics should henceforth determine or at least strongly influence the curriculum—is deeply at odds with the presuppositions of traditional humanistic study.

That of course is the point, as one can see from other areas of "progress" that Professor Showalter cited. Already there is daring "new research" underway, she told us, that promises to result in "new curricular experiments" and "genuine knowledge" of a field. Like what? Well, like the proliferation of current feminist studies of eating

[10] "Yale College Programs of Study," *Bulletin of Yale University,* ser. 84, no. 7 (1 Aug. 1988): 423.

disorders that, among other wonderful things, "creates new interest in the binge/purge syndrome" as it relates to the American poet Sylvia Plath's development. Lest you think Professor Showalter was exaggerating, note that among the many sessions dealing with feminist subjects at the Modern Language Association meeting in 1988 was a panel devoted to "Food and the Construction of Femininity in Drama by Women." Here, for example, one could listen to R. L. Widmann of the University of Colorado, Boulder, deliver a paper called "Sugar Shock in the Plays of Hroswitha and Beth Henley's *Crimes of the Heart,*" in which such evils as "dichotomized sex" and "compulsory heterosexuality" were roundly denounced. Professor Showalter herself did not participate in that session, doubtless because she was busy preparing her talk about George Eliot as a female androgyne and the "delegitimization" of "patriarchal poetics" that she delivered later in the day.

Such a "delegitimization" was high on Professor Showalter's agenda in New Haven, too. Feminism cannot rest content with championing female (one could hardly call it feminine) experience, she told us. Male experience must also be scrutinized. Professor Showalter named "the defamiliarization of masculinity" as "one of the most important tasks facing feminist criticism in the next decade." If male experience has hitherto been understood to be natural and unproblematic, a mode of experience that represents "humanity in general," it must now be exposed as a biased, ideologically laden construction. Men, too—perhaps especially men—must be enlisted in this attempt to "open up the discourse of masculinity." And good news: for those men who have abandoned "the myth of objectivity and transcendence," who have "the courage to become vulnerable" and "realize that they are embodied," this new recognition of masculinity "will be a transformation of volcanic force." "Simply to think about masculinity is to become less masculine oneself," we were assured—and, after all, what could be better than that?

It must not be thought that such ideas are considered aberrant or especially radical in the academy today—quite the contrary. Professors Johnson and Showalter are influential scholars and teachers who enjoy a large following and tenure at premier institutions. But the feminist ideas they espouse are simply the standard fare being dispensed in academic publications and humanities courses across the country. Furthermore, as Professor Showalter enthusiastically proclaimed, her envisioned program implies a complete revolution in the teaching of our literary heritage, a revolution that would also establish gay criticism, black criticism, postcolonial criticism, and so on as equal partners in the academy. In fact, Professor Showalter's proposals provide a sterling illustration of the way in which feminism has provided a kind of blueprint for special interests that wish to appropriate the curriculum to achieve political goals. As Thomas Short pointed out in an excellent anatomy of radical trends in the academy, one result of the academic feminist agenda is a situation in which "every course will be Oppression Studies."[11] For if gender is a "crucial element in the way we all read and write," then why not sexual orientation, race, and class? Why not any political interest? Presumably, the only criticism that would not be nurtured as a minority interest in this feminist utopia is *literary* criticism, tainted as it is by an allegiance to the myth of disinterested inquiry and a notion of scholarship that deliberately strives to transcend political differences.

V • AN INTRODUCTION TO OPPRESSION STUDIES

To understand how the principles at work in Professor Showalter's presentation can be applied by ideologies other than feminism, let us turn to Houston Baker's presentation, titled "The Promised Body," in which the privileged category was race, not gender. Professor Baker, whom we shall have occasion to meet again at the end of this book, began with a bit of ideological throat clearing, invoking Marx to the effect that the canon is determined to some extent by class interests and reminding us that the past is always an "ideologically conditioned version of events gone by." In the American academy today, he told us, the entire fabric of literary study, including the determination of the literary canon, is the function of a biased reading of the recent and the distant past, especially our own past. In his view, the "most penetrating and reverberant" sound in canon formation in the last three decades in the United States is the sound of civil rights

[11]Thomas Short, " 'Diversity' and 'Breaking the Disciplines': Two New Assaults on the Curriculum." *Academic Questions,* vol. 1, no. 3 (Summer 1988): 24.

marchers chanting—and here Professor Baker himself began to chant—"we shall not be moved, we shall not be moved."

This brought Professor Baker to his main point: that the black power and black art movements of the sixties and early seventies challenged dominant white Western cultural values in a uniquely productive and promising way. It was then, he told us, that the black experience "found its way onto the stage of the American academy and the black initiative became a reality for every man, woman, or student, every administrator, professor, resident adviser, security guard, or secretary." Professor Baker's oratory included quotations from Washington and Jefferson meant to portray them as racists, charges that the Constitution of the United States is a racist document (a "Gothic romance," as he memorably put it), readings from the writings of former slaves to show what terrific literature we've missed, and abundant references to what Professor Baker referred to as "the African diaspora."

Although delivered with unusual pathos, all this was in fact the most predictable fare imaginable. But Professor Baker concluded with a twist that was new to me, comparing the black experience in this country to the Roman Catholic Mass. Central to both, he told us, is the notion of a sacrifice and also the "materialization and engorgement of the body as a manifested covenant of a new order." He also liked to describe black Americans as "the African body," noting, among much else, that "the African body emerges as a canonical announcement of a promised or covenanted body." It need hardly be said that the audience was spellbound by Professor Baker's performance, especially by his concluding litany of recent outbreaks of violence and racial prejudice against the African body on several campuses around the country. It has become rare in these quiet days in the academy that your average white, middle-class audience can indulge in such ecstasies of intellectualized liberal shame, and they were clearly grateful to Professor Baker for an opportunity to gorge themselves on it.

Of course, presentations such as those of Professors Showalter and Baker put any respondent at a tremendous rhetorical disadvantage. Anything resembling dissent risked being excoriated as a sexist or racist attack on the voices of freedom. This Professor Holquist must have realized, for when it came time for him to respond he contented himself with a few apologetic mumblings about how "political considerations" had kept black studies from becoming institutionalized as successfully as gender studies. But Professor Hartman did venture a few tentative criticisms. Noting that both presentations exhibited a strong utopian element, he began by remarking the high pitch of his colleagues' rhetoric; he even made bold to ask whether their rhetoric wasn't sometimes "stronger than their concepts." The end they envisioned was generous, he hastily added, but he had to admit that on the "conceptual level" he was "perplexed, even disconcerted."

Although he would seem to have long since given up serious criticism for modish intellectual esoterica, Professor Hartman's remarks reminded one that he has done brilliant, even lasting, work, especially in the field of English romantic poetry, and one was reminded, too, that he was without doubt the most distinguished scholar to participate in the symposium. What worried him was the possibility that the essentially political programs outlined by his colleagues would compromise the freedom and independence of the university, jeopardizing disinterested scholarship. Recognizing that the university is in many respects a place apart, he gently urged caution lest overt political imperatives be allowed to determine the character of university life. He seems, alas, to have underestimated both the extent to which the political infiltration of intellectual life was the frankly acknowledged goal of his more radical colleagues and the enormous strides that infiltration has already made.

V • BOURGEOIS PLOTS AND OTHER PEDAGOGICAL MATTERS

Although it began quietly, the third session of the Yale symposium on literary theory and the curriculum ended by showing just how frankly acknowledged such political imperatives could be. Entitled "The Institution of Criticism: What Should We Be Teaching, and Teaching Future Teachers to Teach?" it included Gerald Graff of Northwestern University and Margaret Ferguson of Columbia University as the session's main speakers; Neil Hertz of Johns Hopkins University and Peter Brooks responded.

Professor Graff's presentation, "What Should We Be Teaching When There's No 'We'?" was by far the most practical paper in the symposium. Whatever one thought of his ideas, it was clear that he had devoted considerable time to thinking about the problems of the classroom. In his view, the basic problem was that, although the "we" of the academy is far more inclusive now than it used to be, there is no agreement on first principles and hence no consensus about what should be taught, or how. His solution was simply to dispense with the ideal of consensus and adopt a model of conflict. We don't need a consensus, he told us, to carry on work in the academy; we can agree to disagree and, as he has put it again and again in subsequent symposia and papers, "teach the conflict."

In some respects, Professor Graff's proposals were reminiscent of the teachings of John Dewey. He tended, for example, to downplay content in favor of process. If many students are going to fail to understand much of what they read anyway, Professor Graff argued (and given the hermetic quality of contemporary academic criticism, who can blame them?), then the content of what they read "hardly matters." What does matter, according to Professor Graff, is the way it feeds into students' experience and engages their interest.

Turning to some practical applications of this insight, he suggested that one might experiment with "teacher swapping" (not to be confused with team teaching), an innovation in which one teacher teaches a course for, say, five weeks, after which another comes in and begins by asking what the first teacher said, probing his presuppositions and prejudices. Despite certain attractive elements in Professor Graff's proposal, in the end it is a prescription for confusion, guaranteed to muddle young minds. If, as he suggests, students often have trouble even assimilating what they read, simply providing them with a diet of conflicting arcane theories is not going to help matters. But the real problem with Professor Graff's vision—as with the progressive ideas from which it derives—is that it ends up purchasing pluralistic concord at the price of intellectual content. It never seemed to occur to Professor Graff that some intellectual positions might be truer or more worthy of transmission than others. While lecturing us about how important it is to keep the discussion going among ideological adversaries, he neglected to ask himself whether cultivating ideologies ("teaching the conflict") is the proper business of the university. If it hardly matters what students read, it will hardly matter what they know or believe.

But Professor Graff appeared as a beacon of moderation and sanity in comparison with his successor, Margaret Ferguson. Although delivered in measured, even demure, tones, her paper, "Teaching and/as Reproduction," was easily the most radical presentation of the symposium. Her thesis was that in liberal bourgeois society teaching must be seen primarily as a means by which the ruling class perpetuates or "reproduces" inequitable class relations. In one sense, certainly, Professor Ferguson is quite right that schools are "sites for social reproduction." That is a principal reason civilized cultures have always put such stock by education. The problem today, however, is not that our schools reproduce the culture and values that support them, but that they are doing the job so poorly.

Yet to hear Professor Ferguson tell it, things are bad indeed in the particular capitalist bourgeois society that she has the misfortune to inhabit and work in. She began by questioning the appropriateness of the word *should* in the title of the session: given the enormous constraints that the university supposedly places on thought and action, what sense does it make to ask what we *should* be teaching when the question of what we *can* be teaching is so pressing? And isn't it problematic, she asked her colleagues, to see ourselves primarily as critics or teachers and only secondarily, if at all, as state functionaries or employees of a major corporation?

But think about it. What is so compromising about being an employee of the state or a corporation, even a "major corporation"? At what point did leftist attitudes so infiltrate everyday language that working for the Post Office or General Foods, let alone a major corporation such as Columbia University, should *ipso facto* seem to carry with it a moral taint? Are we to believe that the citizens of a socialist country are spiritually or physically freer from state control than their counterparts in Western democracies? Odd then, isn't it, that they are rushing the world over to embrace the principles of Western liberal democratic societies. And what dire constraints does Professor Ferguson imagine the university imposes on the thought and action of its employees? One could not help noticing that this tenured radical appeared remarkably unconstrained that afternoon.

That Professor Ferguson's paper should be littered with such contradictions should not surprise us. They represent the standard operating equipment of intellectual Marxists, who are always ready to trump mere empirical evidence with the charge of false consciousness or bad faith, reserving to themselves the determination of what is to count as genuine insight and authenticity. Hence it was only to be expected that Professor Ferguson should describe "capitalist social relations" as "monolithic" and then, by virtue of her criticism, arrogate to herself a place outside that allegedly monolithic totality. And it was simply business as usual that she should rail against the liberal tradition and its ideal of "pluralist accommodation," even though it was only in a society governed precisely by that spirit of pluralist accommodation that criticism of the sort she propounded would be tolerated.

But to get the full flavor of Professor Ferguson's *Weltanschauung,* let us look for a moment at the book that provided her with the inspiration and title for her paper, *Reproduction in Education and Society,* by the French Marxist sociologists Pierre Bourdieu and Jean-Claude Passeron. A work of aggressive impenetrability, *Reproduction in Education and Society* advances the thesis that education in bourgeois societies has the "social function of reproducing the class relations, by ensuring the hereditary transmission of cultural capital."[12] The book consists of a series of highly contentious propositions about social life and education dressed up and elaborated in the abstract, pedantic argot favored by certain academic Marxists. Near the beginning of the book, for example, Bourdieu and Passeron inform us that *"all pedagogic action (PA) is, objectively, symbolic violence insofar as it is the imposition of a cultural arbitrary by an arbitrary power."*[13] Their use of the term *objectively,* recalling as it does an older tradition of "scientific" Marxist analysis, is a touch especially worth savoring. And later on, the authors confide that the corrupted ethos of the bourgeoisie reveals itself in its very language. Hence they distinguish between bourgeois language, which is said to tend to "abstraction, formalism, intellectualism and euphemistic moderation," and working-class language, which

> manifests itself in the tendency to move from particular case to particular case, from illustration to parable, or to shun the bombast of

[12]Pierre Bourdieu and Jean-Claude Passeron, *Reproduction in Education and Society,* trans. Richard Nice, Vol 5, *Sage Studies in Social and Educational Change* (Silver Spring: Sage Publications, 1977), 199.

[13]Ibid., 5. (Emphasis in the original.)

> fine words and the turgidity of grand emotions, through banter, rudeness and ribaldry, manners of being and doing characteristic of classes who are never fully given the social conditions for the severance between objective denotation and subjective connotation.[14]

All this is the sheerest quackery, of course, although it does inspire the droll question whether its authors believe they have achieved anything like the stylistic frankness they claim to admire in working-class language.

Like her mentors, Professor Ferguson displayed a thoroughgoing animus toward the Western democratic tradition. Invoking the Italian Marxist Antonio Gramsci, she castigated the "ideology" of free will propagated by Western bourgeois societies. And on a lighter note, she indulged in ridiculing the authors of an article that appeared in *Commentary* for suggesting that traditional liberal academics attempted "to promote intellectual openness and tolerance through an honest reading of the West's achievements."[15] Naturally, this provoked considerable mirth in the audience, for who in the academy still believes in either the West's achievements or its honesty?

After Professor Ferguson's performance, the responses could hardly help seeming anticlimatic. Neil Hertz maundered on about education as a process of "unmasking" and the desirability of opening up the university "to as many modes of self-dramatization as possible," while Peter Brooks took the occasion to pillory Secretary Bennett for his "reactionary" and "sclerotic" views about education. Reflecting on the title of the session, Professor Brooks noted that he understood "us" to mean "we who are not nostalgic for the old consensus." Even the formal proceedings of the symposium, with its round of speakers didactically addressing an audience from a podium, was too formal and too canonical for his taste. Perhaps he would have preferred a series of spontaneous improvisations?

The discussion that followed, however, proved quite lively. Two exchanges in particular seem worth remarking. In one of the symposium's rare moments of dissension, Professor Graff rose to challenge Professor Ferguson's presentation. Although he assured the audience

[14]Ibid., 116.

[15]Stephen H. Balch and Herbert I. London, "The Tenured Left," *Commentary,* vol. 83, no. 4 (Oct. 1986): 50.

that he considered himself "on the Left," he nevertheless felt that Professor Ferguson had given a distorted picture of the situation in the American academy. Compared to what, he asked, may we complain that our universities are sites of "ideological reproduction"? Ah, yes, "Compared to what?" The question marked the day's single burst of common sense. Where else, Professor Graff asked, would one find the ideas of Marx, Foucault, Althusser, and Professor Ferguson's other heroes taken seriously except in the university? Where else would her presentation not only be encouraged but actually listened to and (one assumes) paid for?

Obviously infuriated by her colleague's impertinence, Professor Ferguson responded but did not really reply to these questions. Instead, she pointed out that success in the university, especially for women and minorities, comes at a tremendous psychic cost. She confided that she herself had had to internalize a code of decorum and manners to succeed in the academy; almost sadly, she assured the audience that she was not going to stand up and swear at us, or at Professor Graff, much as she might want to at the moment; part of the price of being there on the podium was being trained not to do such things. And in case we didn't get it the first time around, she reminded us that she regarded the real problems in the academy as political problems: questions about the canon or pedagogy or education in general were merely fronts for political issues. Not surprisingly, Professor Ferguson's confession was greeted by a loud round of applause.

Professor Graff replied by asking Professor Ferguson what she proposed to do with the many people in the academy who happened not to agree with her. No one, he observed, had addressed himself to that rather elementary question. Nor was anyone going to. Sensing that the moment was ripe, Professor Baker intervened from his place in the audience to charge that Professor Hartman's contribution to the symposium had been a "conservative, possibly racist response." Moreover, he declaimed, Professor Hartman had indulged in "an extraordinary valorization of the university," implying as he did that the life of the mind was a delicate thing that the university ought to take care to protect from the crass exigencies of society at large. This, too, got a rousing round of applause from an audience apparently disgusted with the whole idea of valorizing the university even if they were only too happy to inhabit its protected purlieus. And poor Professor Hartman: "Conservative!" "Racist!" One wondered which epithet stung worse. He made some effort to respond, but it soon became clear that nothing as feckless as a reasoned reply could influence the course of opinion in a room so charged with overheated rhetoric.

VI • THE STANFORD DEBACLE

What is particularly depressing about such spectacles is the thought that, far from being atypical, they represent the dominant current of opinion in our most presigious institutions of higher education. Yale, Harvard, Princeton, Johns Hopkins, Columbia, Brown—the company represented is nothing if not renowned. And, of course, such institutions serve as models for their less prestigious brethren, so that what is chic at Harvard one semester is sure to be aped at the state school or aspiring liberal arts college down the road the next. Nor should one think such antics as were on display at Yale and in the pages of *Salmagundi* are confined to the realm of theory, that they are battles waged only in the pages of obscure academic journals and from the podiums of academic conferences. Indeed, perhaps the most notorious case involving canon revision—the dropping of the Western culture requirement at Stanford University in the spring of 1988—showed how resolutely the debate has moved out of theory and into practice.

The controversy at Stanford dates back to April 1986, when members of the Black Student Union complained that the requirement of a yearlong course for freshmen in Western culture was racist, sexist, and failed to address the needs of minority students and women. It is even reported that one critic of the course declared that it is "not just racist education, it is the education of racists." Racism on our campuses is a subject to which we shall return. But it is worth noting here that at Stanford *racism* is something that apparently is only a problem when directed against certain preselected groups. How else can one understand the letter written in June 1988 to the Stanford student newspaper by the president of the Black Student Uniion, which began by explaining that "it is an unfortunate fact of life that most students at Stanford are white, middle class, privileged, sheltered and apathetic" and went on to confide that "I do not like most white people"?[16] Just imagine the uproar that would have ensued if the student newspaper had printed that same letter with the adjective "white" changed to "black." In any event, these charges and instances of racism provide the appropriate context in which to appreciate one of the most dramatic and telling moments in the controversy: the spectacle of the Reverend Jesse Jackson marching with 500 students at Stanford chanting "Hey hey, ho ho, Western culture's got to go."

For many observers, the Reverend Jackson's sentiments seemed to sum up the issue with all possible clarity. The question was how Stanford, itself a glittering product of Western culture, would respond. The answer came at the end of March 1988, when the Faculty Senate voted 39–4 to abandon its required course in Western culture. Part of the Stanford curriculum since 1980, the Western culture requirement was to be gradually replaced with a new cluster of courses called "Culture, Ideas, Values," a name designed to preserve a hint of civilization in its initials—it is known as "CIV" for short—but without the offending adjective, *Western.* It should be noted that, like its successor, the Western culture requirement did not stipulate that all students take the same course. Rather, students were free to choose among eight yearlong courses with titles such as "Great Works," "Values, Technology, Science and Society," "Philosophy," and "Humanities." Unlike the courses in the "Culture, Ideas, Values" program, however, the eight courses in the Western culture program were all built around a "core list" of sixteen acknowledged masterpieces of Western culture, including selections from the Bible, Homer, Plato, Augustine, and Dante.

Abandoning even that slender basis of commonality in the one required humanities course at the university is disturbing enough. Even more disturbing is the patently political rationale for the change. According to the faculty plan for the program, all the courses in the "Culture, Ideas, Values" program must include "works by women, minorities and persons of color" and at least one work each quarter must address issues of race, sex, or class. As with Professor Showalter and the *Yale Bulletin* entry for women's studies, it is not said whether any of the works must address issues of literary merit, aesthetic excel-

[16]Quoted by Sidney Hook, ed., "Stanford Documents." *Partisan Review,* vol. 55, no.4 (Fall 1988): 662, 664.

lence, philosophical sophistication, or historical importance. Such criteria presumably belong to the racist and sexist heritage of Western culture that Stanford is endeavoring to dispense with. But Donald Kennedy, the university's president, nonetheless proclaimed the change "a substantial improvement."[17]

Not everyone agreed. Kennedy found his supporters, to be sure, but Secretary of Education William Bennett, for example, publicly castigated the change as education by "intimidation." And numerous editorials, reports, and letters in major newspapers across the country regarded the scuttling of the required course in Western culture with dismay. In an effort to counter the negative publicity, the administration did everything it could to downplay the significance of the change: What was all the fuss about? Stanford wasn't throwing out Western culture *tout court,* it was merely opening up the curriculum in the name of *diversity* (a favorite code word) and pluralism. In letters addressed to Stanford friends, parents, alumni, and other potential sources of financial support, various administrative officials from the president on down affirmed that Stanford was still a citadel of liberal learning, that—far from being a step backward—the modification (as the official university documents liked to put it) of the Western culture requirement represented a victory for reason, culture, and tolerance.

Charles Junkerman, the assistant dean of undergraduate studies, was somewhat franker, perhaps inadvertently so, in a letter he wrote to *The Wall Street Journal* defending Stanford's new course. Fifty years ago, Dean Junkerman wrote, John Locke might have had something to tell us about the question "What is social justice?" But now "it may be that someone like Frantz Fanon, a black Algerian psychoanalyst, will get us closer to the answer we need.[18]

So John Locke, one of the chief philosophical sources of political liberalism and perhaps the single greatest philosophical influence on the Constitution of the United States, is to be scrapped in favor of Frantz Fanon. And who was Frantz Fanon? The short, evasive, answer is that Fanon was a French-educated psychiatrist from Martinique. But he is not remembered for his contributions to psychiatry, as Assistant

[17]Lee A. Daniels, "Stanford Alters Western Culture Course," *The New York Times,* 2 Apr. 1988.

[18]Charles Junkerman, "Letter to the Editor," *The Wall Street Journal,* 6 Jan. 1989.

Dean Junkerman's epithet may imply, but for his politics, for what Professor Fox-Genovese called his theory of purging violence. What the good assistant dean was thinking of, but did not say, was that Fanon was stationed in Algeria during the French–Algerian war, was radicalized and became a leader of the Algerian National Front, and delivered himself in the early sixties of a revolutionary screed titled *The Wretched of the Earth.*[19] Available in English with a predictably admiring preface by Jean-Paul Sartre, then in one of his most politically radical phases, *The Wretched of the Earth* is essentially a pep talk for third world revolutionaries committed to achieving decolonialization through the systematic application of violence. "Have the courage to read this book," Sartre advised, "it will make you ashamed, and shame, as Marx said, is a revolutionary sentiment."

Here is a small sample of what Frantz Fanon, the man whom Assistant Dean Junkerman hopes might "get us closer to the answer we need" regarding the question of social justice, has to say about Western culture in the first section of his book, "Concerning Violence": "When the native hears a speech about Western culture he pulls out his knife—or at least makes sure it is within reach."[20] Of course, the primary allusion in this passage is to the statement, variously attributed to Goering and other Nazi party members, that "When I hear the word *culture,* I reach for my gun."

It is worth keeping that allusion in mind as one ponders Fanon's message. For it must not be forgotten that Fanon's book, although cast in the passionately aggrieved rhetoric of political redress, was written as an incitement to murder. It might also be mentioned that though Fanon's main object of attack is Europe, he does not entirely neglect the United States. "Two centuries ago, a former European colony decided to catch up with Europe," he wrote near the end of his book. "It succeeded so well that the United States of America became a monster, in which the taints, the sickness, and the inhumanity of Europe have grown to appalling dimensions."[21] Edifying, is it not, especially when considered as a replacement for John Locke in a

[19]Frantz Fanon, *The Wretched of the Earth,* trans. Constance Farrington, preface by Jean-Paul Sartre (New York: Grove Press, 1963).

[20]Ibid., 43.

[21]Ibid., 313.

required course for freshmen at Stanford?

Assistant Dean Junkerman was also a cosignatory, together with the dean of undergraduate studies, of a mollifying letter addressed to parents of Stanford students. "Unfortunately," they wrote, "outside the immediate campus there has been a good deal of misunderstanding about the changes that were made. . . . Rest assured that our faculty will develop academically challenging and responsible tracks for the new CIV Program. Indeed, one very impressive new track, entitled 'Europe and the Americas,' is already under development."[22]

Let us take a brief look at what this "impressive new track" on Europe and the Americas, first taught in the fall of 1988, offers students. Because faculty are still required to assign some classics, in the first section of the course, titled "Conventions of Selfhood," students are required to read a portion of St. Augustine's *Confessions.* That is in a class called "The Body and the 'Deep' Interior Self." But things get going a few days later with a class devoted to the subject of multicultural selves in the Navaho country, for which students are assigned the film *The Story of a Navaho Family, 1938–1986.* (This is one of several required films for the course.)

The visit with the Navahos is followed the next week by a class called "Our Bodies, Our Sheep, Our Cosmos, Ourselves," featuring a reading from *Son of Old Man Hat* by Left Handed. Naturally, there is the obligatory reading from Karl Marx later in the course. And then, under the rubric "Making Other Cultural Selves," a class devoted to labor, gender, and self in the Philippine uplands, for which the reading is from—are you ready?—Genesis and Revelations. Perhaps the Bible is hard to come by out in Palo Alto, because this assignment, alone among the assignments for this course, is followed by the parenthetical notation, "to be distributed." And lest one think that Assistant Dean Junkerman had bandied about Frantz Fanon's name merely as a hypothetical instance, rest assured, as he might say, that Fanon occupies an honored place in Stanford's new "Europe and the Americas" course. The section on forging revolutionary selves begins with a class called "Violence and the Self" and generous readings from *The Wretched of the Earth.*

[22]Dean of Undergraduate Studies Thomas Wasow and Assistant Dean of Undergraduate Studies Charles Junkerman, letter to parents of Stanford University students: "The Process and the Product: The Inside Story on the Western Culture Debate," Fall 1988.

There are several things that must be said about this curricular debacle at Stanford. First, as President Donald Kennedy noted in a soothing letter of February 15, 1988 to Stanford friends, "the primary voices for change have been the faculty's." He meant by this admission to reassure Stanford's benefactors that charges of intimidation by students had been exaggerated. And, notwithstanding the agitation by members of the Black Student Union and others, he was undoubtedly right: The faculty was, in the end, to blame for the demise of the Western culture course at Stanford. But, of course, this is more, not less, troubling, because it means that the elite body of the Faculty Senate at Stanford—those men and women entrusted with helping to set educational policy at one of our greatest universities—willingly, nay, eagerly, voted 39–4 against preserving even a minimally traditional educational requirement. Now, instead of an introduction to masterpieces, students at Stanford are getting the likes of Frantz Fanon, the movies, and "Our Bodies, Our Sheep, Our Cosmos, Ourselves."

VII • THE TRIUMPH OF LEFT ECLECTICISM

Like most of the reflections in the *Salmagundi* colloquy and the symposium at Yale, the demise of the Western culture requirement at Stanford underscores the predominance in the academy of what the literary critic Frederick Crews has aptly dubbed "Left Eclecticism." As Professor Crews explained, Left Eclecticism is not identical with Marxism, exactly, but represents any of a wide variety of antiestablishment modes of thought from structuralism and poststructuralism, deconstruction, and Lacanian analysis to feminist, homosexual, black, and other patently political forms of criticism. At the heart of Left Eclecticism, wrote Professor Crews, is

> an understanding, ultimately borrowed from the Marxist ethos, that analytic and theoretic discourse is to be judged primarily by the radicalism of its stance. The schools of thought thus favored make sharply divergent claims, yet all of them set themselves against allegedly repressive Western institutions and practices. In dealing with a given painting, novel, or piece of architecture, especially one dating from the capitalist era, they do not aim primarily to show the work's character or governing idea. The goal is rather to subdue

> the work through aggressive demystification—for example, by positing its socioeconomic determinants and ideological implications, scanning it for any encouraging signs of subversion, and then judging the result against an ideal of total freedom.[23]

Taken together, the *Salmagundi* collection, the Yale symposium on the canon, and Stanford's abandonment of its Western culture requirement provide a veritable inventory of the sort of thing Professor Crews has in mind. While there is much more to be said about the influence of Left Eclecticism in the academy, at this point I wish only to underscore the goal Professor Crews identifies of subduing the work "through aggressive demystification." For it is often in the name of radical demystification, of skepticism raised to the highest power, that the assault on the canon proceeds. The idea is, of course, that by shedding inherited beliefs, traditions, and prejudices one thereby frees oneself for more genuine insight. It rarely occurs to the champions of disillusionment that demystification consistently pursued results in its own, particularly sterile, forms of remystification.

That so many of the teachers and scholars we have discussed are apparently prepared to jettison the intellectual principles and, indeed, the moral grounding that have nourished and given meaning to their disciplines is a deeply foreboding sign. And the ominousness of the current situation is only compounded when we realize that many of these same men and women now hold positions of considerable power and influence in the colleges and universities that are charged with educating our youth. The cynicism, devotion to shallow intellectual fashion, and unthinking importation of politics into the humanities that these educators display make it easy to wonder, with Allan Bloom, whether "there is either the wherewithal or the energy within the university to constitute or reconstitute the idea of an educated human being and establish a liberal education again."[24] One must believe that such energy and wherewithal does or could exist. But the radical ethos prevailing in the academy today means that their achievement is not only ever more precarious, but also ever more urgent.

[23]Frederick Crews, *Skeptical Engagements* (New York: Oxford University Press, 1986), 138–139.

[24]Bloom, *The Closing of the American Mind,* 380.

CHAPTER 2

SPEAKING AGAINST THE HUMANITIES

I • THE ACADEMY STRIKES BACK

The assault on the canon has no doubt been the most publicly controversial element in the recent debate over the future of the humanities in this country. But that assault must be understood in the context of the enormous changes that have taken place over the last two decades in the academic understanding of the nature and goals of liberal arts education. Many of these changes, such as the demand that the curriculum be recast to accommodate racial, sexual, or ethnic quotas, are overtly political. Other changes, such as the attack on the ideal of disinterested scholarship or the rise of deconstruction and its progeny, also rest partly on political presuppositions, although often in ways that are not immediately apparent.

Perhaps the best way to begin to appreciate the extent of these changes is to consider the academy's response to its critics. There is no more telling introduction to this subject than the brief report recently issued by the American Council of Learned Societies (ACLS) titled *Speaking for the Humanities.*[1] A slender thirty-eight pages, this pamphlet was written jointly by six prominent academics—including one dean and five directors of humanities centers—and was endorsed by an additional twenty-one professors from

[1]George Levine et al., *Speaking for the Humanities,* American Council of Learned Societies Occasional Paper No. 7, 1989.

across the country.* It is intended partly as a position paper or manifesto, outlining what has come to be the established academic view of the humanities. It is also intended as a concerted response to critics of the academy such as Allan Bloom, William Bennett, and the current director of the National Endowment for the Humanities, Lynne V. Cheney, whose recent report on the state of the humanities[2] takes up where Secretary Bennett's *To Reclaim a Legacy* left off in criticizing the way academy has dealt with the humanities.

The charges that *Speaking for the Humanities* attempts to answer fall roughly into two categories. There is, first, the question of what we might call the statistical health of the humanities. In *To Reclaim a Legacy,* for example, we read that since 1970 the number of students majoring in the humanities has declined by about half, by nearly two-thirds in the case of history, that fewer than half of all colleges and universities require foreign language study for the bachelor's degree—down from 90 percent in 1966—and that a student can now be graduated from 75 percent of our colleges and universities without having studied European history. Similarly, *Humanities in America* reports that between 1966 and 1986—a time when the number of bachelors degrees awarded in this country increased by 88 percent—the number of bachelors degrees awarded in the humanities declined by 33 percent. It also reports that one can be graduated from 80 percent of our four-year colleges without taking a course in the history of Western civilization, from more than 80 percent of our institutions of higher education without taking a course in American history, and from 62 percent without taking a course in philosophy. According to these and other reports, then, in the past two decades American education has suffered a

*The authors of the pamphlet are Peter Brooks, introduced in the previous chapter; Jonathan Culler, professor of English and Comparative Literature and director of the Society for the Humanities at Cornell University; George Levine, professor of English and director of the Center for the Critical Analysis of Contemporary Culture at Rutgers University, who also undertook to orchestrate the writing and editing of the pamphlet; Marjorie Garber, professor of English and director of the Center for Literary and Cultural Studies at Harvard; E. Ann Kaplan, professor of English and director of the Humanities Institute at the State University of New York at Stony Brook; and Catharine R. Stimpson, professor of English and dean of the Graduate School at Rutgers.

[2]Lynne V. Cheney, *Humanities in America: A Report to the President, the Congress, and the American People* (Washington, D.C.: The National Endowment for the Humanities, 1988).

wholesale flight from the humanities.

Speaking for the Humanities responds, in essence, with the time-honored two-step known as backing and filling. It goes something like this: Yes, there has been a nationwide decline in humanities enrollments, but it was not due to the way the humanities were being taught; no, there wasn't such a big decline in enrollments after all, and even if there were, people such as Secretary Bennett and Lynne Cheney don't understand its real significance; OK, there was a precipitous decline in humanities enrollments, but it was because economics suddenly became such a popular subject—again, not our fault; well, possibly there was a decline in humanities enrollments at some institutions, but the number of English majors at Rutgers University did not decline during the last two decades and at Harvard the number of students majoring in the humanities "actually" rose.

One need not be a statistician (or a psychologist) to realize that the authors of *Speaking for the Humanities* are merely temporizing. Nor are they convincing in their responses to the second, more substantive, category of charges: that the humanities have become overspecialized and needlessly obscure, that they have repudiated the ideal of disinterested scholarship to pursue various politicized educational agendas, and that they have in many instances abandoned the study of the great works of the Western tradition to lavish attention on material that is secondary, trivial, or of dubious intellectual importance.

Once again we find the authors of *Speaking for the Humanities* indulging in a good deal of the old two-step: The humanities have not become overspecialized, or if they have it's because "The problems are almost always more complicated than the popular interpretation allows" and, what's more, "to be specialized is not to be trivial."[3] We are told, too, that the humanities have not simply given up the ideal of disinterested scholarship—or if they have it's because (1) there are no such things as disinterestedness and objectivity anyway or (2) if there are such things, they aren't all they have been cracked up to be. (Take your pick.) Besides, why worry about boring things such as objectivity, disinterestedness, or facts when "the humanities are better

[3]Levine et al., *Speaking for the Humanities*, 4, 6.

conceived as fields of exploration and critique rather than materials for transmission,"[4] that is to say, when the intellectual and moral substance of the humanistic tradition is regarded as material for free play ("exploration") rather than a precious legacy worthy of preservation. We also discover that the humanities have not become more politicized; they have simply woken up to the fact that everything is political. Nor, apparently, have the humanities given up great works; they've merely expanded the definition of what counts as great. And so on.

Although written in the sanitized prose that joint authorship imposes, *Speaking for the Humanities* is a disturbing document on any number of levels. For one thing, it exhibits an extraordinary contempt for the nonacademic public. Consider only the assertion that "professionalization makes thought possible"—as if those who are not professionals are therefore incapable of thought. Indeed, this statement reveals a great deal about the patently self-serving spirit that informs *Speaking for the Humanities.* Its authors concede that many unenlightened people seem "frightened" that recent developments in the humanities will "subvert the moral order." But their response is to retreat to the platitude that "to live with uncertainty is one of the conditions of great art."[5] The implication, of course, is that our beleaguered humanists have the rare courage to withstand the existential uncertainties of great art and, therefore, the public must indulge them. What they don't say is that all too often humanities courses in our colleges and universities begin by asserting that what has been acclaimed as great art is really only the product of a biased elite, of no greater value than any other cultural artifact. Nor do they say that everything in their cultivation of specialization and attitude of professionalization conspires against the preservation of great art, tending instead to transform art into fodder for pedantic academic commentary.

In the same vein, they explain that it

> is precisely because the teachers of the humanities take their subject seriously that they become specialists, allow themselves to be profes-

[4]Ibid., 8.

[5]Ibid., 8, 9.

> sionals rather than amateurs—belle lettrists who unselfconsciously sustain traditional hierarchies, traditional social and cultural exclusions, assuming that their audience is both universal and homogenous.[6]

In other words, only your professional academic is canny enough to escape bondage to naïve and intellectually crippling assumptions about social and cultural power. No mere Mencken or Orwell or Auden could do it, you see, because, as amateurs and belle lettrists, they were just too unaware of "traditional hierarchies" to tell us anything of much value.

In addition to the generalized arrogance that *Speaking for the Humanities* communicates, there is the problem of its underlying conception of what constitutes a liberal arts education. At the same time that the distinguished authors of this pamphlet are busy telling us that everything is just fine in the academy, that the criticism launched by Secretary Bennett and others regarding overspecialization "is badly off the mark,"[7] they also confide that

> developments in modern thought . . . have made us alert to what is left out when "the best that has been thought and written" is selected or when discussion focuses on "man." We have learned to ask whether universalist claims do not in fact promote as a norm the concerns of a particular group and set aside as partial or limited those of other groups.[8]

The measured tones of this prose ("developments in modern thought," etc.) conceal a deep if somewhat evasive disregard for the substance of the humanities as traditionally conceived. Perhaps the first question one wants to ask is what developments are the authors of this pamphlet thinking of? They imply they have some sort of evidence for the highly contentious propositions that they put forth: that education should *not* be concerned with the best that has been thought and written, for example, or that the aspiration of the humanities to speak to the concerns of all men and women is only a cover for

[6]Ibid., 6.

[7]Ibid., 5.

[8]Ibid., 16.

one group's interests. But in fact the only development they could point to is the rise of a politicized view of education that requires the redefinition of the curriculum along the lines specified by the "gender, class, and race" lobby.

It is also worth noting how much *Speaking for the Humanities* gives away in its contemptuous dismissal of higher education as an effort to acquaint students with "the best that has been thought and written." The phrase comes from Matthew Arnold, the influential Victorian poet, critic, and man of letters. Arnold had looked to the preservation and transmission of the best that had been thought and written as a means of rescuing culture from anarchy in a democratic society. And, indeed, that a liberal arts education sought the best was one reason college was once referred to as "higher" education: it was higher in the sense not only of providing more education but also in the sense of providing a more profound acquaintance with the formative ideas and values of our culture. Intellectually, its aim was truth; morally, its aim was virtue. These days, however, when such value judgments are looked on with suspicion and all comparisons of quality are considered invidious, Matthew Arnold and everything he stood for are rejected as elitist.

In fact, *Speaking for the Humanities* really speaks for this attitude of rejection, not for the humanities. In this respect, however, it is no different from many other developments in the academy today. One thinks especially of the rapid growth of academic programs devoted to the study of popular culture. It must be understood that, whatever legitimate interest the academic study of popular culture may hold, the study of popular culture has been pursued primarily as a means of attacking the traditional academic concentration on objects of high culture. This can be seen in any number of modish academic movements, but is perhaps most completely exemplified by the movement called Cultural Studies. The latest and most important academic effort to resuscitate Marxist analysis and liberate the humanities from an "elitist" concern with high culture, Cultural Studies had its origin in Britain but has quickly gained an important following in this country. Its adherents are especially numerous at colleges and universities with interdisciplinary humanities centers, which provide a natural roost for Cultural Studies. Richard Johnson, one of the founders of Cultural Studies in Britain, puts the chief issue bluntly in what is generally considered the charter document for the movement, "What is Cultural Studies Anyway?" "Analysts [i.e., teachers and scholars] need to abandon once and for all," he wrote, "both of the two main models of the critical reader: the primarily evaluative reading (is this a good/bad text?) and the aspiration to text-analysis as an 'objective science.' "[9]

What are the implications of this demand to liberate criticism from readings that are "primarily evaluative," that seek "the best that has been thought and written"? One thing it implies is that the highest achievements of civilization are somehow off-limits or inaccessible to certain groups on the grounds that they are not of the appropriate sex, ethnic heritage, or race. It's as if the teachings of Plato, because he was a white European male, were therefore necessarily unintelligible to Chinese women or black men. Indeed, it is important to recognize how deeply exclusionary—one might even say racist and sexist—are the suppositions that stand behind the emancipationist rhetoric one finds scattered throughout *Speaking for the Humanities* and other contemporary academic credos. As is often the case, rhetoric promising greater openness, diversity, and pluralism actually helps to perpetuate the most stringent intellectual conformity.

It is also important to note that the critique of what it pleases the authors of this pamphlet to refer to as "the positivist ideal of objectivity and disinterest" is not a critique at all but simply a generalized animus against the notions that reality is not an invention and that the human mind is capable of apprehending truths that exist apart from the perturbations of subjective fancy. If one wanted to characterize the psychological foundations of this animus, probably the most generous word one could propose would be *adolescent*—after all, what could be more adolescent than this spirit of contempt blended as it is with an almost comic self-absorption?

The political implications are even more forbidding. For behind any cavalier dismissal of truth lies a disdain for empirical reality that can easily be enlisted by tyranny. This was underscored by the influential literary critic and scholar Tzvetan Todorov in his review of *Speaking for the Humanities.* Taking issue with the authors' repudiation

[9]Richard Johnson, "What is Cultural Studies Anyway?" *Social Text: Theory/Culture/Ideology,* vol. 6, no. 1 (Winter 1986/7): 74.

of the ideals of objectivity and disinterestedness—a dismissal that is based, they proudly reminded us, on "the consensus of most of the dominant theories"—Todorov noted how "awkwardly reminiscent" it is of the torturer O'Brien's terrifying speech in George Orwell's *1984:* "You believe that reality is something objective, external, existing in its own right. . . . But I tell you, Winston, that reality is not external. Reality exists in the human mind and nowhere else."[10] As Winston discovered, it was not advantageous to dispute this contention.

There are many other disturbing things about *Speaking for the Humanities.* Some, like the anachronistic "alternative" readings the authors offer, would be downright funny if one didn't know they were being taken seriously and perpetuated as "developments in modern thought." Thus, for example, we discover that *The Tempest* is being widely read as an allegory of imperialist conquest: Caliban is the exploited native, you see, and Prospero the evil imperialistic European. Similarly, *Paradise Lost* is presented as a problem text for feminists because Milton portrays Adam as being "for God only" but Eve as being merely for God in Adam. If such interpretations were critical bagatelles, admired more for their ingenuity than their insight, there would be no need for concern. But, in fact, they are taken very earnestly and, indeed, provide models for a whole range of ideological attacks on the humanities. What a reading of *The Tempest* as an imperialist drama and a reading of *Paradise Lost* as a feminist tragedy have in common is an eagerness to subordinate literature to an extraneous political agenda, the agenda of third world racial concerns on the one hand and feminist restitution on the other. In both cases, what threatens to be lost is not only the integrity of the individual text—bad enough though that is—but the whole idea of literature as a distinctive realm of expression and experience with its own concerns, values, and goals. No one would deny that literature is often about politics; but that is a far cry from maintaining, as do the authors of *Speaking for the Humanities,* that the *essence* of literature is politics.

Equally disturbing is the extent to which *Speaking for the Humanities* is a kind of position paper for that newly refurbished academic

[10]Quoted by Tzvetan Todorov, "Crimes against Humanities," *The New Republic,* 3 July 1989, 28.

entity, the interdisciplinary humanities center. As the authors noted, there are now some 300 such centers at campuses scattered around the country and new ones are opening all the time. Generously funded by universities, corporations, and government agencies such as the National Endowment for the Humanities, these centers have increasingly become, to use a word much in vogue at the moment, "sites" of enormous institutional power and prestige. The authors of *Speaking for the Humanities* place great stock in the promise of this relatively new institution. Yet it is by no means clear that the rise of the humanities center is a beneficent development for the study of the humanities. Far from seeking to preserve the intellectual and moral integrity of the humanities, they have typically become the favored homes of such radical academic movements as the New Historicism and Cultural Studies, among others, movements overtly seeking to politicize the humanities and undermine allegiance to traditional scholarly ideals.

Moreover, existing as they do on the margins of the traditional academic disciplines, such enclaves are typically dedicated to the goal of what Thomas Short referred to as "breaking the disciplines." Thus it is that one often hears talk of "postdisciplinary" studies and programs that seek to transcend the usual divisions between academic subjects so that professors trained in English can pretend to be philosophers, philosophers can pretend to be literary critics, and everyone can absorb large doses of sociology to overcome the ingrained habit of regarding any academic subject as worthy of study in its own right.[11] Indeed, although the authors of *Speaking for the Humanities* are full of praise for both the idea of academic specialization and the proliferation of interdisciplinary humanities centers, nowhere do they mention that one of the most often declared ambitions of the new interdisciplinary movements is to undermine the intellectual and institutional prestige of traditional specialized scholarly work.

II • ROCKING AROUND THE CLOCK

In order to appreciate the kind of alternative subjects that *Speaking for the Humanities* recommends, let us now turn to look briefly at what at least some of its authors regard as worthy objects of attention for

[11]Short, " 'Diversity' and 'Breaking the Disciplines.' "

humanistic study. In many respects, the pamphlet owes its genesis to one of its authors, Professor E. Ann Kaplan from the State University of New York at Stony Brook. It was she who first went to the ACLS to suggest that it sponsor a meeting of directors of humanities centers; and it was out of the meetings that followed that the "need" for an institutional response to recent criticisms of the academy was articulated. There is a great deal in *Speaking for the Humanities* about the sanctity of new "research" being undertaken by contemporary humanists, whose work may be too specialized and professional to be intelligible to the general educated reader, of course, but who are nonetheless avidly pursuing important "developments in modern thought."

What sort of research does Professor Kaplan pursue? Her speciality seems to be Hollywood movies—she has written several books on the subject—although recently she has branched out into the promising field of rock videos. More specifically, her recent book, *Rocking Around the Clock: Music Television, Postmodernism, & Consumer Culture,*[12] is an investigation of MTV with special reference to the rock videos of the pop singer Madonna, "the female star," she writes, "who perhaps more than any other embodies the new postmodernist feminist heroine."[13] In *Rocking Around the Clock,* Professor Kaplan enumerates the five types of rock video she has discerned in the course of her painstaking research into MTV and provides recondite analyses of such landmark works of art as "Smokin' in the Boys' Room," by the rock band Motley Crue, "Rebel Yell," by Billy Idol, and John Cougar Mellencamp's "Hurts So Good," which, we discover, "addresses recent interest in sado-masochism on the part of both young men and women."[14]

Not that her book is intended to be a popular account of this popular entertainment medium. On the contrary, although she is not terribly adept at the practice, she does everything she can to jazz up (or perhaps we should say "rock up") her pages with formidable quotations from Lacan, Derrida, Jameson, and other certified aca-

[12]E. Ann Kaplan, *Rocking Around the Clock: Music Television, Postmodernism, & Consumer Culture* (New York: Methuen, 1987).

[13]Ibid., 117.

[14]Ibid., 114.

demic gurus. For example, in a chapter titled "Gender Address and the Gaze in MTV," she begins by telling us that "we need particularly to explore how far theories of the 'male gaze' apply to watching television," confides the exciting news that "the plethora of gender positions on [MTV] is arguably linked to the heterogeneity of current sex roles and to an imaginary [*sic*] constructed out of a world in which all traditional categories, boundaries, and institutions are being questioned," and concludes that "the romantic video functions in the pre-symbolic dyadic terrain between the illusory merging with the mother and the phallicism that follows the mirror phase."[15] This solecistic use of "imaginary" is typical of Professor Kaplan's gratuitous use of Lacanian jargon. Also typical is her penchant for introducing politically correct persiflage at every opportunity. Early on in the book, for example, we are told that "the racist aspect of MTV . . . reflects aspects of Reagan's America."[16] And near the end of the volume, she muses that

> one could see the effacing in MTV of old boundaries between high and low culture, between past, present, and future, and between previously distinct art forms as an exhilarating move toward a heteroglossia that calls into question moribund pieties of a now archaic humanism. . . . The creativity and energy of rock videos could represent a refusal to be co-opted into the liberalism that has brought America to its present crisis.[17]

The chief merit of this rebarbative nonsense is as a graphic sociological document bearing witness to cultural decadence. Who would have thought it possible that a woman entrusted with teaching college English and directing a humanities center at a major university would make her scholarly reputation writing about "Smokin' in the Boys' Room," the rock videos of Madonna, and "Gender Address and the Gaze in MTV"? And do take note of Professor Kaplan's diction: "moribund pieties," "archaic humanism," "the liberalism that has brought America to its present crisis." One would never know that the real crisis is that words such as *humanism* and *liberalism*—to

[15]Ibid., 89, 90, 95.

[16]Ibid., 31.

[17]Ibid., 147–148.

say nothing of *objectivity, disinterestedness,* and *truth*—have been drained of meaning and are now regarded, precisely, as "moribund" by men and women whose lives were once devoted to the ideals those words named. In one of the most excoriated sections of *The Closing of the American Mind,* Allan Bloom discussed what he believes to be the baneful effects rock music has had on the imaginations of students. Many people found his conclusions extreme. "I believe," Bloom wrote, that rock music "ruins the imagination of young people and makes it very difficult for them to have a passionate relationship to the art and thought that are the substance of liberal imagination."[18] A perusal of *Rocking Around the Clock* makes Bloom's judgment seem like an understatement.

It must be understood that Professor Kaplan's book raises another issue as well. While her performance, bedizened as it is with snippets of obscure theoretical jargon, is more pretentious than many such expositions, in its basic approach and effort to *academicize* popular culture *Rocking Around the Clock* is by no means exceptional. At campuses around the country, and especially in interdisciplinary programs and centers, we have for some time now been witnessing an aggressive effort to erase the qualitative distinction between high culture and popular culture and to introduce the methods, concerns, and subject matter of the social sciences into the humanities. More and more, courses in literature seem like amateur exercises in sociological or anthropological sermonizing. Professor Kaplan's book is merely one of this large and growing genre. We are now at a point almost diametrically opposed to the ideal envisioned by Matthew Arnold. Instead of perpetuating the best that has been thought and said, our new humanists assure each other and their students that *best* is a socially relative term and that, at bottom, one might just as well study the "text" of "Smokin' in the Boys' Room" as bother reading Wallace Stevens, let alone someone as fusty as Matthew Arnold.

III • THE ECLIPSE OF THE SELF

The attack by the academy on fundamental terms and distinctions takes several forms. At the same time that the Professor Kaplans of

[18]Bloom, *The Closing of the American Mind,* 79.

the profession are busy watching MTV and complaining about "the liberalism that has brought America to its present crisis," others are employing more conventional academic tools in an effort to cast doubt on the values and aspiration of traditional humanistic inquiry. A striking example of the latter appeared in 1986, when Stanford University Press published *Reconstructing Individualism: Autonomy, Individuality, and the Self in Western Thought,* a collection of essays drawn from papers presented at a conference of the same title that had been held at Stanford two years previously.[19] Including contributions by such formidable scholars as the art historian Michael Fried, the philosophers Stanley Cavell, Martha C. Nussbaum, and Ian Hacking, the sociologist Niklas Luhmann, the historian Natalie Zemon Davis, the literary critics John Frecero and Stephen Greenblatt, and others of similar academic repute, the volume may be taken as a state of the art interdisciplinary report on recent academic thinking about individualism. And because the notion of individualism has traditionally occupied a central place in the humanities, we may also look to *Reconstructing Individualism* for further insight into the way the more advanced precincts of contemporary academic speculation has "reconstructed" the goals and values of humanistic education.

It has become practically axiomatic in the academy that one cannot invoke so jaded a notion as *individualism* without an elaborate garland of reservations, qualifications, and caveats. Just as Professor Kaplan unself-consciously referred to an "archaic humanism," so any academic discussion of the subject of individualism has to be undertaken with the clear understanding that one is dealing with tainted goods. As we have seen, the very idea that there is something special about the individual is likely to be taken as a red flag by progressive academics for whom individualism is tantamount to racism.[20] Because individualism is widely recognized as one of the bedrocks of Western liberal thought and society, no, as it were, self-respecting (not to say individualistic) academic would dream of taking it "straight," of dealing with it on its own terms as an idea that continues to have a profound claim on us morally and intellectually. *Individualism* in this

[19]Thomas C. Heller et al., eds., *Reconstructing Individualism: Autonomy, Individuality, and the Self in Western Thought* (Stanford: Stanford University Press, 1986).

[20]Kors, "It's Speech, Not Sex, the Dean Bans Now."

sense is only slightly less disreputable in the academy these days than that ultimate term of abuse, *bourgeois.*

Accordingly, we read in the introduction to *Reconstructing Individualism* that the "animating assumption" of the conference and the volume of essays it inspired was that "the concept of the individual, which has played such a central role in the formation of the post-Renaissance world, needs to be rethought in the wake of the severe criticisms which have been directed against it" over the course of the last century. "Developments in the material and social realms," we read, "such as industrialization and the emergence of mass society" have rendered the individual "problematic," have even "altered the ontological foundations of individual identity." By now, having been subjected to the "deconstructive" scrutiny of such critics as Marx, Nietzsche, and Freud—to say nothing of the legions of academics who carry on in their name today—individualism can be made academically palatable only if it is suitably reconstructed. While the particulars of this envisioned reconstruction are never really set forth, it is nonetheless clear that most of these essays are to be seen primarily as attempts to explore alternative, reconstructed versions of individualism—"postcultural" versions, perhaps, to employ a word brandished by one of the essays—versions of individualism sophisticated enough to dispense with anything so embarrassing as particular individuals. "At the volume's close," the introduction cheerfully concludes, "the figure of the individual has not been discredited or dissolved so much as displaced and transposed."[21]

Perhaps. But it must be said that most of the efforts at displacement and transposition collected there also do what they can to discredit the "figure of the individual." In "Toward a Relational Individualism: The Mediation of the Self Through Psychoanalysis," for example, Nancy Julia Chodorow assures us that "psychoanalysis radically undermines notions about autonomy, individual choice, will, responsibility, and rationality, showing that we do not control our lives in the most fundamental sense."[22] Let's think about this for a moment. In what sense has psychoanalysis really *undermined* the ideas

[21]Heller et al., eds., "Introduction," in *Reconstructing Individualism,* 1, 2, 16.

[22]Nancy Julia Chodorow, "Toward a Relational Individualism: The Mediation of the Self Through Psychoanalysis," in *Reconstructing Individualism,* ed. Heller et al., 197.

of will, choice, responsibility, etc.? After all, didn't Professor Chodorow *will* to write this essay? Did she not *choose* to contribute to this volume? Did she not assume the *responsibility* of submitting a manuscript by a certain date and so on? Notwithstanding the voluminous attempts of academic psychoanalysis to convince us that we are creatures of unconscious impulses, do we not in fact bear witness to the cogency and pertinence of these concepts every day?

Among the chief casualties of this brand of criticism are its heroes. Nietzsche has suffered particular indignities at its hands. Typical is Werner Hamacher's long and elliptical essay called " 'Disgregation of the Will': Nietzsche on the Individual and Individuality." Amazingly, he manages to grind all of Nietzsche's trenchant comments on the subject into a murky verbal paste. "The term 'individuality,' " Professor Hamacher tells us, "properly applies only to what transgresses the series of forms and the form of forms (typological knowledge and its objective correlatives), dissociating itself from the rigor mortis of canonical life forms, eluding the subsumptive compulsion to general categories, advancing toward a future that withdraws from every typology and objectification."[23] This is Nietzsche, champion of Dionysus, philosopher of the Anti-Christ? "I shall repeat a hundred times," Nietzsche wrote in *Beyond Good and Evil,* "we really ought to free ourselves from the seduction of words!"[24] Obviously, there are some things you can't say too often.

To speak of "seduction of words" brings us to one of the main features—one might even say "principles"—of the sort of chic academic criticism that *Reconstructing Individualism* specializes in: the attempt to enliven its cruelly abstract, anemic prose with an obsessive concern with sex, preferably perverse sex, the more violent the better. To employ one of its favorite terms, we might even say that such criticism *fetishizes* the erotic. The chief locus of sexual relations is not, of course, between living individuals but within language itself. Perhaps because they have lost interest in particular individuals, these critics of individualism find that language is where the real excitement lies. This makes for some pretty silly speculations, but it does allow

[23]Werner Hamacher, " 'Disgregation of the Will': Nietzsche on the Individual and Individuality," in *Reconstructing Individualism,* ed. Heller et al., 110.

[24]Friedrich Nietzsche, *Beyond Good and Evil* in *The Basic Writings of Nietzsche,* trans. and introduced by Walter Kaufmann (New York: Random House, 1966), 213.

one to throw around lots of terms such as *phallocratic, castration,* and so on. *Reconstructing Individualism* is full of this sort of thing. Stephen Greenblatt, for example, a celebrated champion of the New Historicism in literary studies, bases his entire article, "Fiction and Friction," on the story of a seventeenth-century French hermaphrodite, the insistence that sexual difference is "unstable and artificial," and a theory about the relation between individualism, "sexual chafing," and "the wantonness of language."[25]

Indeed, recourse to the more specialized precincts of the erotic seems to have become a kind of ritual gesture, a verbal tic in the academy. One first says something about language—about how everything is really only a corollary of language, etc.—and then one introduces a sexual twist. Paolo Valesio offers a good example in his essay, "The Beautiful Lie," (the "lie" being individualism, of course). Having told us that individualism is "a poetic concern, a concern with linguistic intensification and shaping," he proceeded to note that here, "as in every intensification of reading, not only the link with the process of writing emerges, . . . but the link of both processes with solitary and self-sufficient love—with the softly existential grounding of solipsism, masturbation."[26]

Or take Christine Brooke-Rose's essay, "The Dissolution of Character in the Novel." In the midst of the usual litany about the death of character—"character," like "individualism," turns out to be in need of "reconstruction"—we read that "characters are verbal structures; they are like our real-life relationships but have no semblance of a referent. More and more swollen with words, like stray phalluses they wander our minds, cut off from the body of the text."[27] Those phalluses! They crop up everywhere these days.

The treatment of sex in such works as *Reconstructing Individualism* highlights one of the great ironies of the whole enterprise: It goes on and on about the importance of reading more carefully, more critically, more openly, and then proceeds to display a quite remarkable

[25]Stephen Greenblatt, "Fiction and Friction," in *Reconstructing Individualism,* ed. Heller et al., 35, 49.

[26]Paolo Valesio, "The Beautiful Lie," in *Reconstructing Individualism,* ed. Heller et al., 165.

[27]Christine Brooke-Rose, "The Dissolution of Character in the Novel," in *Reconstructing Individualism,* ed., Heller et al., 186.

obtuseness about the specific works it addresses. Concentrating on some detail of a text, it misses the whole; isolating verbal similarities, it misses the sense. Often, it seems, this is just the point.

Stanley Cavell's essay, "Being Odd, Getting Even: Threats to Individuality," offers a good example of the procedure. Continuing his recent efforts to champion Emerson's philosophical credentials and to blur the distinction between philosophy and literature, Professor Cavell begins by suggesting that in "Self-Reliance" when Emerson wrote that "Man is timid and apologetic; he is no longer upright; he dares not say 'I think,' 'I am,' but quotes some saint or sage," Emerson was actually quoting Descartes's famous slogan *cogito, ergo sum.* More, he insists that Emerson was up to essentially the same sort of thing that Descartes was up to in the *Meditations.* "One can describe Emerson's progress as his having posed Descartes's question for himself and provided a fresh line of answer, one you might call a grammatical answer: I am a being who to exist must say I exist, or must acknowledge my existence—claim it, stake it, enact it." He goes on to compare the studied, deliberately ratiocinative style of Edgar Allan Poe's story "Imp of the Perverse" to Descartes's prose style, and, in a move that underscores to what extent fundamental distinctions are elided by today's humanists, ends by suggesting that Hollywood melodrama "may be seen as an interpretation of Descartes's cogito."[28]

Professor Cavell's presentation is canny, entertaining—and perfectly unbelievable. We may pass over the details of his exposition. But, speaking of "Imp of the Perverse," it is worth remarking how perverse his essay is. Consider only his treatment of Emerson. " 'Self-Reliance' as a whole," he tells us, "presents a theory . . . of reading."[29] In fact, what Emerson presents, in that essay as elsewhere, are not really theories at all but strongly held opinions. Whatever virtues Emerson possessed, his was not a philosophical mind; he did not argue, he declaimed, he preached. What he wrote was not philosophy but a species of hortatory essay. And to pretend that "Self-Reliance"—that rousing, unsystematic sermon on the virtues of independent thinking—to pretend that it has any intrinsic connection to a seven-

[28]Stanley Cavell, "Being Odd, Getting Even: Threats to Individuality," in *Reconstructing Individualism,* ed., Heller et al., 279, 282, 305.

[29]Ibid., 289.

teenth-century philosophical tract concerned with basic epistemological and theological questions is simply ridiculous.

Professor Cavell's remarks at least have the virtue of being written in something resembling English. This cannot be said of all the contributions to *Reconstructing Individualism.* Many trail off into a vertiginous hinterland of the mind where the words spin themselves out in hopeless, jargon-laden opacity. And it is important to realize that this is precisely the kind of specialization and professionalization that *Speaking for the Humanities* was at pains to defend. One could open *Reconstructing Individualism* pretty much at random for examples, but Niklas Luhmann's reflections on the individuality of the individual contain some choice items. "We may, of course, define emotions as the autopoietic immune system of the autopoietic psychic system; but again: is this emotionally adequate?" Anyone care to answer that? "The most important consequence," Professor Luhmann continued a bit later, "might well be that the theory of autopoietic systems seems to bar all ways back to an anthropological conception of man. It precludes, in other words, humanism. [Yet another term, incidentally, that has been singled out for academic "reconstruction."] . . . This means that we have to invent new conceptual artificialities in order to give an account of what we see when we meet somebody who looks and behaves like a human being. How do we know that he is one?"[30] Hard to say, hard to say.

IV • HUNTING COURBET

All of these faults—deliberately perverse interpretations, verbal obscurity, etc.—are writ large in Michael Fried's contribution to *Reconstructing Individualism:* "Courbet's Metaphysics: A Reading of 'The Quarry.' " It is indeed an exemplary performance, and shows that the new approach to the humanities has infiltrated and perverted the traditional methods and concerns of art history as well as literary studies. The announced subject of Professor Fried's essay is Gustave Courbet's 1856 painting, *The Quarry,* a hunting scene that depicts a moment of rest after a successful hunt. In the left foreground, we see

[30]Niklas Luhmann, "The Individuality of the Individual," in *Reconstructing Individualism,* ed., Heller et al., 323.

the vanquished deer hanging from a branch, its head lolling sideways on the ground. To the right, receding into a shadow, the hunter—generally acknowledged to be a self-portrait—leans back dreamily against a tree. Farther to the right, the *piqueur,* the master of the hounds, sits in a brilliant slip of light blowing a hunting horn. In the right foreground two dogs, also brightly illuminated, frisk playfully. It is well to supply this simple description at the outset, for as Professor Fried proceeds with his interpretation one's grasp of the particulars of Courbet's painting is likely to become shaky.

Among much else, Professor Fried's interpretation indulges heavily in a second main principle—not to say cliché—of fashionable academic criticism: the principle holding that whatever the work (poem, painting, novel, essay, etc.) is ostensibly about, at bottom it is self-referential, being primarily a symbol of the creative activity of painting or writing. The overt subject of the work may initially mislead one into supposing that it is really about something else, something quite tangible in one's physical or emotional experience—a hunting scene, for example. But an adroit practitioner of the new academic criticism easily overcomes such "extrinsic" objections. One powerful, if by now well-worn, aid in this task is the word *symbol* and its fashionable variants: *metaphor, metonymy, synecdoche, trope,* etc. Like the philosopher's stone, skillful use of these terms can transform the base material of reality into the gold of intertextuality. Professor Fried provides us with many wonderful examples of the procedure. We do not have to read far into his essay before we are told that the *piqueur* is really

> another of Courbet's characteristically displaced and metaphorical representations of the activity, the mental and physical *effort,* of painting. Thus the young man's strange, half-seated pose (with nothing beneath him but his folded jacket) may be taken as evoking the actual posture of the painter-beholder seated before the canvas. The hunting horn, held in his left hand, combines aspects of a paintbrush (I'm thinking of the horn's narrow, tubular neck) and a palette (its rounded shape) though strictly resembling neither, and of course a horn being blown is also a traditional image of the fame Courbet forever aspired to win by his art.[31]

[31]Michael Fried, "Courbet's Metaphysics: A Reading of 'The Quarry,' " in *Reconstructing Individualism,* ed. Heller et al., 86.

It's not long, in fact, before Professor Fried concludes that "all three principals—hunter, roe deer, and *piqueur*—are in different respects figurations of the painter-beholder [Courbet himself]."[32] One only wonders what he has against the dogs: why aren't they, too, "figurations of the painter-beholder"? Isn't their playfulness there in the painting's foreground a symbol of the playful dialogue of the creative mind at work—doubled to represent the simultaneous interplay of the productive and critical faculties, tokens of the artist's awareness of his intractable animality? But you see how it works.

Operating on the principle that if something isn't shown, it is more present than if it is, Professor Fried has no trouble populating the canvas with all manner of objects and significances that Courbet somehow forgot to include. Is there no gun depicted in the painting? No problem: "In place of the missing musket there is the *piqueur*'s hunting horn, previously described as symbolizing the painter's tools (and therefore linking those tools with the absent weapons)." *Therefore?* "Therefore" approximately in the sense of "abracadabra," perhaps. But what about sex? We have seen that no such interpretation can be complete without a dash of the erotic, preferably outlandish; but where in this forest scene could one conjure sex? A tired hunter, self-absorbed *piqueur,* two dogs, and a dead deer may not seem much to work with. Not to worry: "I for one," Professor Fried confides, "am struck by the implied violence of the exposure to the hunter's viewpoint of the dead roe deer's underside, specifically including its genitals."[33]

One has to admire's Professor Fried's brass. And his well-developed sense of just how far he can intrude on the reader's credulity without making concessions to common sense. "The last observation may seem excessive," he allows.

> For one thing, I am attaching considerable significance to a "side" of the roe deer *we cannot see as well as to a bodily organ that isn't actually depicted.* For another, the hunter isn't looking at the roe deer but faces in a different direction. But I would counter that we are led to imagine the roe deer's genitals or at any rate to be aware of their existence by the exposure to our view of the roe deer's anus,

[32]Ibid., 94.

[33]Ibid., 87.

a metonymy for the rest. . . . I would further suggest that, precisely because the roe deer's anus stands for so much we cannot see—not simply the roe deer's genitals and wounded underside but an entire virtual face of the painting—such an effect of equivalence or translatability may be taken as indicating that the first, imaginary point of view is more important, and in the end more "real," than the second.[34]

The imaginary point of view is more important and in the end more real than the point of view discerned with one's eyes: This sums up Professor Fried's method. But wait, there is more. In a long footnote to this passage, he tells us that

My suggestion that *The Quarry* calls attention to the roe deer's undepicted genitals and to their exposure to the hunter or at least to his point of view invites further discussion in terms of the Freudian problem of castration. Now what chiefly characterizes the painting's treatment of these motifs (if I may so describe them) is the absence of any signs of special or excessive affect and in particular of anxiety, which may seem to indicate that for the painter-beholder the implied threat to the roe deer's genitals was simply that, an objective menace, not the expression of a primal insecurity. On the other hand, the absence of affect ought perhaps to be seen as a further expression of the splitting of the painter-beholder into passive hunter and active *piqueur:* that is, it would be a further index of the hunter-painter's manifest passivity, which itself might be described as a sort of castration.[35]

Consider: The roe deer's genitals are undepicted, therefore the painting "invites" discussion in terms of the Freudian notion of castration. The hunter isn't looking at the deer: No matter, the deer's genitals are exposed "at least to his point of view" (i.e., if he only turned his head, he would see them). Despite this alleged threat of castration, the hunter displays no special signs of affect or emotion, quite the opposite, in fact—never mind: Being passive may itself be described as "a sort of castration" (on which account I suppose that a painting of a man asleep or unconscious or dead would provide an even more dramatic index of preoccupation with castration). Poor Courbet!

[34]Ibid., 88. (Emphasis added).

[35]Ibid., 337.

Even to raise objections would risk complicity with Professor Fried's undertaking, granting it a measure of credibility it can never have. For the suggestion that *The Quarry* has anything to do with castration—indeed, that it has anything to do with sexual violence period—is ludicrous. If any of the theories of Sigmund Freud has a bearing on the matter, it is not his conjectures about castration anxiety or "displacement" but his method of free association: here at any rate we may have a clue to Professor Fried's own critical method.

Professor Fried's speculations about the hidden sexual current in Courbet's painting are perhaps the most outrageously absurd aspect of his interpretation of *The Quarry.* But in many ways even more absurd—because it touches directly on the core of Courbet's painting—is the end to which Professor Fried's complex hermeneutical apparatus tends. This is summed up in the title "Courbet's Metaphysics," probably the drollest piece of unintentional wit in the whole of *Reconstructing Individualism.* Drawing in part on an obscure work by the obscure nineteenth-century French philosopher Felix Ravaisson, Professor Fried concluded that "the project of Courbet's Realism—of his metaphysics—was above all to represent" the "indemonstrable ideality" of nature.[36] Well, Professor Fried is certainly right that the ideality of Courbet's artistic project is indemonstrable; but then untrue propositions do tend to have that inconvenient aspect. Nevertheless, one cannot help but admire Professor Fried's sly apposition of *realism* and *metaphysics* here, as if these opposing terms really meant more or less the same thing.

Of course, the truth is that in the repertoire of Courbet's beliefs, there is nothing that can even remotely be described as a metaphysics. Indeed, few painters can have been more overtly *anti*metaphysical than Gustave Courbet. In part, that is what the usual description of him as a realist intends. Courbet himself put the matter with admirable clarity in 1861 in a letter to his students.

> I also believe that painting is an essentially CONCRETE art and can only consist of the representation of REAL AND EXISTING objects. It is a completely physical language that has as words all visible objects, and an ABSTRACT object, invisible and nonexistent, is not part of painting's domain. Imagination in art consists in know-

[36]Ibid., 99.

> ing how to find the most complete expression of an existing object, but never in imagining or in creating the object itself.[37]

So much for Professor Fried's contention that the "imaginary point of view is more important, and in the end more 'real,' than the second."

V • IT'S ONLY A GAME

> *The Glass Bead Game is a mode of playing with the total contents and values of our culture; it plays with them as, say, in the great age of the arts a painter might have played with the colors on his palette. All the insights, noble thoughts, and works of art that the human race has produced in its creative eras, all that subsequent periods of scholarly study have reduced to concepts and converted into intellectual property—on all this immense body of intellectual values the Glass Bead Game player plays like the organist on an organ.*
>
> —HERMANN HESSE,
> *The Glass Bead Game*

Like many of the essays in *Reconstructing Individualism,* Professor Fried's interpretation of Courbet's painting brings considerable erudition and an even more considerable ingenuity to bear on his subject. We read about Courbet's method of composing a painting by joining separate strips of canvas, are privy to considerations of the evidence of pentimento, and witness the rehearsal of a stunning array of scholarship. But to what end? As in Hesse's *Glass Bead Game,* the matter at hand is merely the occasion, the raw material for an elaborate interpretive exercise. What we see throughout those essays is an extraordinary amount of learning and analytical talent engaged in what is at bottom a narcissistic game. Whether the occasion be Nietzsche, or Augustine, or psychoanalysis, or an obscure account of hermaphroditism in seventeenth-century France, individualism is only the theme on which the players execute their hermeneutical arabesques—not to illuminate the idea but to embellish the pages of their critical text. "The whole secret," as Kierkegaard once put it in an analysis of this sort of aestheticism, "lies in arbitrariness. . . . You consider the whole of existence from this standpoint; let its reality be stranded

[37]Gustave Courbet, letter to his students, Dec. 25, 1861, in *A Documentary History of Art,* Vol. 3, ed. Elizabeth Gilmore Holt (New York: Doubleday, 1966), 352. (Emphasis in the original.)

thereon."[38] And the fact that the notion of individualism is assumed to be bankrupt only makes the game more piquant. The task then becomes finding a way of reconstructing individualism without precisely reinstating or legitimating it; and in this task, at least, it must be said that most of the essays excel.

What Michael Fried has in common with Stanley Cavell, Stephen Greenblatt, Werner Hamacher, and most of the other contributors to the volume is the almost casual cynicism characteristic of an age that, to quote Kierkegaard again, *"leaves everything standing but cunningly empties it of significance."*[39] (emphasis in original.) In itself, the performance of the writers collected in *Reconstructing Individualism* is nothing out of the ordinary. The players are more skilled than many, but in essence it is simply business as usual in the academy these days. Particularly dispiriting is the thought that many of these men and women are among the brightest, most talented scholars in their respective fields. That they should have chosen to abandon anything like a traditional humanistic approach to their subjects and have given themselves up shamelessly to the latest intellectual fashions is an ominous sign of the malaise suffered by the humanities at even our most prestigious institutions. But of course what is most disturbing is the thought that the defiant hermeticism and gratuitous triviality represented by *Reconstructing Individualism* are not only being pursued as research by our humanists, but are also being broadcast as genuine humanistic inquiry in the classroom and lecture hall. That constitutes a slander on tradition and a fraud against students.

VI • THE END OF A COMMON CULTURE?

To get a more tangible sense of what humanistic inquiry means in the environment of today's academy, let us return to the Whitney Humanities Center at Yale University to consider some of the presentations that were given at a daylong public symposium in the spring of 1986 titled "The Humanities and the Public Interest." The purpose of the event, in the words of a university press release, was "to

[38] Søren Kierkegaard, *Either/Or,* Vol. 1, trans. David F. Swenson and Lillian Marvin Swenson, rev. Howard A. Johnson (Princeton: Princeton University Press, 1971), 295.

[39] Søren Kierkegaard, *The Present Age,* trans. Alexander Dru (New York: Harper & Row, 1962), 42.

re-examine the traditional association between the study of the humanities and the guardianship of humanistic values in the context of contemporary American society." Peter Brooks, who as director of the Whitney Humanities Center presided over this event as he had presided over the symposium on the canon discussed above, expanded on this. "The symposium will ask whether the case for the humanities can rest on traditional assumptions," he was quoted as saying, "or whether a new rationale is needed if the humanities are to claim a major place in contemporary modes of thought and analysis."*

The symposium opened with some introductory remarks by Professor Brooks, who noted that the original impetus for the symposium was his favorite reading material, former Secretary of Education William J. Bennett's report on higher education in the humanities, *To Reclaim a Legacy.* As we have seen, this report defends precisely those "traditional assumptions" of the humanities that Professor Brooks hoped the Yale symposium would question. For himself, Professor Brooks declared his "profound disagreement" with the conclusions and general outlook of Secretary Bennett's report, taking issue especially with what he described as its "intellectual fundamentalism." Professor Brooks's opening remarks were very brief, but in many ways they established the tenor for the day's discussion, and because he identified Secretary Bennett's report as the catalyst for the symposium, we may begin by returning to take a closer look at the report's argument.

To Reclaim a Legacy begins by reaffirming the traditional role of the humanities as the chief instrument of our cultural self-definition. Its presiding deity is Matthew Arnold, whose faith in the ennobling effects of high culture, of "the best that has been thought and said," is patent throughout the report. Elaborating Arnold's famous phrase, Secretary Bennett describes the humanities as "the best that has been said, thought, written, and otherwise expressed about the human experience." The humanities are important, he wrote, because

> they tell us how men and women of our own and other civilizations have grappled with life's enduring, fundamental questions: What is justice? What should be loved? What deserves to be defended? What is courage? What is noble? What is base? . . .

*Unless otherwise noted, all quotations in this section are taken from the presentations and responses delivered at this symposium.

> These questions are not simply diversions for intellectuals or playthings for the idle. As a result of the ways in which these questions have been answered, civilizations have emerged, nations have developed, wars have been fought, and people have lived contentedly or miserably.[40]

But the real source of the controversy surrounding Secretary Bennett's report lies not so much in such general observations as in his prescriptions for "reclaiming" the legacy he finds threatened and, in the end, in his understanding of the substance and definition of that legacy. In the simplest terms, he calls for a reshaping of undergraduate study "based on a clear vision of what constitutes an educated person." In his view, the goal of the humanities should be a common culture rooted in the highest ideals and aspirations of the Western tradition.

Nevertheless, it is important to note that, despite accusations to the contrary, Secretary Bennett does not advocate restoration of a previous state of affairs. He insists that the solution to the current crisis in the humanities "is not a return to an earlier time when the classical curriculum was the only curriculum and college was available to only a privileged few." Given the charges of elitism and the reaction that his proposals have brought forth, especially from the most elite of our universities, it seems well to emphasize the point. "American higher education today serves far more people . . . than it did a century ago," Secretary Bennett wrote.

> Its increased accessibility to women, racial and ethnic minorities, recent immigrants, and students of limited means is a positive accomplishment of which our nation is justly proud. . . . But our eagerness to assert the virtues of pluralism should not allow us to sacrifice the principle that formerly lent substance and continuity to the curriculum, namely, that each college and university should recognize and accept its vital role as a conveyor of the accumulated wisdom of our civilization.[41]

It is of course this final affirmation that has angered Secretary Bennett's opponents. For one thing, who decides what counts as "the accumulated wisdom of our civilization"? In Arnold's terms, why

[40]Bennett, *To Reclaim a Legacy,* 3.

[41]Ibid., 2, 4, 29.

should the humanities be concerned primarily with the *best* that has been thought and said? Does that not exclude a large portion of human experience? And does not that mass of experience deserve equal time in our institutions of higher education? Here again, who is to say what counts as best? Perhaps the Arnoldian injunction has been interpreted too narrowly, too ideologically, too exclusively? Furthermore, why should the humanities focus so intently on the past? Why should they not concern themselves as much with the *creation* as with the *preservation* and *transmission* of culture? Such questions are at the heart of Professor Brooks's profound disagreement and charge of intellectual fundamentalism—a charge that has been loudly echoed in the academy and that was to be advanced with great zeal that Saturday at Yale's Whitney Humanities Center.

It was not, however, until the second, and most publicized, session, "The Social Mission of the Humanities," that the subject of the humanities and the public interest really came into focus. This session featured a dialogue between the late A. Bartlett Giamatti, who had not yet given up the presidency of Yale University to become commissioner of baseball, and Norman Podhoretz, the critic and editor of *Commentary* magazine. Responding to President Giamatti and Podhoretz were Henry Rosovsky, former dean and now professor of social science at Harvard, and Cornel West, a professor of the philosophy of religion at the Yale Divinity School. It was in this session that the real issues facing the humanities in contemporary America society were most clearly set forth.

Podhoretz spoke first. The humanities, he said, cannot be justified on practical grounds. Because the knowledge and culture they represent are "good in themselves," their ultimate justification is simply their intrinsic value. From this it follows that the humanities cannot directly help us in the formulation of public policy, nor do they yield any particular political position; nor, indeed, does acquaintance with the humanities necessarily make us morally more upright or more humane—think only of the cultivated Nazi commandants who savored Mozart. Echoing the sentiments expressed in Secretary Bennett's report, Podhoretz identified the chief function of the humanities to be the creation of a "common culture." Central to this view of the humanities is the idea of a more or less generally recognized canon of works that define that common culture and preserve its traditions.

Podhoretz admitted that there will always be disagreement about the composition of the canon at, as it were, its edges; but he claimed that, at least until recently, there has been a widely shared consensus about the core body of works that constitute "the best that has been thought and said."

In one sense, this view of the humanities can be said to be exclusive or elitist, because it presupposes a rigorously defined notion of what it means to be an educated person. But in another sense, it is deeply democratic for it locates authority not in any class or race or sex, but in a tradition before which all are equal. As Podhoretz observed, to the extent that the humanities are crucial to the maintenance of civilized life, it is essential that as many people as possible have the opportunity to steep themselves in the great works of the canon: only thus is high culture preserved and transmitted. Furthermore, as the transmitter of the canon, of what Podhoretz described as our "intellectual patrimony," the humanities have traditionally instilled a sense of the value of the democratic tradition we have inherited. And it is in this respect, he noted, that the humanities *do* have a political dimension, insofar as they rest on a belief in the value and importance of Western culture and the civilization that gave birth to it.

With the social and political upheaval of the sixties and early seventies, Podhoretz continued, this entire conception of the humanities came under radical assault. Not only the idea of a common culture founded on a recognized canon of great works, but the very notion of a politically autonomous realm of culture was dismissed as naïve, ethnocentric, or somehow repressive. Even the fundamental belief in the value of Western culture and civilization—the value, that is to say, of the whole humanistic enterprise—was undermined. And while it is true that the more extreme manifestations of this revolt have disappeared, Podhoretz maintained that the radical attitudes espoused in the sixties and seventies live on in attenuated form in the academy—even, or rather especially, in the humanistic disciplines, in the values and assumptions that typically inform the teaching and study of the humanities. For the most part, he said, a study of the humanities now tends at best to encourage a feeling of "mild contempt" for culture as traditionally defined and at worst to inspire outright hatred of our civilization and everything it stands for. And because of this sedimented radicalism in the academy, the humanities, however much they may still add to an individual's enlightenment and culture, no longer really contribute to the common good.

Not surprisingly, Podhoretz's diagnosis was met with great hostility. I overheard the idea of a common culture, for example, variously described as "moribund," "imperialistic," and "fascist." It was considered to be equally "sexist," I gathered, judging from the knowing looks that his use of the phrase *intellectual patrimony* occasioned. President Giamatti began by telling us that he found Podhoretz's talk "internally contradictory," for is there not a contradiction between asserting the essentially private nature of the humanities and then lamenting that they no longer conduce to the commonweal? In fact, though, President Giamatti's charge depended on distorting Podhoretz's description of the humanities. It is one thing to say that the humanities cannot be justified on instrumental grounds, as Podhoretz did, quite another to say that they are a private affair entirely without social consequence, which no one but President Giamatti thought to propose.

The president of Yale University, who at one time was known as a scholar of Renaissance literature, also came out strongly against the idea of a canon. Instead, he thought that the humanities should encourage "modes of thinking that would discipline the imagination without pretending to direct it"—the idea being, I suppose, that it doesn't much matter what one learns so long as one learns something.* President Giamatti even claimed that this was the "Greek view" of education. Perhaps he meant the view current in contemporary Greece; certainly, the idea that education should seek "to discipline the imagination without pretending to direct it" is completely foreign to the classical ideal of *paideia,* of formative education, as well as the teachings of Plato and Aristotle. One thinks, for example, of the quite definite ideas that Plato expressed about what should and should not be taught in his discussion of education in the third book of *The Republic.* But leaving the Greek view of education to one side, President Giamatti's reservations about the importance of the canon do help us understand his central charge against Podhoretz: that his view of the humanities is "solipsistic" and "spiritually selfish." Basically, President Giamatti presented Podhoretz as an elitist who wanted to

*Perhaps this is what Professor Graff had in mind?

keep culture for himself. But the real difference between them was that Podhoretz wanted the *substance* of the humanities to be as widely available as possible, whereas President Giamatti was happy with what we might call universal schooling—the substance, the content, of what was taught was for him incidental.

If nothing else, President Giamatti exemplified the strategy that Henry Rosovsky, the session's first respondent, identified as the prime imperative for academic administrators: "Be vague." Professor Rosovsky went on to suggest that the hallmark of the humanities was "an eternal dissatisfaction," that the humanities ought in fact to "engender a kind of dissatisfaction," and hence that they "should not be conservative." Against Podhoretz's vision of a common culture, Professor Rosovsky sided with President Giamatti in questioning the desirability of adhering to a canon and in extolling as an alternative to this the ideal of a "multiculture" nourished by disparate sources and traditions. It is worth noting that the word *multiculture* and its variants have become code words for an approach to the humanities that is in effect *anti*cultural—at least anti–high cultural. Part of the rhetoric of "pluralism" and "diversity," the elevation of *multicultural* experience cloaks the abandonment of traditional humanistic culture. It belongs with prattle about the humanities instilling dissatisfaction and the desirability of undermining the traditional canon. Such sentiments are heard everywhere in the academy today, but it did seem odd coming from the lips of a man who in the early seventies, when he was a dean at Harvard, had been a staunch supporter of the canon and one of the chief architects of Harvard's now-dismantled core curriculum. In 1974, faced with the prospect of curricular anarchy, Professor Rosovsky publicly deplored the loss of "an older community of beliefs and values";[42] now he looks to the loss of those beliefs and values as a prelude to the establishment of a multicultural paradise. *Autres temps, autres moeurs.*

VII • GENDER, RACE, AND CLASS

But the most articulate, as well as the most histrionic, response to Podhoretz came from Cornel West. Professor West's performance

[42]Quoted by Gilbert Allardyce, "The Rise and Fall of the Western Civilization Course," *American Historical Review,* vol. 87, no. 3 (June 1982), 696–697.

combined something of Houston Baker's appeal to race with aspects of Margaret Ferguson's generalized discontent with Western liberal society to produce a potent rhetorical effect. Approximating the fervor of a political rally or revival meeting, he clearly won the hearts and minds of the Yale audience. They thrilled to his rhetoric, punctuating his impassioned speech with enthusiastic applause. Professor West warmed up with a few words about "decolonization," "the eclipse of European dominance" in the world, and the disintegration of "white, male, WASP hegemony" in the academy. (I had thought that WASPs were white by definition, but no matter, "white, male, WASP hegemony" has an edifying ring to it.) He pictured the evolution of the humanities in recent years as a reflection of a worldwide struggle for freedom against what it has pleased him to describe elsewhere as "the final fruits of bourgeois humanism: North Atlantic ethnocentrism."[43]

In Professor West's view, the "collapsing consensus" that Podhoretz spoke of tokened not decline but liberation. The sixties, far from being a debacle, were a "watershed" for the humanities. For one thing, the "onslaught" of popular culture that began then has helped undermine elitist notions of high culture. Then, too, the attention lavished on the history and literature of blacks, women, peasants, and other groups has revealed the traditional canon to be the biased, ethnocentric construction that it is. Hence the "self-contempt" that Podhoretz said a study of the humanities tended to instill these days is really "a deeper self-critique" that mirrors important changes in the world ("the eclipse of European dominance," etc.), changes that must be recognized and accommodated "if we are not to blow up the planet."

I hasten to add, though, that in criticizing Podhoretz, Professor West by no means sought to align himself with President Giamatti. On the contrary, he criticized both men for their "lack of historical sense" and their conservatism. (One notes that in the academy the word *conservative* has degenerated into a term of abuse.) Distinguishing between the "battle-ridden neoconservatism" of Podhoretz and the "more charming" conservatism of President Giamatti, Professor West

[43]Cornel West, "Afterword: The Politics of American Neo-Pragmatism," in *Post-Analytic Philosophy,* ed. Cornel West and John Rajchman (New York: Columbia University Press, 1985), 259–275.

wondered whether the "dynamism" championed by President Giamatti didn't at bottom merely represent "the recovery of high-brow classical humanism." He can rest easy on that score, at least.

The real clue to Professor West's view came with his celebration of the incorporation of the New Left into the university. Among other things, he championed the New Left for creating "combat zones" that could challenge the entire ethos of bourgeois humanism that stands behind the humanities as traditionally conceived. And taking issue with Podhoretz's criticism of the intellectual, moral, and political effects of the New Left, Professor West described writers such as Herbert Marcuse and the post–World War II French Marxists as "the best of Western civilization."

It is important to consider Professor West's identification of Herbert Marcuse and the French Marxists as representatives of the best of Western civilization. Just what do these writers and thinkers stand for? What have they contributed to furthering the fundamental principles of the humanities? Consider Louis Althusser, one of the most influential of the French Marxists whom Professor West admires. In an interview that he gave in 1968, this example of the best of Western civilization explained that he had come to philosophy through his attempt to "become a Communist militant" during and after World War II. Having finally understood that "philosophy is fundamentally *political,*" more specifically, that it is a tool of "class struggle," Althusser also realized that "it was not easy to resist the spread of contemporary 'humanist' ideology, and bourgeois ideology's other assaults on Marxism." Being an intellectual, a philosopher, made things especially difficult, he confided. "Proletarians have a 'class instinct' which helps them on the way to proletarian 'class positions.' Intellectuals, on the contrary, have a petty-bourgeois class instinct which fiercely resists this transition."[44] Most would agree, however, that Althusser succeeded rather well in overcoming the specified resistance, even if he finally fell prey to "contemporary humanist ideology" when he confessed to murdering his wife in a fit of insanity in 1980.

Then there is Marcuse. One could turn to any number of his

[44]Louis Althusser, "Philosophy as a Revolutionary Weapon," in *Lenin and Philosophy and Other Essays,* trans. Ben Brewster (New York: Monthly Review Press, 1971), 11–22.

works for an introduction to his view of the value of the humanities—to the "Political Preface" that he added to the 1966 edition of *Eros and Civilization,* for example, where he calls for a thoroughgoing revolt against "the political machine, the corporate machine, the cultural and educational machine" of "affluent western society."[45] What he calls for, in short, is a revolt against just those political, social, and intellectual traditions that define the humanistic endeavor. But perhaps the best précis of Marcuse's thinking about such matters is to be found in his notorious 1965 essay, "Repressive Tolerance."[46] Unable to deny that modern Western democracies offer their citizens an unparalleled degree of personal and political liberty, Marcuse is nevertheless able to denounce the West as essentially "totalitarian" by the simple device of declaring its brand of liberty "repressive" and a product of "false consciousness." (What a versatile tool of obfuscation the notion of "false consciousness" has been, utterly exempt as it is from subservience to mere "empirical reality"!) Indeed, he offers a simple formula for distinguishing between the "repressive tolerance" that expresses itself in the real world in such phenomena as freedom of assembly and the "liberating tolerance" that would seems to occur chiefly in his imagination: "Liberating tolerance," he wrote, "would mean intolerance against movements from the Right, and toleration of movements from the Left."

In brief, then, what Marcuse wants is "not 'equal' but *more* representation of the Left," and he blithely sanctions "extralegal means if the legal ones have proved to be inadequate." In one of the more extraordinary passages of the essay, Marcuse admitted that "extreme suspension of the right of free speech and free assembly is indeed justified only if the whole of society is in extreme danger," but continued immediately to note that

> I maintain that our society is in such an emergency situation. . . . Different opinions and "philosophies" can no longer compete peacefully for adherence and persuasion on rational grounds: the "marketplace of ideas" is organized and delimited by those who de-

[45]Herbert Marcuse, *Eros and Civilization: A Philosophical Inquiry into Freud* (Boston: Beacon Press, 1966), xvii.

[46]Herbert Marcuse, "Repressive Tolerance," in *A Critique of Pure Tolerance,* by Robert Paul Wolff, et al. (Boston: Beacon Press, 1969), 81–123.

> termine the national and the individual interest. In this society, for which the ideologists have proclaimed the "end of ideology," the false consciousness has become the general consciousness—from the government down to its last objects.

There is no escape, apparently—unless, that is, one happens to be blessed, as Marcuse apparently believed himself to be, with the privileged insight, what we might call the "true consciousness," that allows one to penetrate such nearly universal mendacity.

It is in the context of such ideas that we must understand the conception of freedom that underlies Professor West's view of the humanities. Like his heroes, Professor West finds the "ideology of pluralism" suspect because it "domesticates" radical thought. And like them, too, he questions the traditional bourgeois notion of the citizen as a bearer of rights. Instead, he lobbies for an idea of citizenship that would incorporate "collective action," that would "undermine the liberal protection of rights" in favor of a more encompassing ideal—an ideal that aspires to nothing less than coercive control of all thought and expression.

We can begin to appreciate some of the practical effects of Professor West's position by considering the controversy over the issue of free speech that is erupting on many campuses today. There have lately been moves by college and university administrations across the country to circumscribe or prohibit speech and behavior that is considered racially or sexually "insensitive." In an important article on the subject, Chester Finn, former assistant secretary of education, adduces numerous examples: a six-page "antibias code" replete with stiff penalties for violators recently issued by the University of Wisconsin, or the University of Michigan's prohibition of speech that "stigmatizes or victimizes an individual on the basis of race, ethnicity, religion, sex, sexual orientation, creed, national origin, ancestry, age, marital status, handicap" or—my favorite item—"Vietnam-era veteran status."[47] Nor is such legislation limited to state schools. Emory University in Atlanta, the University of Pennsylvania, and Stanford, for example, have all instituted bans on what has come to be called *ethnoviolence.* These restrictions on the kinds of things can be said and talked about

[47]Chester E. Finn, Jr., "The Campus: 'An Island of Repression in a Sea of Freedom,' " *Commentary,* vol. 86, no. 3 (Sept. 1989): 17.

apply inside as well as outside the classroom and they have had, in the words of a brief by the Michigan American Civil Liberties Union, a "chilling effect on the free expression of ideas" in the university.[48]

One event that seemed particularly indicative of the recent trend against free speech in the academy was a weeklong program of panels and workshops that took place at Harvard University under the rubric "AWARE," an acronym that stands for Actively Working Against Racism and Ethnocentricism. Robert Detlefsen, who reported on the AWARE symposium for *The New Republic,* recounted many extreme positions adopted by participants. A former dean at Dartmouth College, for example, suggested that Dartmouth and Harvard were "genocidal in nature" because of their attitudes toward racial issues. But somehow among the most disturbing things in Detlefsen's article is the account of a talk by a Harvard professor of ichthyology who told the AWARE audience that one should never "introduce any sort of thing that might hurt a group" because "the pain that racial insensitivity can create is more important than a professor's academic freedom."[49]

Now we may well want to deplore speech and action that hurts the feelings of others. But what does it mean that the university, traditionally a bastion of free speech and a place where controversial ideas may freely circulate, has begun to encroach even on these ideals in the name of a certain vision of political rectitude? What does it mean, for example, that Dean Hilda Hernandez-Gravelle, whose Office of Race Relations and Minority Affairs at Harvard originated the AWARE program, called for a ban on fifties nostalgia parties because racism was rampant in America in the 1950s? Or that Barbara Johnson, that champion of radical feminism whom me met in the last chapter, should declare at the AWARE symposium that "professors should have less freedom of expression than writers and artists, because professors are supposed to be creating a better world"?

What makes such statements so obnoxious is not simply the extraordinary odor of superior self-righteousness they exude, as if professors and academic deans have some special purchase on creating a better world. There is also the fundamental constitutional issue that

[48]Quoted by Kors, "It's Speech, Not Sex, the Dean Bans Now."

[49]Robert R. Detlefsen, "White Like Me," *The New Republic,* 10 Apr. 1989, 20.

these antiharassment policies violate the right to free speech guaranteed by the First Amendment. As one of the leaders of the Stanford student government admitted, "What we are proposing is not completely in line with the First Amendment. But I'm not sure it should be. We at Stanford are trying to set a different standard from what society at large is trying to accomplish."[50] It is a sobering irony that what began as an appeal by the Left for free speech at Berkeley in the sixties has ended with an equally fervent appeal by the Left for the imposition of censorship. A further irony, as Chester Finn has noted, is that now, when most colleges and universities have given up attempting to act *in loco parentis,* when they are busy installing condom dispensers in dormitories and distributing "safe sex" kits to freshmen, they should suddenly act to curtail radically this one aspect of personal behavior.

The politically motivated origins of this campaign against unpopular ideas is not hard to discern. At a time when the student population at many colleges and universities is becoming increasingly conservative, it is nothing less than an effort by left-leaning faculties and administrations to impose the politics and mind-set of the sixties by fiat. As Alan Charles Kors has noted,

> "harassment policies" at a growing number of universities have used the real need to protect students and employees from sexual and racial abuse as a partisan pretext for . . . "privileging" one particular ideological agenda, and for controlling speech deemed offensive by those designated as victims of American society (including those "victims" about to receive Ivy League degrees!).[51]

Moreover, it is important to note how corrosive unfounded charges of racism, sexism, and the like can be. Sidney Hook got to the heart of the issue when he observed that

> as morally offensive as is the expression of racism wherever it is found, a false charge of racism is equally offensive, perhaps even more so, because the consequences of a false charge of racism enable an authentic racist to conceal his racism by exploiting the loose

[50]Felicity Barringer, "Drives by Campuses to Curb Race Slurs Pose a Speech Issue," *The New York Times,* 25 Apr. 1989.

[51]Kors, "It's Speech, Not Sex, the Dean Bans Now."

> way the term is used to cover up his actions. The same is true of a false charge of sexism or anti-Semitism. This is the lesson we should all have learned from the days of Senator Joseph McCarthy. Because of his false and irresponsible charges of communism against liberals, socialists, and others among his critics, many communists and agents of communist influence sought to pass themselves off as Jeffersonian democrats or merely idealistic reformers. They would all complain they were victims of red-baiting to prevent criticism and exposure.[52]

It is worth pondering Hook's remarks as one attempts to digest the professoriate's smug and unending charges of racism, sexism, elitism, and the rest. What Professor Kors wrote about the University of Pennsylvania's attitude can be applied equally to other institutions intent on mandating virtue for their students and faculty: "In short, Penn is a tolerant and diverse community, and if you do not agree with its particular notions of tolerance and diversity, it will gladly reeducate you."[53]

VIII • A NEW RATIONALE FOR THE HUMANITIES?

Because the second session of Yale's symposium on the humanities and the public interest had sought to dispose of the traditional rationale for the humanities, it seemed only appropriate that the final session should address itself to the question of formulating a new rationale for its discredited predecessor. The session was moderated by Professor Brooks, and featured presentations by Jonathan Culler, one of the authors of *Speaking for the Humanities* and a professor of English and comparative literature at Cornell University, and Vincent Scully, professor of the history of art at Yale. Among the respondants to Professors Culler and Scully was Carolyn G. Heilbrun, an influential academic feminist and professor of English at Columbia University.

Anticipating a central argument of *Speaking for the Humanities,* Professor Culler began by criticizing the traditional rationale for the

[52]Hook, "Stanford Documents," 655.

[53]Kors, "It's Speech, Not Sex, the Dean Bans Now."

humanities as "universalist" and "foundationalist." As we have seen, this is practically de rigueur for right-thinking academics. The pretension to be universalist, he said, was primarily a political consideration: The humanities as traditionally conceived had presumed to speak universally to the human condition, but had in fact represented a narrow "white male" viewpoint. The attempt to be foundationalist involves epistemological considerations: The humanities had pretended to provide a foundation for both thought and values, but radical criticism in the last decades had exposed the fictional, and ideologically motivated, ground of that pretense. Professor Culler did not, however, attempt to formulate the new rationale for the humanities that he demanded, but instead offered a list of "divided imperatives" that he thought the humanities ought to heed. It seems that he may be better at deconstruction than construction, however: the list he offered was fairly vague, even banal. The humanities ought to "assume unity" but also assert the value of other cultures, and so on, although it must be admitted that Professor Culler did sprinkle his talk with appropriately combative rhetoric and wonderful-sounding, Nietzschean proclamations such as the suggestion that thought really becomes valuable "only when it is extreme."

As an example of the kind of retrograde thinking he disparaged, Professor Culler cited a letter he had recently received from a dean at St. John's College in Annapolis, Maryland, inviting him to lecture there. St. John's offers a traditional "great books" curriculum—tailored to include classic developments in modern science and mathematics—and the dean, explaining the nature of the curriculum, described it as based on the "greatest books" of the Western tradition. This Professor Culler and his audience found quite risible, for after all what did the dean from St. John's mean by the "greatest books"? Only books written by "white Western males before 1900," of course, something that for Professor Culler seemed to demonstrate how parochial, not to say ethnocentric and sexist, his correspondent's notion of education must be. (For the record, it should be noted that students do read some women and twentieth-century authors at St. John's.) Professor Culler never really specified his own idea of a good college curriculum, but one can bet that it wouldn't be ethnocentric. Indeed, it's not even clear that it would be anthropocentric, because Professor Culler wondered in passing whether a view of the humanities based exclusively on a study of mankind wouldn't be guilty of "speciesism."

Mercifully, Professor Culler did not pursue this absurdity, although it was taken up by Vincent Scully, who began his talk by suggesting that what we needed was not so much a new rationale for the humanities as a new rationale for "animality." Professor Scully then treated us to a slide show that opened, as such slide shows must, with a picture of the snow shovel Marcel Duchamp presented as a work of art in 1915. What won't be taken as a work of art today? Professor Scully asked, and then went on to share with his audience a number of other truly novel ideas: that the movies and television have emerged as the dominant style of modern life, for example, or that the artist must be "open-minded, pluralistic, poised for surprise."

Carolyn Heilbrun began her response on a melancholy note by observing that even now, even at a symposium on the humanities at Yale in 1986, she was the only woman on the panel. And I was surprised, I must confess, that Professor Brooks could have made this blunder. Surely he must have known that such a discrepancy in numbers would be held up for criticism. And as an academic administrator, he must also have known that the important thing in such situations is not to get the appropriate speakers for the occasion but to assemble a panel with the correct ethnic, social, and sexual mix. In any case, Professor Heilbrun went on to note that, although she was also the oldest person on the panel, it was the symposium's youngest representatives, Professors Culler and West, who spoke for her. She, too, believed that college should "teach us to be dissatisfied" and that thought is really valuable only when it is extreme. In addition, as the panel's official feminist, she also told us that it is the questions that women can ask about the canon that are the important questions. While she did not specify what the important questions might be, one got a pretty good idea of the kind of thing she had in mind when she criticized Professor Scully for presenting Michelangelo's depiction of the creation of man as representative of the human condition. After all, both God and Adam were—well, there's no getting around it—they were depicted as male, and how universal can that be?

This session, and the symposium, ended with a few comments and questions. Particularly important were Professor Heilbrun's assertion that our reading of texts is inescapably "ideological" and Professor Brooks's concluding observation that, because the humanities are "inherently subversive," the recent developments in the academy that people such as Secretary Bennett and Podhoretz bemoan actually ought to be taken as signs of health. Together, these comments seemed to epitomize the proceedings in New Haven that day, and are worth examining more closely.

The idea that all reading is ideological has gained great currency in literary studies in recent years. Among other things, it implies that we are imprisoned by our point of view, that our language, our social or ethnic background, or our sex inescapably determine the way we understand things. But are we so imprisoned? Granted that such contingencies *influence* our point of view, do they finally determine it? We shall return to this question in Chapter Six. But for the moment, let us merely ask what it might mean to say that "all reading is ideological." It is important to realize that ideologies are not simply a set of guiding opinions; rather, as the social philosopher Hannah Arendt pointed out some years ago, they are "isms which to the satisfaction of their adherents can explain everything and every occurrence by deducing it from a single premise."[54] In this sense, Arendt noted, an ideology differs from a simple opinion "in that it claims to possess either the key to history, or the solution for all 'riddles of the universe,' or the intimate knowledge of the hidden universal laws which are supposed to rule nature and man."[55] Yet it is precisely this sort of distinction that the contention that all reading is ideological dismisses. It dismisses, in other words, the critical distinction between a point of view and an ideology, between an individual perspective on the world—which *as* a perspective is open to challenge, accommodation, correction—and an *idée fixe.*

And in this context, given that Matthew Arnold has been so consistently castigated by champions of "new rationales" for the humanities, it is worth noting that in his once-celebrated essay "The Function of Criticism at the Present Time" (1865) Arnold identified "disinterestedness" as the chief mark of responsible criticism. In describing criticism as disinterested, Arnold did not mean that it presumes to speak without reference to a particular point of view, although critics of the idea often so caricature it. Rather, he meant a

[54]Hannah Arendt, *The Origins of Totalitarianism* (New York: Harcourt Brace Jovanovich, 1973), 468.

[55]Ibid., 159.

habit of inquiry that keeps "aloof from what is called 'the practical view of things' . . . by steadily refusing to lend itself to any . . . ulterior, political, practical considerations about ideas."[56] In contemporary terms, we might say that Arnold looked to criticism to provide a bulwark *against* ideology, against interpretations that are subordinated to essentially political interests. The ideal of such disinterested criticism is rejected by many contemporary critics as naïve (or worse), although the criticism they practice is no more astute than Arnold's but only, alas, more ideological.

Arnold is also relevant in considering the oft-voiced contention that education ought to instill dissatisfaction or, to use Professor Brooks's more dramatic formulation, that the humanities are "inherently subversive." Such sentiments are so widely shared in fashionable academic circles today that it is almost taken for granted that the function of education is not to impart knowledge but to subvert, to excite dissatisfaction. Thus it is that *Speaking for the Humanities* assures us that "the humanities are better conceived as fields of exploration and critique rather than materials for transmission." Behind this idea is a deep suspicion of authority, a suspicion that would have us collapse another critical distinction: the distinction between authority and authoritarianism—between, that is to say, *legitimate* power whose aim is unity and *arbitrary* power whose aim is domination. In the wake of this collapse, the very idea of authority has become suspect. In a thoughtful article titled "The Future of Tradition," David Bromwich, a professor of English at Yale, suggests that a humanist is someone who "rejects authority" but "respects tradition."[57] But this tidy slogan misses something important; it is doubtful whether the humanities can survive in any recognizable form without accepting the authority of tradition. It is indeed for this reason that, in "The Literary Influence of Academies," Arnold praised the willing "deference to a standard higher than one's own habitual standard in intellectual matters" as the result of a "sensitiveness of intelligence."[58] And thus it is, too, that Hannah Arendt suggested that "conservatism, in the sense of conser-

[56]Matthew Arnold, "The Function of Criticism at the Present Time," in *The Portable Matthew Arnold,* Lionel Trilling ed. (New York: Viking Press, 1972), 248.

[57]David Bromwich, "The Future of Tradition: Notes on the Crisis of the Humanities," *Dissent,* vol. 36, no. 4 (Fall 1989), 542.

[58]Matthew Arnold, "The Literary Influence of Academies," in *The Portable Matthew Arnold,* Lionel Trilling ed. (New York: Viking Press, 1972), 273.

vation, is of the essence of the educational activity, whose task is always to cherish and protect something." "The real difficulty in modern education," Arendt wrote,

> lies in the fact that, despite all the fashionable talk about a new conservatism [Arendt was writing in 1958], even that minimum of conservation and the conserving attitude without which education is simply not possible is in our time extraordinarily hard to achieve. . . . The crisis of authority in education is most closely connected with the crisis of tradition, that is with the crisis in our attitude toward the realm of the past. . . . The problem of education in the modern world lies in the fact that by its very nature it cannot forgo [*sic*] either authority or tradition, and yet it must proceed in a world that is neither structured by authority nor held together by tradition.[59]

"Neither structured by authority nor held together by tradition"—in the end, this would seem to describe the goal of the new rationale for the humanities envisioned at Yale and elsewhere. And, of course, the real casualties are the students and junior faculty, who often haven't the foggiest notion of the value of the tradition they have been taught to disparage. The senior faculty at least are generally old enough to recognize what it is they are abandoning. Champions of the new rationale like to pretend that they are merely thinking more critically than the tradition had allowed. In fact, though, they have often degenerated from the rigors of criticism to a rootless and sharply politicized nihilism. A closer look at the language and the guiding ideas of some of those proposing such new rationales will give us fuller appreciation of what is at stake when tradition and authority are rechristened as the enemies rather than the preservers of culture.

[59]Hannah Arendt, "The Crisis in Education," in *Between Past and Future: Eight Exercises in Political Thought* (New York: Penguin, 1978), 192–193, 195.

CHAPTER 3

THE OCTOBER SYNDROME

I • THROUGH A GLASS EYE, DARKLY

Few things have contributed more to the debasement of contemporary intellectual and cultural life, especially in the academy, than the honored place now accorded to deliberate obscurity. Deconstruction and semiology, structuralism and poststructuralism: These and kindred obfuscatory theories imported from the Continent are favored staples in much of what passes for intellectual discourse today. Combined with the unexamined assumption that the realm of high culture—indeed, that the very *idea* of high culture—is irredeemably tainted by political interests, this triumph of opacity has largely succeeded in transforming serious discussion—as well as the teaching—of art, literature, and culture into a congeries of hermetic language games.

In our academic journals, university classrooms, and even in our museums' exhibition catalogs, arcane, pseudophilosophical jargon and radical sentiment compete to forestall genuine engagement with aesthetic or intellectual issues. Alas, only the radical sentiment receives clear and frank expression. As we have seen, even as clarity and intelligibility are spurned as simpleminded, the traditional ideal of disinterested scholarship is bluntly dismissed as a cover for class or ethnic privilege and Western culture itself is pilloried as a bastion of unacknowledged sexist and imperialistic attitudes. Given this intellectual climate, it is hardly surprising that criticism should degenerate into a species of cynicism for which nothing is properly understood until it is exposed as corrupt, duplicitous, or hypocritical. Nor is it surprising that the ideal of art or literature as a relatively autonomous endeavor—an endeavor, that is to say, that is free from direct political imperatives—should be ridiculed as a fantasy perpetrated by the entrenched and parochial interests of bourgeois taste. Today, while criticism—or what generally goes under the more impressive-sounding name of "critical theory"—pursues its polysyllabic hunt for suppressed political motives, many artists and writers have likewise adapted themselves to the prevailing *ethos* and have more and more come to see themselves primarily as purveyors of politically correct attitudes and politically approved notions of social enlightenment.

There can be little doubt that the primary source of these evils is the academy. For it is precisely the predominance of aggressively opaque rhetoric and political posturing in the humanities departments of our colleges and universities that has validated and, as it were, underwritten the proliferation of such practices. In seeking to understand the origin of this cultural debacle, however, one must not underestimate the role played by those multitudinous and influential props of university life: academic journals devoted, at least ostensibly, to the arts and the humanities. *Diacritics, Critical Inquiry, Tel Quel, New Literary History, Representations, Yale French Studies:* these are a few of the more influential academic organs peddling politicized obscurantism. It is in the pages of such journals that the latest personalities, chic theories, and critical vocabularies are auditioned and, if found acceptable, are trotted out over and over again until they become verbal tics, part of the atmosphere of academic exchange and requisite equipment for any graduate student or assistant professor with his eye on the grail of tenure. Lacan, Benjamin, Derrida, de Man, Bataille, Jameson, Althusser, Barthes, Foucault—these and a few other names from the current pantheon are scattered like confetti through their pages; "logocentric," "phallocentric," "imperialist," "aura," "strategy," "marginalization," "text," "signifier"—these are some of the more attractive terms that one finds repeated *ad nauseam.*

This is not to suggest that these journals—and their number, be assured, is legion—are all of a piece. Each has its own identifying wrinkle, its distinctive editorial personality. Yet while none is in any sense popular or widely read, some few have emerged as peculiarly influential and representative of the spirit of politicized obscurantism under which our cultural life labors. Of these representative few, none is more political, more opaque, or more influential in certain "advanced" circles than the quarterly *October.* So consummately does *October* epitomize these qualities, and so successful has it been in combining fashionable academic jargon with radical political ideology, that one is tempted to single it out as a specimen case. The recent publication of *October: The First Decade, 1976–1986*[1] provides a good opportunity to consider the magazine in some detail, to catalog its salient features, and to discuss some of its recurrent themes. The more closely one examines its contribution to current intellectual and artistic debate, the more one is tempted to regard *October* not simply as a magazine but as a *syndrome,* a set of symptoms typifying a somewhat amorphous but nonetheless unmistakably prevalent malaise affecting intellectual life in and out of the academy.

II • THE OCTOBER SYNDROME

Started in the spring of 1976, *October* soon established itself as a cynosure of approved opinions in the confusing firmament of advanced literary and artistic taste. In many respects, the *October* syndrome was already in full flower in the inaugural issue. Here readers were treated to a tortuous lead essay by the much revered Michel Foucault on Magritte's famous drawing *Ceci n'est pas une pipe.* (Surrealism and semiotics: what a perfect combination with which to begin *October!*) Among other delicacies included in that first issue were an essay by Rosalind Krauss on the video "art" of Vito Acconci, Lynda Benglis, and others. Here is a sample sentence: "One could say that if the reflexiveness of modernist art is a *dédoublement* or doubling back in order to locate the object (and thus the objective conditions of one's experience), the mirror-reflection of absolute feedback is a process of bracketing out the object."[2] There were also some notes on filmmaking by Hollis Frampton ("The mode we call reading entails a correct extrapolation of the axiomatic substructure from the artist's immediately apprehensible tradition,"[3] etc.) and the first part of a three-part essay by Jeremy Gilbert-Rolfe and John Johnston that pretended to

[1] Annette Michelson, Rosalind Krauss, Douglas Crimp, and Joan Copjec, eds., *October: The First Decade, 1976–1986* (Cambridge: M.I.T. Press, 1987). Unless otherwise noted, quotations in this chapter are from this volume.

[2] *October* 1 (Spring 1976): 57.

[3] Ibid., 106.

discover thematic similarities between Thomas Pynchon's novel *Gravity's Rainbow* (1973) and Robert Smithson's massive "earth work," *Spiral Jetty* (1969–1970). "In *Gravity's Rainbow,*" we discover in that essay, "digression becomes the whole through an approach to writing which, again as in Cézanne, unifies all data by insisting on a model which substitutes redistribution for climax."[4]

October's influence and distinctive character owe much to two of its founding editors, Rosalind Krauss, the well known art critic and Distinguished Professor of Art History at Hunter College and the Graduate Center, City University of New York, and Annette Michelson, the veteran critic and professor of "cinema studies" at New York University. (The other founding editor, the critic and painter Jeremy Gilbert-Rolfe, left the magazine after three issues.) Professor Krauss, especially, has been a moving force in the world of academic art criticism. The recipient of many honors, her extraordinarily hermetic writings as well as her teaching and editorial proclivities have exerted a great influence on contemporary academic art criticism, helping to shape the substance and style of the work of many students, art critics, and professors of art history.

In the introductory note to their first issue, the editors reveal that the journal was named partly in "celebration" of the heyday of the Russian avant-garde that was inaugurated by the Bolshevik revolution of October 1917, partly in commemoration of Sergei Eisenstein's 1928 film *October* (better known as *Ten Days That Shook the World*), which itself was made to commemorate that wonderful event. Indeed, in bringing *October* to the world, they hoped to replicate and abet for our own time that fusion of avant-garde art and revolutionary politics that has been one of the abiding dreams of certain utopian Marxists for much of this century. Despite a promise to include work that is "at times idealist" as well as work that is "materialist," they frankly acknowledged that *October* was inspired by a commitment to the Marxist dictum that art and culture are essentially reflections of economic processes. "*October*'s strong theoretical emphasis will be mediated by its consideration of present artistic practice," the editors assured us. "It is our conviction that this is possible only within a sustained awareness of the economic and social bases of that practice, of the material

[4]Ibid., 58.

conditions of its origins and processes, and of their intensely problematic nature at this particular time."

The *October* syndrome not only involves a loving embrace of cultural Marxism (it embodies in the purest form imaginable what Frederick Crews identified as Left Eclecticism), but also, as a kind of corollary, a violent attack on middle-class culture and society, especially in its American varieties. The phrase "intensely problematic at this particular time" already points in that direction, for what the editors mean to imply is that contemporary artistic practice in America is crippled by being insufficiently aware of its social and economic bases. And that's only the beginning. It is a prominent feature of the *October* syndrome that, whenever possible, the discussion of art or ideas should be extended to include an indictment of Western capitalist society. Again, the editors' note in their inaugural issue provides a preliminary taste of the procedure. *October,* they write,

> is a reference which remains, for us, more than exemplary; it is instructive. For us, the argument regarding Socialist Realism is nonexistent. Art begins and ends with a recognition of its conventions. We will not contribute to that social critique which, swamped by its own disingenuousness, gives credence to such an object of repression as a mural about the war in Vietnam, painted by a white liberal resident in New York, a war fought for the most part by ghetto residents commanded by elements drawn from the southern lower-middle-class.[5]

The contention that "art begins and ends with a recognition of its conventions" is something we shall have occasion to consider more closely below; it, too, is an essential feature of the *October* syndrome. (As indeed is the description of a work of art as "an object of repression" and the blithe rejection of the controversy over Socialist Realism, as if that Stalinist interdiction of art were some negligible disturbance in an otherwise glorious cultural and social renaissance.) But the editors' concluding observation is one especially worth pausing over. "Elements drawn from the southern lower-middle-class"? One wonders what these connoisseurs of contempt would have said had they discovered such snobbery and class prejudice in, say, the writings

[5]Ibid., 4–5.

of other white liberal residents of New York.

In any event, *October: The First Decade* provides an even more splendid showcase for the *October* syndrome. The opacity, the radical pronouncements, the obsession with violence and perverse sexuality, the assumption that art should be primarily a form of political activism: It's all vividly displayed in this collection of two dozen pieces. Consisting mostly of essays, *October: The First Decade* also includes interviews, portfolios of photographs, translations of historical documents, and a translation of a long poem about sex and language by the German writer Peter Handke. Its contents are arranged under six categories: "The Index," "Historical Materialism," "Critique of Institutions," "Psychoanalysis," "Rhetoric," and "The Body." The tenor of the volume can be gleaned by sampling the titles of its contributions: "Index of the Absent Wound (Monograph on a Stain)," "Mimicry and Legendary Psychasthenia," "From Faktura to Factography," "The Judgment Seat of Photography," "Of Mimicry and Man: The Ambivalence of Colonial Discourse," and "On the Eve of the Future: The Reasonable Facsimile and the Philosophical Toy." Speaking of "The Index," one could have wished that the editors or M.I.T. Press had seen fit to provide the book with one—and that they had provided some identifying material on the contributors.

Before turning to the particular works anthologized here, however, we must sample the prefatory remarks supplied by the editors. Alluding once again to Eisenstein's film *October* and the revolutionary ethos of the Russian avant-garde after 1917 as the magazine's inspiration, they declare that "*October* is emblematic for us of a specific historical moment in which artistic practice joined with critical theory in the project of social construction." In other words—although, of course, they never put it like this—the term *October* commended itself because of its association with a moment in which art was enlisted in the service of Communist ideology and propaganda. In this context—the context of an "artistic practice" joining with "critical theory in the project of social construction"—they note that the legend appearing on the cover of every issue of the magazine, "Art | Theory | Criticism | Politics," expresses the "conjunction" they seek to realize in the material they publish. A more truthful advertisement for the contents of *October,* however, would be "Art = Theory = Criticism = Politics."

Like so many people affected by the *October* syndrome these days, the editors of *October* look especially to Russian constructivism as a model in their struggle against the depredations and superficialities of contemporary Western culture. The deliberate blurring of the boundary between aesthetics and politics, the intoxication of succumbing to vanguard revolutionary sentiment, the rejection of cultural activities not amenable to the cause of the socialist renovation of society: All this recommended constructivism to the editors of *October.* Unfortunately, that golden revolutionary moment was difficult to sustain. After one of their frequent assurances that their fondness for postrevolutionary Russia is not colored by nostalgia (a prime bourgeois vice, nostalgia), the editors explain that "we wished to claim that the unfinished, analytic project of constructivism—aborted by the consolidation of the Stalinist bureaucracy, distorted by the recuperation of the Soviet avant-garde into the mainstream of Western idealist aesthetics—was required for a consideration of the aesthetic practices of our own time."

Please note the argument: Constructivism was both "aborted by the consolidation of the Stalinist bureaucracy" as well as "distorted" by being assimilated "into the mainstream of Western idealist aesthetics." Let's leave to one side the dubious claim that the achievements of Russian constructivism—think only of artists such as Malevich and Rodchenko—can be said to have been "distorted" by being assimilated to the idealist tradition of Western art. For our understanding of the *October* syndrome, the important thing is the principle that any criticism of Stalinism or totalitarianism must be ritually followed up with a criticism of the United States or Western culture or capitalist (actually, I believe the required phrase is "late capitalist") society.

One of the central appeals of the *October* syndrome, the feature that perhaps more than any other ensures its great contemporary relevance, is its contention that the art and activist politics of the 1960s and early 1970s marked an exuberant reflowering of the kind of revolutionary spirit that enlivened the constructivist movement in the early years of the Bolshevik revolution. "The 1960s," we are told, "had witnessed . . . extraordinary developments in the visual and temporal arts: in painting, sculpture, dance, performance, and film." But to understand and perpetuate these extraordinary developments, we are now urged to resuscitate "the kind of critical theory" that burgeoned in the Soviet Union sixty or seventy years ago. Precisely this is the task that the editors of *October* set for themselves.

Continuing "the unfinished project of the 1960s" has not, one gathers, been an easy task. For one thing, just when the "extraordinary developments" of the sixties and seventies were beginning to get going, bang, a period of reaction set in. Then, too, the dazzling, promiscuous display of new styles and pseudostyles that marked the period has been misunderstood by others. "We did not see this juncture as that of the vaunted 'death of the avant-garde' and a new 'pluralism.' We saw it rather as that of late capitalism, a time of continued struggle to radicalize cultural practices, and of the marginalization of those attempts through the revival of traditional artistic and discursive tendencies."

In the face of this nefarious attempt to exclude ("marginalize") certain artistic practices and to revive "traditional artistic and discursive tendencies"—such tendencies, it is worth noting, as easel painting, figure drawing, and writing intelligible prose—the editors of *October* considered their work on the magazine to be "the necessary response to what was *once again* a consolidation of reactionary forces within both the political and cultural spheres." (Emphasis added.) "Once again"? The previous "consolidation of reactionary forces," remember, referred to Stalinism; this time it refers to . . . well, to American society under the leadership of Jimmy Carter and Ronald Reagan.

To appreciate just how bad things are under the jackboot of American democracy in the late twentieth century, one need only attend to the plaintive cry of the editors' peroration. It brings together so many of the political features of the *October* syndrome that it is worth quoting at some length. "We in New York," they wrote

> saw our community forced out of the SoHo they had helped to create, forced in turn to collaborate in the eviction of even more marginal populations from the Lower East Side, as the creation of a new art district was conscripted as a wedge for real-estate development. . . . We saw, at the same time, the very artistic experimentation that we had associated with the SoHo community abandoned in favor of the production of luxury objects for consumption and investment, often now by multinational corporations. . . . We watched

> in dismay as art institutions resurrected the claims of disinterestedness. . . .
>
> Our attention also had to be directed toward the operations within these institutions [the artist's studio, the gallery and museum, the corporate patron, the discipline of art history] of a system of privilege that rewarded the masculine and ignored the rest, that addressed itself to a male subject that it took as adequate indicator of the universal. A radical ignorance with respect to sexual difference had to be confronted. Women had to be written into historical and contemporary cultural practices as producers and as addressees. This task would entail, however, more than a simple retrieval of women from neglected historical archives or the support of contemporary women's work. It would also entail a reconception of the scotoma that kept women from sight not as an impediment to be removed but as a process of vision itself.[6]

So many complaints in so little space! SoHo became expensive; the fledgling galleries of New York's Lower East Side were dupes of the real estate developers; some of the young artists of the sixties grew up and began making money (and, what is worse, selling their art not only to corporations but, evil of evils, to *multinational* corporations—Margaret Ferguson, where are you?); some museums turned away from the politicization of art and attempted once more to deal with art "disinterestedly," i.e., as art instead of as a form of political activism; and on and on. Obviously we are dealing with a late-capitalist plot of terrifying dimensions.

But while we are on the subject of abandoning "experimentation" in "the SoHo community . . . in favor of the production of luxury objects for consumption and investment," perhaps we should reacquaint ourselves with the beginning of Janet Malcolm's 1986 profile of Ingrid Sischy in *The New Yorker.* Sischy was then the editor of *Artforum,* a journal with fewer scholarly pretensions than *October,* but no less a dispenser of opaque and fashionably politicized cant about art and culture. Malcolm's article dilates not only on Sischy's career at *Artforum* but the whole superchic downtown art scene. With unerring journalistic instinct, Malcolm opened her article by recounting a visit to Rosalind Krauss. "Rosalind Krauss's loft, on Greene Street," Malcolm began,

[6]Michelson et al., eds., *October: The First Decade,* x–xi.

> is one of the most beautiful living places in New York. Its beauty has a dark, forceful, willful character. Each piece of furniture and every object of use or decoration has evidently had to pass a severe test before being admitted into this disdainfully interesting room—a long, mildly begloomed rectangle with tall windows at either end, a *sachlich* white kitchen area in the center, a study, and a sleeping balcony. An arrangement of geometric dark-blue armchairs around a coffee table forms the loft's sitting room, also furnished with, among other rarities, an antique armchair on splayed, carved feet and upholstered in a dark William Morris fabric; an assertive all-black Minimalist shaped-felt piece; a strange black-and-white photograph of ocean water; and a gold owl-shaped Art Deco clock.[7]

Could it be that even Rosalind Krauss has been "conscripted as a wedge for real-estate development"? Or is this merely an illustration of the old adage that living well is the best revenge?

III • RATS, CAPITALISM, AND OTHER ARTISTIC PHENOMENA

Unfortunately, a full appreciation of the *October* syndrome requires that one consider more than these rather programmatic statements about *October*'s predecessors and aspirations. One must also examine some of its chief arguments, recurrent themes, and stylistic habits. Perhaps the single most important contention advanced by the *October* set is the idea that "art begins and ends with a recognition of its conventions." No doubt this statement is susceptible to a variety of interpretations. But when considered as part of the *October* syndrome, it means that our chief interest in art should not be in the art itself—in whatever special perception of beauty or sudden insight it might be capable of communicating—but rather in the "strategies" (to use that indispensable critical term) that the art employs to question its own formal and social presuppositions. In this sense, art becomes a kind of *meta-art,* art whose chief concern is with its social, economic, and conceptual presuppositions, just as criticism becomes meta-criticism, criticism that is concerned more with its own methodology than with the aesthetic substance of art.

Douglas Crimp provides a sterling example of one aspect of this

[7] Janet Malcolm, "Ingrid Sischy." *The New Yorker,* Oct. 20, 1986, 49.

procedure in his essay "The Art of Exhibition." Discussing the Documenta Exhibition of 1982, Crimp expresses his outrage that credence is given to an idealizing view of art, a view of art that values art for its aesthetic or even its spiritual qualities. (As Professor Krauss put it in another *October* essay, one not included in this volume, "by now we find it indescribably embarrassing to mention *art* and *spirit* in the same sentence."[8]) For his part, Crimp combats the idealization of art by reminding his readers of the large number of homeless people in New York City and the large number of rats found in a lot next to his apartment building. This provides an occasion to castigate former Mayor Edward Koch ("the most reactionary mayor in New York's recent history," etc.) and, of course, ex-President Reagan, and to praise artists such as Christy Rupp, who specializes in producing images of attacking rats, and Jenny Holzer, whose art consists of slogans pasted on city walls, engraved on stone benches, or immortalized in the flashing lights of electronic signboards.

Both artists, Crimp assures us, stand outside the nasty, inequitable system of established galleries and museums, and both produce "works manufactured cheap and sold cheap, quite unlike the paintings and sculptures within museum buildings." Well, Crimp is surely correct that their works are "quite unlike" the paintings and sculptures one *used* to find in museums. I wonder, though, if he has been following Holzer's career lately—since, for example, she was selected by a panel of distinguished museum directors and curators to represent the United States at the 1990 Venice Biennale (the first woman so honored), since her photograph appeared on the front page of *The New York Times,* since her electronic signboards have been fetching (at last count) between $30,000 and $50,000 apiece, since the Solomon R. Guggenheim Museum in New York mounted a large installation of her work late in 1989? "Protect Me From What I Want," "Abuse of Power Should Come As No Surprise": these are some of the artistic masterpieces that have made Holzer famous. She calls them "mock clichés," but I believe she is altogether too modest: they are the real thing, and one only wonders how well she—or her champion Crimp—feels she is doing at resisting the depredations of museums "whose

[8]Rosalind E. Krauss, "Grids," in *The Originality of the Avant-Garde and Other Modernist Myths* (Cambridge: M.I.T. Press, 1985), 13.

real but disguised condition is that of the international market for art, dominated increasingly by corporate speculation"?

There is a good deal about corporate speculation and real estate in the *October* reader. Instead of an examination of the *art* of New York's Lower East Side, for example, we find an essay about the social and economic effects of the gentrification of the area. And instead of an examination of the artist's studio as a place where art is made, we find a dissection of the studio as the "material presupposition" of art "production." In "The Function of the Studio" we learn that "analysis of the art system must inevitably be carried on in terms of the studio as the *unique space* of production and the museum as the *unique space* of exposition. Both must be investigated as customs, the ossifying customs of art." Why, you might ask, are the customs (presumably, the author means "conventions") of art necessarily ossifying? We are never told, but we do discover that "the studio is a place of multiple activities: production, storage, and finally, if all goes well, distribution. It is a kind of commercial depot." Yes, sure, an artist wants to sell his works. But what is of permanent interest about an artist's studio is precisely what *distinguishes* it from a commercial depot. And about that side of studio life, the aesthetic side, *October* has nothing to say.

The large-scale shift away from a concern with the aesthetic substance of art helps explain a number of salient features of the *October* syndrome, not least its obsession with photography and film. (There are more pieces devoted to photography and film in *October: The First Decade* than to any other medium.) The favored place accorded to photography and film in certain critical and artistic circles today is a complex subject well worth meditating on. Professor Kaplan has shown us that even trash such as MTV rock videos can serve as grist for the academic grinder. Professor Krauss, who has not yet supplied us with an interpretation of rock video, tends to prefer avant-garde videos and photography, in which she finds a deeper (and, I daresay, darker) sexual charge than most of us could have ever imagined. For example, in another of her *October* essays that does not appear in this reader, she meditates on the "phallicism" implicit in two photographs: a self-portrait by Florence Henri and Man Ray's *Monument to de Sade,* a photograph of a woman's buttocks on which is superimposed the outline of an inverted cross. But more remarkable than the discovery of "phallicism" where it exists only by dint of ingenious hermeneutical imputation are the conclusions that Professor Krauss draws from her discovery. For the phallicism that is said to be implicit "in the whole photographic enterprise of framing and thereby capturing a subject . . . can be generalized way beyond the specifics of sexual imagery to a structural logic."[9] Among much else, then, Professor Krauss would have us believe that photography is itself an act of sexual conquest, that composing an object in the viewfinder and clicking the shutter are somehow analogous to sexual intercourse.

The attraction of film, video, and photography for those cynical about the claims of traditional art and infatuated with the exhibitionism and surface glitter of "performance art" goes beyond Professor Krauss's rather specialized taste, however. The important thing to grasp is that the appeal of these fashionable art forms has little to do with any specifically *aesthetic* or *artistic* potential they may have. On the contrary, the chief appeal of photography, film, and video is that their "mechanical reproducibility" (to adapt a phrase from Walter Benjamin's adored essay "The Work of Art in the Age of Mechanical Reproduction") promises to demystify both the work of art as a uniquely valuable object and the artist as a uniquely talented, individual sensibility. In other words, one reason photography and film are so highly touted by the *October* set is because they promise to reduce art and artistic creation to the status of an industrialized process. As Professor Krauss puts it near the end of "Notes on the Index: Seventies Art in America," photography "demands that the work be viewed as a deliberate short-circuiting of issues of style. Countermanding the artist's possible formal intervention in creating the work is the overwhelming physical presence of the original object."[10]

A similar set of concerns motivates Benjamin H. D. Buchloh's lugubrious essay "From Faktura to Factography." Buchloh begins by criticizing the founding director of the Museum of Modern Art, Alfred H. Barr, for being blind to the true revolutionary content of Soviet avant-garde "production," especially photography. (This, by the way, is another tic that the *October* syndrome has inherited from the rhetoric of Marxism and Russian constructivism: Instead of speak-

[9]Rosalind E. Krauss, "The Photographic Conditions of Surrealism," in *The Originality of the Avant-Garde and Other Modernist Myths* (Cambridge: M. I. T. Press, 1985), 91.

[10]Rosalind E. Krauss, "Notes on the Index: Seventies Art in America," in *October: The First Decade,* ed. Michelson et al., 14.

ing of making or, heaven forfend, of *creating* art, one speaks of artistic or cultural "production.") Never mind that Alfred Barr did more than any other single individual to bring the art of the Soviet avant-garde, including the art of photomontage that Buchloh so admires, to the attention of the American public: His unforgivable mistake was to view it as, yes, as *art,* not as a form of political propaganda.* In Buchloh's view, the real value of the avant-garde photography that emerged from constructivism was that it "had deliberately and systematically disassociated itself" from the framework of modernism "in order to lay the foundations of an art production that would correspond to the needs of a newly industrialized collective society."[11] Hence, what's so wonderful about a certain species of avant-garde photography is that it allows one to forget about art and get on with the business of "social production."

Buchloh's essay is also useful as yet another example of how the *October* syndrome requires that every mention of totalitarianism implicate Western capitalism and the United States in the general infamy. He begins by lamenting that El Lissitzky and Walter Benjamin's "media optimism . . . prevented them from recognizing that the attempt to create conditions of a simultaneous collective reception for the new audiences of the industrialized state would very soon issue into the preparation of an arsenal of totalitarian, Stalinist propaganda in the Soviet Union. What is worse," Buchloh continued,

> it would deliver the aesthetics and technology of propaganda to the Italian Fascist and German Nazi regimes. And only a little later we see the immediate consequences of Lissitzky's new montage techniques and photofrescoes in their successful adaptation for the ideological needs of American politics and the campaigns for the acceleration of capitalist development through consumption. *Thus, what in Lissitzky's hands had been a tool of instruction, political education, and the raising of consciousness was rapidly transformed into an instrument for prescribing the silence of conformity and obedience.*[12]

*It is worth noting that *October* devoted a large part of its Winter 1978 issue to the diary Barr kept while traveling in the Soviet Union in 1927 and 1928. Thus while the *October* crowd is prepared to honor Barr as a kind of pilgrim to the anointed land, in the end they criticize him for failing to understand the true, i.e., Marxist, cultural, and political significance of his own experience.

[11]Benjamin H. D. Buchloh, "From Faktura to Factography," in *October: The First Decade,* ed. Michelson et al., 102.

[12]Ibid., 103. (Emphasis added.)

That is, the adoption of montage and kindred techniques in America has been used to prescribe "the silence of conformity and obedience." And if the message was not clear enough the first time around, Buchloh recapitulates his main point in his concluding sentence: "at the cross-section of politically emancipatory productivist aesthetics and the transformation of modernist montage aesthetics into an instrument of mass education and enlightenment, we find not only its imminent transformation into totalitarian propaganda, but also its successful adaptation for the needs of the ideological apparatus of the culture industry of Western capitalism."[13] No doubt we must be grateful to the courageous Buchloh for breaking the silence and conformity prescribed by the "needs of the ideological apparatus of the culture industry of Western capitalism." But then shouldn't he and his colleagues at *October* be grateful to such organs of "the ideological apparatus of the culture industry" as the National Endowment for the Arts and the New York State Council on the Arts, both of which have been longtime supporters of *October?* Perhaps a future issue of the magazine will be devoted to explaining why *October* deigns to avail itself of funds from government agencies representing a political system they consistently vilify.

IV • GENDER, RACE, AND CLASS

The contributions of Crimp, Buchloh, and others provide good examples of one side—what we might call the old-time anticapitalist side—of the *October* syndrome. But while that certainly helps account for *October*'s cachet in the academy and among advanced artistic circles, it is by no means the whole story of its charms. Equally important is the more "philosophical" and "cultural" side of the *October* syndrome, a side for which Professor Krauss certainly sets the tone but that has attracted a number of able imitators.

Of course no such collection as this would be complete without a large measure of feminist rhetoric. One finds it scattered throughout the volume, but the most amusing—although perhaps also the most frightening—instance is provided by Mary Ann Doane in her essay on feminist filmmaking, "Woman's Stake: Filming the Female Body."

[13]Ibid., 112.

Complaining that "cinematic images of woman [note the singular] have been so consistently oppressive and repressive that the very idea of a feminist filmmaking practice seems an impossibility," Doane proceeded to explore the ways in which a self-respecting feminist might go about the business of making films. It's a tough job. For one thing, because in Doane's view "the essence of femininity is most frequently attached to the natural body as an immediate indicator of sexual difference, it is this body which must be refused."

Yes, it is difficult to film women—or Woman—without a body. Or is it? Doane assures us that "The body is always a function of discourse," so perhaps one could fill up the screen with words? But the real problem, one gathers, is that the very mechanical process of making films is a threat to a woman's sexuality. As Doane explained, "A machine for the production of images and sounds, the cinema generates and guarantees pleasure by a corroboration of the spectators's identity. Because that identity is bound up with that of the voyeur and fetishist, because it requires for its support the attributes of the 'noncastrated,' the potential for illusory mastery of the signifier, it is not accessible to the female spectator, who, in buying her ticket, must deny her sex." Doane notwithstanding, it does seem odd that a journal that has, shall we say, "fetishized" photography and film should publish an essay proclaiming a trip to the movies as something so fraught with ideological danger.[14]

The cultural side of the *October* syndrome is not confined to feminism, however. For sheer pretension, one of my favorite pieces was Georges Didi-Huberman's essay on the Shroud of Turin, "Index of the Absent Wound (Monograph on a Stain)." "What we need," mused Didi-Huberman,

> is a concept of figurative *Aufhebung.* We would have to consider the dichotomy of its field and its means, and how they deploy a dialectical mimesis as initiation of absolute knowledge; how it attempts to transform sensible space and to begin a movement (Hegel would have said automovement) in the direction of certitude, figural certitude. An absolute seeing that would transcend the scansion of seeing and of knowing; an absolutely reflexive representation. . . .

[14]Mary Ann Doane, "Woman's Stake: Filming the Female Body," in *October: The First Decade,* ed. Michelson et al., 327, 330

> We have to look at this stain again, but this time with the "foresight" of such figural certainty in mind, or its "phantasm," its *phantasia* in the Hegelian sense; for Hegel considered *Phantasie* an *Aufhebung,* and spoke of the movement of truth as a delirium of absolute translucidity.[15]

Lest the reader be puzzled by this, Didi-Huberman obligingly supplies an explanatory reference: "Cf. Georg Wilhelm Friedrich Hegel, *The Phenomenology of Spirit.*" The translator and publication data are listed, but no page number. Students of Hegel will perhaps hazard that Didi-Huberman had in mind the passage from the preface to the *Phenomenology* where Hegel speaks of "the true" being "the bacchanalian whirl in which no member is not drunk."[16] But who knows? Didi-Huberman, at least, is never troubled to say.

This sort of thing is standard practice in the pages of *October.* As in so much academic writing these days, arcane references and wild generalizations are thrown around wholesale. One soon realizes that the footnote to Lacan, the invocation of Foucault, of Freud, of Benjamin, the entire (dare one say it?) superstructure of "scholarship" erected in these essays is intended not to further knowledge but to dazzle the reader. Why, for example, does Joel Fineman feel called on to parade the first line of *The Iliad,* unidentified and untranslated, as an epigraph to his essay, "The Structure of Allegorical Desire"? How many of his readers will be able to read the Greek? Not many, of course, but that is perhaps just as well because the line is slightly miscited, as indeed are several of the Greek words with which Fineman decorates his essay.

Or consider as a final example Homi Bhabha's "Of Mimicry and Man: The Ambivalence of Colonial Discourse," an essay that, we are told, was first presented in 1983 at the Modern Language Association. Warming up with some reasonably benign reflections on "the discourse of post-Enlightenment English colonialism," and so on, Bhabha quickly gets down to business: "Within that conflictual economy of colonial discourse which Edward Said describes as the tension between the synchronic panoptical vision of domination—the demand

[15]Georges Didi-Huberman, "Index of the Absent Wound (Monograph on a Stain)," in *October: The First Decade,* ed. Michelson et al., 43.

[16]G. W. F. Hegel, *The Phenomenology of Spirit,* trans. A. V. Miller (Oxford: Oxford University Press, 1977), 27.

for identity, stasis—and the counter-pressure of the diachrony of history—change, difference—mimicry represents an *ironic* compromise. If I may adapt Samuel Weber's formulation of the marginalizing vision of castration . . . "—but, no, let's leave *that* formulation to one side and continue with some of Bhabha's concluding remarks.

> In the ambivalent world of the "not quite/not white," on the margins of metropolitan desire, the *founding objects* of the Western world become the erratic, eccentric, accidental *objets trouvés* of the colonial discourse—the part-objects of presence. It is then that the body and the book loose [*sic*] their representational authority. Black skin splits under the racist gaze, displaced into signs of bestiality, genitalia, grotesquerie, which reveal the phobic myth of the undifferentiated whole white body.[17]

There is something terribly pathetic about this sort of display, composed as it is of nothing but clichés and phrases echoing the likes of Melanie Klein, Edward Said, Roland Barthes, and our old friend Frantz Fanon—although whether Bhabha is fully aware of his sources is unclear. Indeed, the cruelly ironic thing about this essay on mimicry and colonialism is that it is itself nothing but a poor mimicry of the clotted academic rhetoric that passes for scholarship in our universities and journals. That this rubbish should have been presented as a "paper" at the Modern Language Association is a somber reminder how far that venerable organization has degenerated in recent years.

There are many choice tidbits that I have left out of account here. But readers who find their appetites whetted can turn to the *October* reader to relish such marvels as Georges Bataille's jolly discussion of the Aztec practice of human sacrifice ("Death, for the Aztecs, was nothing," Bataille tells us) or Maria-Antonietta Macciocchi's meditations on the murder of the poet and filmmaker Pier Paolo Pasolini. In Macciocchi's piece, "Pasolini: Murder of a Dissident," we learn that "the death of the opposition sexualizes intensely the life of an entire society, from the dark bowels of fascism to the violence whose language is expressed . . . by the deadly call to aphasia. Is the social link paranoiac?"[18] Who can say?

[17]Homi Bhabha, "Of Mimicry and Man: The Ambivalence of Colonial Discourse," in *October: The First Decade* ed. Michelson et al., 318, 324–325.

[18]Maria-Antonietta Macciocchi, "Pasolini: Murder of a Dissident," in *October: The First Decade,* ed. Michelson et al., 441, 140.

In a recent issue of *October,* the confusion of culture and politics takes a further step in a large special issue devoted entirely to AIDS. The example it provides of how even a disease may be politicized and recruited to serve the cause of radical politics merits careful attention. Once again, Crimp, who edited the issue, managed to produce one of the issue's more extraordinary comments when he argued, in a discussion of "safe sex," that "they insist that our promiscuity will destroy us when in fact *it is our promiscuity that will save us.*" How exactly salvation is to be effected through promiscuity is difficult to say, but Crimp obviously has great faith in "gay male promiscuity . . . as a positive model of how sexual pleasures might be pursued by and granted to everyone if those pleasures were not confined within the narrow limits of institutionalized sexuality."[19] (emphasis in the original.)

V • WHAT DOES IT ALL MEAN?

Although *October* is often opaque and unintelligible, it is not utterly bereft of sense. If one has sufficient patience, something resembling a consecutive argument can often be wrested from the tangled, jargon-ridden prose favored by its contributors. It is difficult, at any rate, to mistake *October*'s enemies.

On the cultural side, one chief target of the *October* set's scorn is the legacy of modernist art and modernist criticism. The emphasis on individual creativity, the seriousness with which art and indeed the entire realm of high culture were regarded, the faith in the spiritually enriching potential of art, even, or rather especially, in a secular age—all this is fundamental to the modernist ethos. And it is all systematically castigated by the writers and editors of *October.* At bottom, the *October* set's rebellion against modernism is the rebellion of the disappointed enthusiast. Like so many others, the editors and contributors to *October* had once seen modernism as a handmaiden of radical politics. The problem is that modernism's affirmation of individuality and high culture turned out to be thoroughly incompatible with the dream of radical social transformation. Yet it was precisely on that dream that modernism's credentials as avant-garde had to a

[19]*October* 43 (Winter 1987): 253.

large extent depended. When it became clear that modernism was not acting to realize that dream, it had to be stripped of its avant-garde status and exposed as an agent of reaction. Thus at the end of the title essay of her last collection, Professor Krauss argues that "the historical period that the avant-garde shared with modernism is over," and urges on us "a demythologizing criticism and a truly postmodernist art, both of them acting now to void the basic propositions of modernism, to liquidate them by exposing their fictitious condition."[20]

When one turns to political matters—matters, I mean, involving elected officials, government policies, and the like (because everything is regarded as political by the *October* set, the distinction is important)—the *October* syndrome obviously tends to be about as direct, but unfortunately about as unconvincing, as the harangues of a soapbox preacher. Western bourgeois society, individualism, capitalism, high art: these are its enemies. Its ideals are radical socialism and anything that works to subvert the existing cultural and political order. Reading through so many pages of *October* brought to mind a remark made years ago by the distinguished English intellectual historian Basil Willey. Discussing the work of Sir Thomas Browne, Willey observed that Browne's literary style "was the incarnation of his sensibility."[21] Style, indeed, is often the incarnation of sensibility. And reflecting on the style of the *October* syndrome—on its opacity, its humorlessness, its pretension, its utter disregard for common sense—one cannot help concluding that, like so many manifestations of academic life today, it is a sensibility for which art and culture exist and have value only as appendages to political ideology.

It is part of the syndrome that *October* exemplifies that the realm of politics, like everything else, exists primarily as a cerebral phenomenon. To appreciate what happens when this essentially abstract, academic radicalism intersects with politics in the everyday sense of the term, let us turn to the strange case of the Belgian-born literary critic and deconstructionist Paul de Man.

[20]Rosalind E. Krauss, "The Originality of the Avant-Garde," in *The Originality of the Avant-Garde and Other Modernist Myths,* 170.

[21]Basil Willey, *The Seventeenth Century Background: The Thought of the Age in Relation to Religion and Poetry* (London: Chatto & Windus, 1950), 46.

CHAPTER 4

THE CASE OF PAUL DE MAN

It is no longer certain that language, as excuse, exists because of a prior guilt but just as possible that since language, as a machine, performs anyway, we have to produce guilt . . . in order to make the excuse meaningful. Excuses generate the very guilt they exonerate.

—PAUL DE MAN,
Allegories of Reading

I • EXCUSES, EXCUSES

December 1, 1987 was an unpleasant day for academic literary critics bewitched by the tenets of deconstruction. That morning, *The New York Times* reported that a young Belgian scholar named Ortwin de Graef had recently discovered that in the early 1940s—at the very moment when Hitler's power was at its zenith and his conquest of Europe seemed assured—the celebrated literary deconstructionist Paul de Man was busy writing articles and reviews, at least one of which was patently anti-Semitic, for Belgian newspapers supporting the Nazi cause. Understandably, the news sent shock waves through the academic literary community, shock waves that have continued to reverberate to this day.

Perhaps the most damaging of de Man's articles appeared in the collaborationist newspaper *Le Soir* on March 4, 1941, under the title "The Jews in Contemporary Literature." "There would not have been grounds for much hope for the future of our civilization," de Man wrote,

> if it had allowed itself to be invaded without resistance by a alien force. In preserving—despite the Semitic meddling into all aspects of European life—its originality and character intact, it has shown that its nature was essentially healthy. Moreover, one thus sees that

> a solution to the Jewish question which envisions the creation of a Jewish colony isolated from Europe would not involve deplorable consequences for the literary life of the West. It would lose, all told, a few personalities of mediocre value and would continue, as in the past, to develop according to its own great evolutionary laws.[1]

In other articles he explained that after the fall of France "the German conquerors were more praiseworthy, just, and humane than the French were in 1918,"[2] assured readers that "the fascist regime [in Italy] leaves the poet completely free to seek his source of inspiration wherever he wants,"[3] and in another article praised "the totalitarian regime," Germany this time, for having overcome the "vague anarchy" of bourgeois French society, replacing it with "definite obligations and duties to which everyone must adapt his talents."[4] He also found occasion to extol "the present war" as "the beginning of a revolution that aims to reorganize Europe in a more equitable fashion"[5] and observe that

> the war will only bring about a more intimate union of two things that have always been close, the Hitlerian soul and the German soul, until they have been made one single and unique power. This is an important phenomenon, because it means that one cannot judge the fact of Hitler without judging at the same time the fact of Germany and that the future of Europe can be envisioned only within the framework of the possibilities and needs of the German spirit. It is not a matter only of a series of reforms but the definite emancipation of a people which

[1]Paul de Man, "Les Juifs dans la Littérature actuelle," in *Wartime Journalism, 1939–1943,* ed. Werner Hamacher, Neil Hertz, and Thomas Keenan (Lincoln: University of Nebraska Press: 1989), 45. (First published in *Le Soir,* Mar. 4, 1941.) This facsimile collection of de Man's wartime writings in French and of English translations of his wartime writings in Dutch was hastily cobbled together in an effort to mollify the public outcry that followed the revelation of de Man's connection with Nazi newspapers. Translations from the French are mine.

[2]Paul de Man, "Brochures flamandes sur le III Reich," in *Wartime Journalism,* 66. (First published in *Le Soir,* Apr. 12–14, 1941.)

[3]Paul de Man, "La troisième conference du professeur Donini," in *Wartime Journalism,* 32. (First published in *Le Soir,* Feb. 18, 1941.)

[4]Paul de Man, "Chronique littéraire: Voir la Figure," in *Wartime Journalism,* 159. (First published in *Le Soir,* Oct. 28, 1941.)

[5]Paul de Man, "Notre Chronique littéraire: Dans Nos Murs," in *Wartime Journalism,* 138. (First published in *Le Soir,* Aug. 26, 1941.)

finds itself called upon to exercise, in its turn, a hegemony in Europe.[6]

What does the strange case of Paul de Man tell us about the way politics has corrupted the humanities? Even more than Professor de Man's own behavior, the academy's response to these articles—subsequent digging revealed that the number was nearly 200—and to de Man's later failure to acknowledge his activities, was predictably evasive and temporizing. While the popular press, from *Newsweek* to *The Nation* and *The Village Voice,* condemned de Man, literary academics, with a few notable exceptions, immediately closed ranks and began manufacturing excuses. Already in October 1987, when the news of de Graef's discovery had begun to leak out, a summit meeting of about twenty deconstructionists—including, *ex officio,* as it were, J. Hillis Miller and Jacques Derrida—convened in Tuscaloosa, Alabama, to examine copies of the offending articles and decide on a policy of what many writers have subsequently termed "damage control."

One early example of the procedure was given by Christopher Norris—himself a prominent second-rung deconstructionist who made his reputation championing de Man—in a long and tortuous examination for *The London Review of Books* early in 1988.[7] Professor Norris offers numerous possible extenuations of de Man's behavior: the articles in question had been "mined for passages" by de Man's enemies to show him in a bad light, he was under political pressure to write the articles, etc. But Professor Norris's chief point seems to be that de Man's early brush with totalitarianism was a kind of learning experience that helped make his postwar writing a model of skeptical rigor.

This in fact was a theme often repeated by academics who weighed in to defend their idol. The famed Jonathan Culler, for example, explained in an article for *The Chronicle of Higher Education* that the discovery of de Man's wartime writings "adds a new dimension to his later writings" and then goes on to tell us that de Man's

[6]Paul de Man, "Chronique littéraire: Voir la Figure," in *Wartime Journalism,* 159. (First published in *Le Soir,* Oct. 28, 1941.)

[7]Christopher Norris, "Paul de Man's Past," *The London Review of Books,* Feb. 4, 1988, 7–11.

later critiques now appear "as a critique of ideas and [*sic*] underlying fascism and their deadly quest for unity and the elimination of difference."[8] In Professor Culler's view, this somehow implies that deconstruction, being deeply skeptical of language, emerges as a formidable opponent of Nazism and totalitarianism. Presumably it follows that de Man, although he wrote collaborationist articles for collaborationist newspapers, is an exemplary anti-Nazi, after all. Obviously, deconstruction is a wonderful thing to have on your side.

Among the early responses, at least, the first prize for mystification must go to Jacques Derrida's extraordinary sixty-page eulogy *cum* jeremiad, which appeared in the academic quarterly *Critical Inquiry.* It begins as follows:

> Unable to respond to the questions, to all the questions, I will ask myself instead *whether responding is possible* and what that would mean in such a situation. And I will risk in turn several questions *prior to* the definition of a *responsibility.* But is it not an act to assume in theory the concept of responsibility? One's own as well as the responsibility to which one believes one ought to summon others?[9]

And it more or less concludes with this exercise in wistfulness:

> As for the accused himself, he is dead. He is in ashes, he has neither the grounds, nor the means, still less the choice or the desire to respond. We are alone with ourselves. We carry his memory and his name in us. We especially carry ethico-political responsibilities for the future. Our actions with regard to what remains to us of de Man will also have the value of an example, whether we like it or not. To judge, to condemn the work or the man on the basis of what was a brief episode, to call for closing, that is to say, at least figuratively, for censuring or burning his books is to reproduce the exterminating gesture against which one accuses de Man of not having armed himself sooner with the necessary vigilance.[10]

[8]Jonathan Culler, "It's Time to Set the Record Straight About Paul de Man and His Wartime Articles for a Pro-Fascist Newspaper," *The Chronicle of Higher Education,* July 13, 1988, sec. 2, p. 1.

[9]Jacques Derrida, "Like the Sound of the Sea Deep within a Shell: Paul de Man's War," *Critical Inquiry* 14 (Spring 1988), trans. Peggy Kamuf, 590.

[10]Ibid., 650–651.

"The exterminating gesture"? What Derrida seems to be saying is that criticizing Paul de Man for writing collaborationist articles is somehow to repeat the savage butchery of the Nazis.

In one way or another, this bizarre idea surfaced often in the academic response to Paul de Man. Another prime example was the invective penned by deconstruction's faithful mascot, J. Hillis Miller, for *The Times Literary Supplement.* Professor Miller explains that de Man "was by no means in these early writings *totally* fascist, antisemitic and collaborationist."[11] Well, OK. Shall we say then that he was only half-fascist, anti-Semitic, and collaborationist? In any event, what Professor Miller found "most terrifying" about the press treatment of de Man "is the way it repeats the well-know totalitarian procedures of vilification it pretends to deplore." I suppose this means that to point out that someone has written collaborationist pieces for newspapers under control of a totalitarian government is itself an example of totalitarianism. The one element of comic relief in Professor Miller's performance was his complaint that journalists (no more opprobrious epithet exists in an academic's vocabulary) had scrambled the facts. For what one saw in Professor Miller's complaint was the spectacle of a man who had spent the last decade or so of his professional life insisting on the indeterminacy of language and denying that there is any such thing as a fact loudly complaining that the mean-spirited press had gotten the facts all wrong. It did seem like poetic justice.

No doubt to help set the facts straight, what we might call the Tuscaloosa Committee decided to arrange for the publication of all de Man's wartime journalism and related documents as well as to organize a volume of responses from various academics concerned with the controversy. After numerous delays, both volumes have appeared. Facsimiles of the 169 pieces de Man wrote for *Le Soir* in French and translations of the 10 articles he wrote in Dutch for *Het Vlaamische Land* appeared along with a few other pieces in spring 1989 in a volume edited by Werner Hamacher, Neil Hertz, and Thomas Keenan.[12] This triumvirate also edited a long volume of responses, which includes a chronology of de Man's early years and some 40 articles by

[11]J. Hillis Miller, "NB" column, *The Times Literary Supplement,* June 17–23, 1988, 676, 685. (Emphasis added.)

[12]Paul de Man, *Wartime Journalism.*

sundry academics eager to have their say about the early de Man.[13] That volume includes a small handful of dissenting pieces. But the vast majority, after a bit of preliminary handwringing, seem to come down squarely on the side of de Man and against his condemnation by the press. I say *seem* here because, in typical deconstructivist fashion, many of the essays are models of obscurantist obfuscation. In addition to a revised version of Derrida's classic response, we also have such gems as Timothy Bahti's "Telephonic Crossroads: The Reversal and the Double Cross," Jeffrey S. Libert's "From the Authority of Appropriate (De)form(ation) to—: Toward de Man's Totalitarian Acts," and Andrzej Warminski's "Terrible Reading (preceded by 'Epigraphs')." And lest the reader conclude that such titles are mere ornaments to more reasonable responses, consider this typical passage from Warminski's contribution:

> A certain self-immolating self-reflection—a self-ironization—takes place here as . . . de Man's [words] about Montherlant say one thing and mean another. But ironies do not end here—indeed, irony, once it begins (and it has always already begun), never just ends, at least not just here. No matter how self-immolating it may be, the act of self-reflection always leaves remainders, traces, ashes—a *reste* or a *restance du texte,* as Derrida might put it, that resists the totalization of any oblivion, that insures a certain memory for every forgetting, even "the most total." . . . The only memory for *those* remainders is the same journalistic "memory" of the present, the one that "remembers" only the present and hence has neither past nor future (and hence does not happen, is not an event, is not historical)—or only *the* past and the future of total oblivion.[14]

II • THE MAKING OF A CRITICAL GENIUS

To understand why the academy should have rallied so vigorously to excuse, explain, and extenuate the wartime journalism of Paul de Man, it is necessary to understand that he was no ordinary college professor. Having come to the United States as an unknown translator

[13]Werner Hamacher, Neil Hertz, and Thomas Keenan, eds., *Responses: On Paul de Man's Wartime Journalism* (Lincoln: University of Nebraska Press, 1989).

[14]Andrzej Warminski, "Terrible Reading (preceded by 'Epigraphs,')" in *Responses: On Paul de Man's Wartime Journalism,* Werner Hamacher, Neil Hertz, and Thomas Keenan, eds. (Lincoln: University of Nebraska Press, 1989), 386.

and journalist after the war in 1947, he did graduate work at Harvard in the early fifties (part of the time as a Junior Fellow in Harvard's prestigious Society of Fellows) and emerged in the mid-seventies as one of the most sought-after literary theorists in the country. Indeed, by the time he died, in 1983 at the age of sixty-four, Professor de Man was considered by some to be one of the most brilliant critical minds of his generation.

With the possible exception of Jacques Derrida—who deserves the appellation of the chief theoretical architect of deconstruction—Professor de Man did more than anyone to institutionalize the "demythologizing" tenets of deconstruction in the literature departments of American universities. Although he in fact published very little, during his years teaching at Johns Hopkins and, later, as Sterling Professor of the Humanities at Yale University, he inspired colleagues and graduate students alike to abandon the methods of traditional literary criticism for the allegedly more rigorous approach of deconstruction—an approach characterized by doctrinaire skepticism and infatuation with the thought that language is always so compromised by metaphor and ulterior motives that a text never means what it appears to mean. "The relationship between truth and error that prevails in literature cannot be represented genetically," he assured us in one typical passage, "since truth and error exist simultaneously, thus preventing the favoring of one over the other."[15] Even today, Professor de Man's teachings and catchphrases are parroted in departments of English and comparative literature across the country. While neither the man nor his theories were universally beloved, we have seen that both inspired fierce devotion from the many partisans of deconstruction, who since his death have been at pains to eulogize his personal virtues as a colleague, teacher, and friend as well as to praise his intellectual gifts and scholarly accomplishments.

That this paragon of chic academic achievement should stand revealed as the author of anti-Semitic articles for pro-Nazi publications at the height of Hitler's power has been a major embarrassment for his many epigones. The reason is obvious: the frequently heard charge that deconstruction is essentially nihilistic has now acquired existential

[15]Paul de Man, *Blindness and Insight: Essays in the Rhetoric of Contemporary Criticism* (New York: Oxford University Press, 1971), 165.

support of the most damaging kind. Not that those early anti-Semitic articles exactly *prove* that deconstruction is nihilistic; but it is a rum thing when the patron saint of a literary movement that has so arrogantly proclaimed itself a champion of freedom is brutally exposed as having trafficked with a political force whose very essence was the denial of freedom.

Judging by the storm of articles and testimonials that have appeared, the ritual of exoneration proceeds roughly as follows: First, yes, it's regrettable that Paul de Man wrote those articles, but after all, he was very young at the time, only in his early twenties; youth is impetuous and often blinded by romantic enthusiasms. Second, it's unfortunate that the prominent newspapers *Le Soir,* where the majority of his early journalistic efforts appeared, and *Het Vlaamische Land* should both have been openly collaborating with the Nazi line; still, de Man was ambitious and naturally seized the opportunity to write for the prestigious papers. Besides, only a few of his articles were explicitly anti-Semitic, most were simply reviews or notices of current cultural events. Third, it's true that he wondered in an article that appeared in March 1941 in *Le Soir* whether the Jews polluted modern literature, and that he envisioned the establishment of a Jewish colony isolated from Europe.[16] We must remember, however, that this was not as vicious as much anti-Semitic writing circulating at the time and that, as far as we know now, he stopped writing for *Le Soir* near the end of 1942, before most people knew about the Nazi death camps. Fourth, while it's lamentable that he never acknowledged his deeds—that he went so far as to claim on at least one occasion that he had been part of the "Belgian resistance" to the Nazis during the war—perhaps his difficulty in coming to terms with his own past helps explain his tough-minded resistance to the bewitchments of language later in life . . .

But, still, besides, however—the qualifications proceed to infinity, almost transforming guilt into innocence, or at least so numbing the mind that the distinction between guilt and innocence begins to blur, begins, in good deconstructionist fashion, to seem merely *linguistic,* merely rhetorical, a matter utterly divorced from the demands of moral judgment. Or as Professor de Man himself put it in a much

[16]De Man, "Les Juifs dans la Littérature actuelle."

admired essay on Rousseau, "the main point of the reading has been to show that the resulting predicament is linguistic rather than ontological or hermeneutic."[17]

III • PROFESSOR HARTMAN RECONSTRUCTS DE MAN

Although the pieces collected in *Responses* provide exacting competition, perhaps the single most extraordinary—if not, finally, the most opaque—attempt at damage control that appeared in the wake of the revelations about Paul de Man's wartime journalistic activities surfaced in the weekly journal of opinion *The New Republic.* Titled "Blindness and Insight" after the title of Professor de Man's influential 1971 collection of essays,[18] this exercise in critical legerdemain was written by his former colleague, Geoffrey H. Hartman, the Karl Young Professor of English and comparative literature at Yale University, whom we met in Chapter One. Himself a still-glittering cynosure of academic fashion, Professor Hartman is admired in advanced literary–critical circles for his work on Wordsworth and other romantic poets and for his impishly convoluted theoretical works. Unfortunately, almost everything about his article must give us pause: its place of publication, the identity of its author, and not least its content and implications. Because it is emblematic of the academy's top-drawer treatment of de Man, Professor Hartman's reconstruction of his late colleague is worth pondering in some detail.

For example, what does it mean that *The New Republic*—a journal that under its current editorship has made such a show of castigating anti-Semitism and supporting Jewish causes—should publish an essay that coyly fudges the significance of Professor de Man's collaborationist articles by reinterpreting them from the perspective of his later deconstructionist writings? What does it mean that this task should have been undertaken by Geoffrey Hartman? Certainly, one could hardly ask for a better pedigree for the job of moral damage control that Professor Hartman undertook in his article. In addition to his

[17]Paul de Man, *Allegories of Reading: Figural Language in Rousseau, Nietzsche, Rilke, and Proust* (New Haven: Yale University Press, 1979), 299.

[18]Geoffry H. Hartman, "Blindness and Insight." *The New Republic,* Mar. 7, 1988, 26–31. Unless otherwise noted, quotations from Geoffrey Hartman are from this article.

regular academic appointment, he is also an advisory committee member of the Judaic Studies Program at Yale as well as an adviser to the Video Archive for Holocaust Testimonies at the Yale library. And what does it mean that this man who fled Germany as a child in the late thirties because (as he put it in a 1985 interview) "of the persecution of the Jews" should now devote his considerable rhetorical skills to arguing that "in the light of what we now know, however, [de Man's] work appears more and more as a deepening reflection on the rhetoric of totalitarianism"? And finally, what does it tell us about the state of contemporary literary criticism that one of its most distinguished practitioners should be so enthralled with the tenets of deconstruction that he should blithely distill one of this century's most rebarbative historical realities into an example of what he at one point calls "linguistic pathos"?

Professor Hartman devotes the first third of his article to a more or less straightforward presentation of the facts, so far as they were then known, of Professor de Man's early journalistic career. His account, I believe, is essentially accurate. But his tone—sorrowful rather than outraged—is decidedly exculpatory, and he does everything he can to mitigate the offense. For example, he speaks of "*an* anti-Semitic piece" and the "one" article that "engaged explicitly with the ideology of anti-Semitism." (Emphasis added.) But suppose we concede that only one article "explicitly engaged with the ideology of anti-Semitism"—that is, was blatantly anti-Semitic: that still says nothing about the scores of other articles that, simply by virtue of appearing in *Le Soir* in 1940, 1941, and 1942, *implicitly* condoned the Nazi's more explicit brand of anti-Semitism, as well as the policies and programs that were instituted on its behalf.

Professor Hartman admits that his late colleague's "formulations" "show all the marks, and the dangerous implications, of identifying Jews as an alien and unhealthy presence in Western civilization." He admits, too, that given the times, his writings were "more than a theoretical expression of anti-Semitism." (Meaning, perhaps, that a merely theoretical expression of anti-Semitism isn't such a bad thing?) What he nowhere acknowledges is the explicit relation those writings bore to the regnant political force of the Nazis. Instead, his basic tack is to console us with the thought that Professor de Man did not behave as badly as he might have done. It is true that Professor de Man envisioned the creation of a Jewish colony isolated from Europe, but he did not demand the extermination of the Jews; he did hail the rise of National Socialism as the "definite emancipation of a people called upon to exercise, in its turn, a hegemony in Europe," but, according to Professor Hartman, his "relation to fascist ideology was not a simple matter." Moreover, Professor Hartman assures us that, "by the terrible standards of the day," an article such as "The Jews in Contemporary Literature" was not really "vulgar anti-Semitic writing" and that it "stands out [from the other collaborationist writings, including those of his uncle, Hendrik de Man] by its refusal to engage directly with political matters." The idea is, I suppose, that simply not descending to the vicious racial slurs of a Goebbels merits commendation.

IV • THE CULT OF THEORY

There is something extraordinarily depressing about the spectacle of a scholar of Professor Hartman's distinction and personal history struggling to find extenuating circumstances for writings undertaken on behalf of an ideology and political movement that were bent on his own destruction. But somehow even more depressing is the *way* in which Professor Hartman has chosen to go about his task. For whereas the first third of his article provides us with an overview of Professor de Man's collaborationist writings, the balance of the piece attempts to rehabilitate Professor de Man by viewing those writings through the lens of deconstruction. The result is a sterling—if not a Sterling Professor's—example of vindication through obfuscation.

Perhaps out of deference to the gravity of the subject, Professor Hartman forbears to indulge his penchant for elaborate, punning wordplay in this article. But as in his other critical writings from the past decade or so, he proceeds not so much by argument as by a display of maddeningly imprecise verbal arabesques. Not surprisingly, he begins by defending deconstruction against the charges of its enemies. "Deconstruction is neither nihilistic nor cynical," he wrote,

> when it questions whether there exists an arena for testing ideas other than the uncontrollable arena of activist politics; or when it demonstrates that philosophy and literature express the impasse

> from which ideas spring, as well as those ideas themselves. . . . What is neglected by de Man's critics, who are in danger of reducing all to biography again, is the intellectual power in his later work, the sheer power of critique, whatever its source, that he deploys against the claims of philosophy and theory.

Leaving the particulars of this passage to one side, how does it answer the charge of nihilism or cynicism? Does it provide us with anything more than an unsupported assertion? And as for the vaunted "intellectual power" of de Man's later work, of what does it really consist? Confining ourselves to Professor Hartman's own examples, we learn that "according to de Man, we are always encountering epistemological instabilities, the incompatibility or disjunction between meaning and intent, or between what is stated and the rhetoric or mode of stating it." Translated out of the forbidding argot, what this seems to mean is that deconstruction helps us realize that there is often a difference between appearance and reality, that language forever falls short of expressing exactly what we mean. But isn't this an insight that any thoughtful high-school student should have when reflecting for the first time on the way language works? Professor Hartman is certainly correct when he observes,

> Those previously suspicious of deconstruction have seized on the revelations. Their sense of deconstruction as morally unsound and politically evasive seems to stand confirmed. They condemn it as untrustworthy because it seeks to avert the reality, and therefore the culpability, of error. That is how they interpret deconstruction's emphasis on the indeterminacy of meaning, and on the complexity of a medium that seems to "speak" us [*sic*] instead of submitting fully to our control.

"Such a judgment is superficial," Professor Hartman assures us, "and divorces deconstruction from its context in the history of philosophy." Really? One need hardly be a deconstructionist to agree that language refuses to submit "fully to our control." In fact, does anyone who has given language a moment's thought believe that it does? Again, Professor Hartman is right that those critical of deconstruction take exception to its "emphasis on the indeterminacy of meaning." But that of course is the central question: Is meaning as expressed in language so indeterminate that we are unable reliably to decipher it? What about Professor Hartman's own assertion that meaning is indeterminate? Would he say that the meaning of that statement, too, is indeterminate? Like so many deconstructionists, Professor Hartman has rather a dualistic view of the matter. He assumes that if one has not abandoned the belief in the intelligibility of language and adopted the skepticism that deconstruction preaches, one must be a kind of cartoon Cartesian, holding that language is a perfectly transparent medium that renders our thoughts about the world without loss or ambiguity. The possibility of a middle ground between nihilistic skepticism and naïve belief never seems to occur to him, perhaps because he has been so deeply impressed by deconstructionist caveats such as this question de Man asks about Rousseau's *Confessions:* "How are we to know we are indeed dealing with a *true* confession, since the recognition of guilt implies its exoneration in the name of the same transcendental principle of truth that allowed for the certitude of guilt in the first place?"[19] How indeed?

And as for deconstruction's "context in the history of philosophy"—well, given Professor Hartman's own intractable hostility to anything resembling philosophical analysis (something that is evident throughout his own theoretical writings), I am sure that it would be most amusing to have him enlighten us about that. As it is, we must be content with his suggestion that deconstruction takes up "the age-old problem" of the relation of language and meaning and his cryptic allusion to the German neo-Kantian philosopher Ernst Cassirer. Cassirer, we are told, "observed that while language wished to overcome 'the curse of mediacy,' it was itself part of the problem it tried to resolve."

Now I doubt that Professor Hartman could have picked a less appropriate figure than Ernst Cassirer to support his brief for deconstruction. Cassirer, another refugee from Hitler's Reich, would be rolling over in his grave if he knew that his name was invoked to support the radically skeptical contentions of deconstruction. In the foreward to *The Philosophy of Symbolic Forms,* his *magnum opus,* Cassirer reviewed the intellectual climate of the 'teens and early twenties, warning that "at times, language seemed to be becoming the principal

[19]De Man, *Allegories of Reading,* 280.

weapon of skepticism rather than a vehicle of philosophical knowledge"[20]—a remark that stands up rather well as a characterization of deconstruction *avant la lettre.* As he put it later in the same volume, "skepticism seeks to expose the nullity of knowledge and language—but what it ultimately demonstrates is the nullity of the *standard* by which it measures them."[21] That is to say, skepticism exposes the nullity of the standard of absolute transparency, the standard that deconstructionists falsely impute to anyone who continues to believe in the possibility of stable meanings and the intelligibility of language.

The point is that philosophical analysis is little more than intellectual window dressing for Professor Hartman. In fact, given his view of language, it is *necessarily* little more than intellectual window dressing for the simple reason that he denies the power of language to communicate effectively through concepts. It has long been clear that for Professor Hartman *concept* is a highly suspect term, implying as it does that thought can meaningfully transcend the particularities of language and rhetoric. This suspicion of philosophy and of the cogency of rational analysis are among the chief reasons that he values deconstruction so highly. For deconstruction provides a handy way of appearing to transform philosophy into a species of literature, reducing concepts to so many rhetorical "tropes" and viewing the whole notion of truth as an unfortunate fictional construct.

It is in this sense that Professor Hartman can offer deconstruction as a defender of the imagination and literature against the supposedly unimaginative depredations of philosophy and science. "Deconstruction is," he explained,

> a defense of literature. It shows, by close reading, (1) that there are no dead metaphors, (2) that literature is often more self-aware than those who attack it, (3) that literary texts contain significant tensions that can be disclosed, but not resolved, by analysis. Any mode of analysis, therefore, that sees the text as an organic unity, or uses it for a totalizing purpose (as when the right or the left speaks for history), is blind, and the text itself will subvert or "deconstruct" such closures.

[20]Ernst Cassirer, *The Philosophy of Symbolic Forms,* Vol. 1, *Language,* trans. Ralph Manheim (New Haven: Yale University Press, 1955), 70.

[21]Ibid., 188.

There is a great deal that one might say about this passage, which blends the highly questionable with the portentously trite. The idea that there are no dead metaphors can be refuted by anyone who ever uttered the phrase "that depends" and bothered to consider its etymology: The metaphorical sense of something "hanging down" is indeed "dead" in most everyday uses of the word. I'm not sure what it means to speak of literature *itself* as being "more self-aware than those who attack it"; no doubt Professor Hartman means to remind us that he has read Heidegger's orphic remarks about "language speaking." But if Professor Hartman is suggesting that many who repudiate the charms of literature are philistines, who would disagree? And as for the contention that "literary texts contain significant tensions that can be disclosed, but not resolved, by analysis," here I should think it all depends on what one means by *resolved.* In one sense, certainly, it is a statement with which scarcely a single literate individual would disagree. But the real point of this passage is that deconstruction is superior to other modes of interpretation because it provides especially "close readings" of texts, readings that reveal nasty things such as the "totalizing" impulses of authors, i.e., their desire for unity and sense.

But one wonders: Is deconstruction better at "close reading" than traditional literary analysis? Let's consider an example of close reading that Professor Hartman cites in his apology for Professor de Man.

> It is indeed hard to associate the young journalist (aged 21) with the distinguished theorist (aged 47) who wrote so critically, and so effectively, against Husserl's *The Crisis of European Humanity and Philosophy.* De Man accused Husserl of blindly privileging Western civilization ("European supremacy") at the very time (1935) that Europe "was about to destroy itself as center in the name of an unwarranted claim to be the center." But of de Man, too, it can now be said that "as a European it seems that [he] escaped from the necessary self-criticism that is prior to all philosophical truth about the self."

First of all, one might well ask why Professor Hartman bothered to introduce Professor de Man's discussion of this late lecture by the philosopher Edmund Husserl. One reason that springs to mind is that it gives him the opportunity to speak of "blindly privileging Western civilization," a charge that is as common (one might almost say obligatory) among fashionable academics these days as the diction is deplorable. But then how "effective" is Professor de Man's own criticism? It is odd, to say the least, that he should charge Husserl with illegitimately "privileging" Western civilization when the main point of the lecture in question was to criticize the "mistaken rationalism" or "objectivism" that in Husserl's view had precipitated a major crisis in Western values—a crisis that he could see unfolding around him in 1935 with the ascension of Hitler and institution of Nazi ideas throughout German society. (Indeed, Husserl, as a Jew, was just then being ostracized from the academic community at Freiburg where he had taught for many years.)

One notes, too, that in the essay to which Professor Hartman refers, Professor de Man archly remarks that "why this geographical expansion [of philosophical reflection] should have chosen to stop, once and forever, at the Atlantic Ocean and the Caucasus, Husserl does not say." But Husserl does not say for the simple reason that he never suggests that the spirit of scientific rationality that he discusses in "Philosophy and the Crisis of European Man" (as the lecture is usually translated) *is* bounded "once and forever" by the Atlantic Ocean and the Caucasus. Quite the contrary. Near the beginning of the lecture, he notes that in invoking the spiritual image of Europe he

> does not mean Europe geographically, as it appears on maps, as though European man were to be in this way confined to the circle of those who live in this territory. In the spiritual sense it is clear that to Europe belong the English dominions, the United States, etc., but not, however, the Eskimos or Indians of the country fairs, or the Gypsies, who are constantly wandering about Europe. Clearly the title Europe designates the unity of a spiritual life and a creative activity—with all its aims, interests, cares, and troubles.[22]

It is a small point, to be sure, but it gives one a good indication of the kind of "close reading" one can expect from our premier deconstructionists.

[22]Edmund Husserl, "Philosophy and the Crisis of European Man," in *Phenomenology and the Crisis of Philosophy,* trans. Quentin Lauer (New York: Harper & Row, 1965), 155.

V • THE LINGUISTIC NATURE OF THE PREDICAMENT

Of course, Professor Hartman did not treat the readers of *The New Republic* to the *longueurs* of deconstruction simply to provide them with another example of the theory at work. His exposition of the putative virtues of deconstruction was part and parcel of his effort at reconstructing Professor de Man in the face of his early journalistic career. "The discovery of these early articles must make a difference in the way we read the later de Man," Professor Hartman admits.

> The new disclosures imbed a biographical fact in our consciousness, a fact that tends to devour all other considerations; it does not spare the later achievement, whose intellectual power we continue to feel. One crucial and hurtful problem is that de Man did not address his past. We do not have his thoughts. Did he avoid confessions . . . and instead work out his totalitarian temptations in a purely intellectual and impersonal manner?

Leaving aside the euphemistic circumlocutions ("imbed a biographical fact in our consciousness," etc.), we may begin by considering the subterfuge contained in Professor Hartman's concluding question—as if the issue were a problem for psychotherapy: working out a totalitarian temptation. More basically, one might ask: How does Professor Hartman handle the troubling fact that his subject never owned up to his past? That in the one semiofficial acknowledgment Professor de Man made of his past—a letter he wrote to the Harvard Society of Fellows in 1955 in response to rumors about his wartime activities—he fudged the extent of his association with *Le Soir,* complaining that "I hear now that I myself am being accused of collaboration. In 1940 and 1941 I wrote some literary articles in the newspaper "le Soir" and, like most of the other contributors, I stopped doing so when nazi [*sic*] thought-control did no longer allow freedom of statement. During the rest of the occupation, I did what was the duty of any decent person."[23] Not surprisingly, Professor Hartman handles all this by deconstructing it: "It is possible to link the intellectual strength of the later work to what is excluded by it, to what, in surging

[23]De Man, *Responses,* 476.

back, threatens to diminish its authority. . . . But the postwar writing may constitute an avowal of error, a kind of repudiation in its very methodology of a philosophy of reading."

What this jewel of opacity would appear to mean is that the critical power of deconstruction provides Professor de Man with an intellectually sophisticated substitute for any mere straightforward "avowal of error." The implication is that in the intellectual empyrean inhabited by Professors de Man, Hartman, and company one can dispense with anything so pedestrian as a frank admission of guilt. After all, has not Professor de Man assured us that "excuses generate the very guilt they exonerate"? But what Professor Hartman's peroration really reveals is how the deconstructionist habit of intellectualizing reality results in a deviousness that willingly forsakes the most basic moral distinctions in its pursuit of ever more clever rhetorical constructs. As Professor Hartman explains it, "Even to say, quite simply, 'I was young, I made a mistake, I've changed my mind' remains blind if it overlooks the narrative shape of this or any confession." "Narrative shape"? Reading Professor Hartman's exegesis, it is easy to forget that we are not talking about Keats's "To Autumn" but a collection of reviews and articles that appeared in pro-Nazi publications. To invoke the "narrative shape" of confession is not to render the issue any clearer or more morally compelling, but merely to insinuate a new element of intellectualized mendacity into the discussion.

And this—the application of ever-more sophistical layers of intellectualized mendacity—is what is finally most troubling about Professor Hartman's essay. While he began with Paul de Man's numerous contributions to collaborationist newspapers, by his second or third page Professor Hartman has transformed the entire discussion into a debate about language. "De Man always asks us to look beyond natural experience or its mimesis to a specifically linguistic dilemma. He claims that the relation between meaning and language is not in our subjective control, perhaps not even human." The idea being what? That because we are to look beyond "natural experience" to a "linguistic dilemma" and because language is reputedly not under our control we are not responsible for the blunders and evil we perpetrate in the realm of "natural experience"? Does it mean that we are henceforth relieved of the obligation to speak and write straightforwardly about such blunders?

To get the full flavor of Professor Hartman's style of thought, it is worth quoting his exposition at some length. "There is no compensation for the failure of action in the perfection of art," he wrote, musing on the relation between art and action in Professor de Man's later writings.

> The fields of critical philosophy, literary theory, and history have an interlinguistic, not an extralinguistic, correlative; they are secondary in relation to the original, which is itself a previous text. They reveal an essential failure of disarticulation, which was already there in the original. "They kill the original, by discovering that the original was already dead. They read the original from the perspective of pure language [*reine Sprache*], a language that would be entirely freed of the illusion of meaning."

"Interlinguistic," you understand, not "extralinguistic"; in other words, in Professor Hartman's view, neither philosophy, nor literary theory, nor even history refers to the real world (i.e., has an "extralinguistic correlative"). How comforting to know that the atrocities we read about are merely literary phenomena, referring not to the sufferings of real people, real "originals," but only to "a previous text"!

Professor Hartman then goes on to tell us that

> this talk of killing the original, and of essential failure, is strong stuff. Knowing today about the writings of the young de Man, it is not possible to evade them as merely a biographical reference point: the early writing *is* an "original" to which the later writing reacts. De Man's method of reading implies that the relation between late and early is interlinguistic only, that the position he had abandoned, one that proved to be a failure and perhaps culpably blind, is not to be used to explain his eventual method; but the biographical disclosure may hurt de Man's intelligibility. Though his method insists on excluding the biographical ("extralinguistic") reference, I do not believe that we can read him without identifying the "original" in his case as the mediated and compromised idiom of his early, journalistic writings. . . .
>
> The earlier self is not off the hook, but the emphasis shifts to the way language operates. The later self acknowledges an error,

> yet it does not attribute it to an earlier self, . . . because that would perpetuate its blindness to the linguistic nature of the predicament.

"The linguistic nature of the predicament"? This is the culmination of Professor Hartman's extraordinary display? What happened to the concern about racism that was so loudly voiced at the Yale conference we examined, at Stanford, and elsewhere? Is collusion with racist forces acceptable if it is later papered over with a suitably radical veneer of critical obfuscation? Furthermore, what does it mean to describe Professor de Man's "predicament" as "linguistic"? If nothing else, it is to suggest that the historical reality of his involvement with *Le Soir* and the other fascist papers was at bottom a kind of linguistic, not a moral, lapse. And note, too, Professor Hartman's conjecture that "the biographical disclosure may hurt de Man's intelligibility," when what is at stake is not his "intelligibility" (which remains untouched by the disclosure of his early writings) but his character. It is symptomatic of the real blindness of deconstruction—and of the many literary academics who continue to embrace it—that it should fail to have any insight whatsoever into this fundamental distinction. How troubling it is, then, that the tenets, methods, and governing spirit of deconstruction should be expanding beyond their original home in departments of literature and making great inroads into other, even the most pragmatic, disciplines. To get a sense of just how far this process of expansion has gone, let us next consider an important example of how deconstruction has installed itself in a discipline and trade that—or so one might have thought—would be constitutionally resistant to such an airy brand of abstract skepticism.

CHAPTER 5

DECONSTRUCTION COMES TO ARCHITECTURE

The dream has become a kind of nightmare.
—MARK WIGLEY,
Deconstructivist Architecture

I • THE DISEASE SPREADS

In his description of what he calls Left Eclecticism, the critic Frederick Crews speaks of "a given painting, novel, or piece of architecture" being susceptible to the "aggressive demystification" that is now passed off as criticism in the academy. Novels, of course, are prime candidates for the demystifying mystifications of deconstructionists, poststructuralists, and the like. And we have seen that even the paintings of Courbet can be scanned, as Professor Crews put it, "for any signs of subversion." But architecture? Surely architecture, that most public and undeniably *material* of the arts, must be exempt from the misty, politicized attacks of academic critical theory?

The answer, unfortunately, is no. Even architecture has fallen prey to the opaque and ideologically charged academicization that has triumphed in other fields. No less a spokesman for the academic vanguard than Jacques Derrida has lately turned his attention to architecture. In various essays and even collaborations with architects, he has seduced many students and practitioners of the craft with his hermetic word-play and warnings that architecture is the last stronghold of Western metaphysics and logocentricism.[1]

[1]See especially Jacques Derrida, "Point de la folie—maintenant l'architecture," in *Psyche: Inventions de l'autre* (Paris: Galilee, 1987), 477–493.

No doubt it had to happen sooner or later. The tenets, attitudes, and techniques of deconstruction have long since metastasized from their home in departments of English and comparative literature and have invaded virtually every branch of humanistic endeavor. Neither the theory nor practice of architecture has proved to be immune. Indeed, the current situation in certain advanced precincts of architectural education provides a splendid example of the way in which Left Eclecticism has spread throughout the humanities, infecting even so stable and straightforward (or so one would have thought) a discipline as architecture.

Now it is obvious to anyone interested in contemporary architecture that the last ten or fifteen years have been a time of tremendous ferment, energy, and, above all, confusion for the profession. While a handful of star architects continue to bask in glamour and celebrity, there is widespread suspicion that the profession as a whole is in disarray. The carousel of architectural styles that one has seen whiz past with dizzying rapidity, the succession of pretentious, aggressively mediocre buildings that litter our cities' skylines, the plethora of arcane theories advanced to explain every conceivable species of architectural practice—all this has left the world of architecture a bit stunned and uncertain where to turn for direction. The confident rise of postmodernism in the seventies and early eighties has been succeeded by a period of doubt and reassessment. Not that there is much indication that the paraphernalia of postmodernism is losing popularity. On the contrary, postmodernist grandiosity remains the order of the day among most corporate clients and ambitious home builders hoping to make an architectural "statement." But neither architects, nor their clients, nor the public at large seem quite so sure these days that the answer to the failings of modernist architecture is to be found in skyscrapers bedizened with Chippendale tops and pastel facades or in houses decked out with pseudo-Palladian windows and slapdash historicist ornamentation.

The resulting atmosphere is one of frenetic indecision. Amid talk of the death of postmodernism and speculation about the next wave of architectural fashion, vanguard spokesmen for the profession seem deeply divided: apologetic and querulous by turns, longing to proselytize yet lacking a compelling vision of the future. The entire radical agenda of Left Eclecticism has promptly established itself in the resulting vacuum. One thinks, for example, of such manifestations as the journal *Zone,* an erratically published collection of neo-Marxist and poststructuralist meditations on architecture and urban design. But more troubling than such radical ephemera is the extent to which many mainstream institutions of architectural education have embraced the ethos of Left Eclecticism. Three recent events—a symposium on architectural education at Princeton University, a debate sponsored by the Parsons School of Design in New York City, and the Museum of Modern Art's exhibition of deconstructivist architecture—offered a good sampling of how far this corruption of architectural education has proceeded in elite architectural circles. Taken together with a handful of books recently published by some of the participants at those events, they may be said to epitomize the politicized spirit of contemporary architecture.

II • THE CULT OF THEORY: A PRIMER FOR ARCHITECTS

Let us begin with "Architecture and Education: The Past Twenty-Five Years and Assumptions for the Future," a daylong symposium sponsored by the Princeton School of Architecture in the spring of 1988.* Convened to honor Princeton's premier postmodernist architect, Michael Graves, on the occasion of his twenty-fifth year teaching at the university, the symposium drew an enthusiastic audience of several hundred students, faculty, and interested outsiders, who crowded into Princeton's elegant McCosh Hall to witness the proceedings. One has not heard quite so much about Graves lately. But the man who brought us The Portland (Oregon) Public Service Building; the Humana building in Louisville, Kentucky; the proposal to expand the Whitney Museum of American Art in New York City; and sundry other delights (an exhibition of drawings and models by Graves was on view next door to remind us of his contributions to architecture) continues to occupy a central place in the architectural limelight. And as limelight is attracted by limelight, it was not surprising that the symposium's participants included other such luminaries from the

*Unless otherwise noted, quotations in the following paragraphs are drawn from the presentations delivered at this symposium.

academic world as Peter Eisenman, Robert Venturi, Robert A. M. Stern, Alan Colquhoun, and Frank Gehry.

The festivities began with some brief remarks by Robert Maxwell, dean of the School of Architecture. Looking back over the changes that had taken place in architectural education during the last twenty-five years, he spoke enthusiastically about the stewardship of his predecessor, Robert Geddes, made some obligatory criticisms of modernist architecture, and praised what he called the "semiotic revolution" in architecture—that university-born revolution that encourages us to treat architecture as a kind of "text" to be deciphered that went hand and hand with the flowering of postmodernism. As Dean Maxwell rightly noted, the application of semiotics to architecture began in the sixties and was given a tremendous boost by *Learning from Las Vegas,* Robert Venturi's notorious 1972 manifesto glorifying the semantic richness of the urban strip. Venturi "crossed semiotics with communications and produced postmodernism," Dean Maxwell told us with undisguised pride.

Despite this revolution, however, the good dean also assured us that education at Princeton's School of Architecture had not changed nearly so much as had the practice of architecture over the last quarter century. At Princeton, there was still an "unchanging emphasis on history and theory and a continuing search for a dialogue that will give meaning to practice." An "unchanging" emphasis, it should be noted, that nevertheless has brought with it all manner of "semiotic" innovations, including the newest wrinkle in architectural theory, "deconstructivism." This barbarous neologism—which derives from the more familiar barbarism *deconstruction*—denotes a theory and practice of architecture motivated largely by various ideas and catchphrases appropriated from chic literary theory. One thus sees architects obsessed with language, rejecting traditional aesthetic values such as clarity, order, and harmony, and designing buildings that seek to undermine or deconstruct such conventional "prejudices" as the desire for comfort, stability, and commodiousness. Hence it turns out that the great thing about the pluralistic ethos that Dean Maxwell extolled at Princeton is that it can embrace a theory that is utterly at odds with everything traditional architectural pedagogy taught and yet somehow, miraculously, remain unchanged.

Although his remarks were generously laced with the good-humored, self-congratulatory platitudes that academic administrators are expected to emit on such occasions, Dean Maxwell did obliquely touch on two points that have come to be absolutely central to most contemporary academic thinking about architecture and that were much in evidence at Princeton that day: (1) the contention that modernist architecture was a social and artistic failure that postmodernism has begun to remedy and (2) the view that architecture is essentially a "narrative" art. One could not be certain that Dean Maxwell appreciated the troubling implications of these ideas, especially the second. One sensed, indeed, that his avuncular, jokey style and what we might call his academic ecumenicism effectively insulate him from having to contemplate the intellectual or artistic consequences of the ideas he routinely bestows his blessing on as dean; but it soon became clear that several of his distinguished colleagues grasped the radical drift of these two ideas with all possible clarity.

Anthony Vidler, for example, who teaches the history of architecture at Princeton and who made a name for himself in avant-garde architectural circles for his contributions to the prestigious architecture magazine *Oppositions* in the seventies, provided us with an astringently academic lecture on the history of architecture and architectural theory in the university. Professor Vidler's lecture aimed to show that, once they had been ensconced in the university, the main task of history and theory of architecture was to uncover the hidden premises of the profession and to spark students "to interrogate the limits of their own practice." Supported by a mélange of quotations from or allusions to writers as various as the architectural historian Colin Rowe, the literary critic Harold Bloom, the philosophers Charles Sanders Peirce and Michel Foucault, Professor Vidler championed the contemporary role of architectural history in the university because it made students "uncomfortable" and helped them to "think past" the traditional models of architecture (to what?), because it encouraged them to investigate "the politics of discourse" that was entrenched in the profession, and because it led them to question the unfortunate "hegemony" of the reigning educational system. Here again we can see the extent to which fashionable ideas from departments of English and comparative literature have seeped into architectural theory: Professor Vidler's talk was hardly more than a tapestry of clichés bemoaning the ideological nature of traditional educational hierarchies and the essentially subversive nature of history and theory.

But while he adhered strictly to the orthodox academic position that orthodoxy must be questioned and exposed, Professor Vidler's lecture was no match, either in entertainment value or in defiant insouciance, for the contributions of Peter Eisenman, who spoke next and who made it his business to speak often from the floor as the day went on. Now Mr. Eisenman is a curious case. Excepting Philip Johnson and maybe one or two others, he is as well known and greatly honored as any living American architect. He has taught at Princeton, Harvard, Yale, Cooper Union, and many other institutions; his fame is international: scarcely a panel of American architects is drawn up for a foreign legation in which his name does not figure. And he is one of only seven architects whose work was chosen to appear in Philip Johnson's much publicized and influential exhibition "Deconstructivist Architecture" at the Museum of Modern Art in the summer of 1988.

But on what does Eisenman's reputation rest? A founder and for several years the director of the fabled Institute for Architecture and Urban Studies in New York, he was also an editor and guiding force of *Oppositions* for many years and was consequently in a position to influence the course of intellectual debate about architectural matters. Although recently he seems to have become interested in building again, his roster of built works is quite small: a few houses in the sixties and seventies, a fire station, and most recently, a biology center for the University of Frankfurt and a visual arts center for Ohio State University in Columbus. Not a great deal more. But Eisenman has something else that has catapulted him into the forefront of architectural celebrity: he is a tireless theorist, and in his use of modish theory he is adamantly, famously, extravagantly obscure. Indeed, judging from the respectful laughter of his audience at Princeton, his audience, expecting him to be unintelligible, want him to be *outrageously* unintelligible—the idea being, one assumes, that if he is going to be obscure he may as well be amusingly so.

And Eisenman can be quite amusing. There is something of the intellectual agent provocateur about him: he delights in stirring up controversy and strife. Accordingly, he began his extemporaneous remarks with a couple of anecdotes whose main intent would seem to have been to insult his colleagues. The first was mildly obscene and not worth repeating; but the second had a peculiar pertinence to the proceedings at hand and deserves to be recounted. When visiting the zoo in Cambridge, England, Eisenman told us, he especially liked to see the tea party put on Friday afternoons by the monkeys. Dressed up in the appropriate clothes, some would be coaxed to play maid and go through the motions of serving, while others would sit around as master and mistress. There they were, playacting, chattering away to themselves, Eisenman observed, "but they never knew what they were saying." This might, he suggested, have some relevance to what was going on that day at Princeton.

He was right. The uncanny aptness of Eisenman's anecdote was brought home again and again as the day wore on, not least during the course of his own presentation. Beginning with the charge that "we are all nostalgics" and that the symposium itself was an event of "enormous nostalgia"—*nostalgia,* remember, is a prime vice in the opinion of the academy these days—he castigated postmodernism's reactionary penchant for adopting historicist ornamentation. He then went on to predict that the generation of students from 1975 to 1985 would usher in a new era of architectural practice, a "theoretical practice energized by an idea of history." The rise of such a practice could afford us the first opportunity to articulate a theory—as distinct from a mere history—of modernism, Eisenman told us. This new theory of modernism would not traffic in any nostalgia for the avant-garde but, on the contrary, would be

> a theory of the center, that is, a theory which occupies the center. I believe only when such a theory of the center is articulated will architecture be able to transform itself as it always has and as it always will. . . . But the center that I am talking about is not a center that can be the center that we know is in the past, as a nostalgia for center. Rather, this not new but [this] other center will be . . . an interstitial one—but one with no structure, but one also that embraces as periphery in its own centric position. . . . A center no longer sustained by nostalgia and no longer sustained by univocal discourse.

Eisenman was speaking off the cuff, and it's possible that my tape recorder did not catch every last word, but there is no denying that this is an expostulation of formidable elusiveness. Nor is Eisenman's more considered prose always more intelligible. His opaque verbal shenanigans—what the critic Charles Jencks has called his "rhetoric machine"—are in top form in the essay he contributed to *Houses of Cards,*[2] for example, a recent book on his work that also includes essays by those other masters of impenetrability, the Marxist architecture critic Manfredo Tafuri and the art critic and editor of *October* Rosalind Krauss. In *Houses of Cards,* Eisenman presents the six houses he designed (of which only four have been built) in the sixties and seventies more or less as demonstration pieces to illustrate his theories about narrative architecture and unsettling the traditional meaning of "home." Appropriately, the houses are not named after their owner or location but are bluntly titled House I, House II, and so on. The book gives an unusually good sense of Eisenman's style of thought, and it is worth taking a bit of a detour to consider some of its more memorable highlights.

Noting that the book was assembled from fragments, Eisenman correctly observes that "it promises and prohibits access; it directs and meanders." In the three essays collected here, he wrote, "as in the house, the ideas transform and decompose. In fact, I ask that the reader augment a traditional reading of this book by also treating the texts and the book as a whole as objects, and by reading the houses, individually and in ensemble, as texts."[3] Presumably to help the reader augment a "traditional reading" of the book, Eisenman has included numerous sketches, drawings, and photographs of the houses, as well as photographically reproduced copies of some of his rough notes on the houses—ostentatiously crumpled, torn, and patched-together notes, full of emendations and crossings out. I suppose we are meant to regard these salvaged scraps (if indeed they *are* salvaged scraps and not carefully manufactured mementos) as the leavings of genius. They do contribute to one's regarding the book as an "object" rather than a text, but they do nothing to deepen one's appreciation of the architecture they are meant to comment on. From the bits on House IV, for example, we learn that

[2]Peter Eisenman, "Misreading," in *Houses of Cards,* with essays by Rosalind Krauss, Peter Eisenman, and Manfredo Tafuri (New York: Oxford University Press, 1988).

[3]Peter Eisenman, "Preface," in *Houses of Cards.*

> this work is an attempt to transcend our traditional view of
> designing
> seeing
> understanding
> our environment
> it is an attempt to alienate the individual from the known way in which he perceives and understand his environment.[4]

But the notes are nothing compared to Eisenman's essay. Grandly informing us that "the essence of the act of architecture is the dislocation of an ever-reconstituting metaphysic of architecture," Eisenman tells us that the six houses that form the subject of his book are all "governed by the intent to define the act of architecture as the dislocation of consequent reconstitution of an ever-accruing metaphysic of architecture." What, you ask, is "an ever-accruing metaphysic of architecture"? Eisenman never says, but it is clear that he has a special liking for the word *metaphysic.* In addition to the "metaphysic of architecture" that he is fond of invoking, we also encounter the "metaphysic of the center," the "metaphysic of the house," even "the metaphysic of dining."[5]

Concerning the last, for example, we learn that Houses III and IV explore

> an alternative process of making occupiable form, . . . a process specifically developed to operate as freely as possible from functional considerations. From a traditional point of view, several columns "intrude on" and "disrupt" the living and dining areas as a result of this process. . . . Nonetheless, these dislocations . . . have, according to the occupants of the house, changed the dining experience in a real and, more importantly, unpredictable fashion.

Please note that Eisenman does not assert that the occupants claim that his ill-placed columns have done anything to make "the dining experience" more *pleasant.* Nor would he want them to. For one of the main goals of Eisenman's architecture (and his writing, too, one suspects) is to subvert anything so bourgeois as comfort or intelligibility. As he puts it, his houses "attempt to have little to do with the traditional and

[4]Ibid., 150.

[5]Ibid., 167, 169, 174, 181.

existing metaphysic of the house, the physical and psychological gratification associated with the traditional form of the house, . . . in order to initiate a search for those possibilities of dwelling that may have been repressed by that metaphysic."[6]

In fact, if Eisenman can be said to have a thesis, it is the standard academic chestnut that the threat of modern technology, and especially of nuclear weapons, has rendered the traditional notion of the home—more, the traditional notion of man—otiose. "With the scientifically orchestrated horror of Hiroshima and the consciousness of the human brutality of the Holocaust," Eisenman gravely intones, "it became impossible for man to sustain a relationship with any of the dominant cosmologies of the past; he could no longer derive his identity from a belief in a heroic purpose and future. . . . Man now lives in an *in extremis* condition."[7] The most wonderful thing about this apocalyptic vision (which is much in evidence in architectural theory these days) is that it licenses the most extraordinary claims. For if man now really lives *in extremis,* then of course everything can be questioned, everything overturned, with impunity, not least the traditional "anthropocentric" function of architecture. Here, in one of his clearer expostulations, is Eisenman on the notion that one important function of architecture is to provide shelter:

> But as shelter also exists in the mind as an idea, in its metaphysical state architecture is a conceptual reflection on physical presence, an "absence" in a material sense. From this perspective, what was earlier described as a traditional architectural history founded on dominant vectors of truth can also be seen as an ideological effort to screen architecture's intrinsic absence behind an emphasis on its physic [*sic*]. It could be said that this screening is a sign of the endurance of anthropocentrism's privileging of presence and centeredness, even beyond its own crisis.[8]

If the issue is architecture considered as a "physic," I suppose one could admit that there is something emetic about this passage. But what, finally, is Eisenman getting at here? Forget about the decon-

[6]Ibid., 169, 172.

[7]Ibid., 170, 172.

[8]Ibid., 182.

structivist curlicues and non sequiturs—the prattle about the "metaphysical state of architecture," the illogical suggestion that "a conceptual reflection on physical presence" is somehow the same as "an 'absence' in a material sense": all that is simply part of the verbal static that automatically crackles through his speech and writing. And don't be put off by the formidable talk of "dominant vectors of truth" or "privileging of presence and centeredness." It's nonsense, but I'm quite sure that Eisenman can't help writing it: his prose has always been like this, laden with half-digested ideas and jargon culled from whatever abstruse academic theories happen to be making the rounds. Perhaps it has something to do with those monkeys he studied in Cambridge. But do consider the final sentence, the one suggesting that traditional architectural history is faulty because it blindly indulges in various "anthropocentric" habits. At bottom, it is nothing more than a simpleminded inversion of every tried-and-true tenet about the function of architecture, an inversion that is finally as ridiculous as it is initially shocking. Immersed in Eisenman's chatter, it is sometimes easy to forget that architecture is essentially about building habitable buildings, buildings that we live and work in, play and worship in, not that we struggle to decode.

There is a great deal more that one could say about Eisenman's essay. Perhaps most amusing is his admission, near the end of the piece, that his houses were not as radical as he had hoped because they turned out to be "grounded in the very anthropocentric metaphysic that they were intended to contravene."[9] Too bad! Although in truth I have confidence that Eisenman's current love affair with the nihilistic presuppositions of deconstruction will prove to be a great aid in expunging anything resembling an "anthropocentric metaphysic" from his architecture and his theorizing.

III • THE DEAN SPEAKS UP

If few of the speakers at Princeton were as radical as Eisenman, none were as dazzlingly obscurantist. In fact, after Eisenman's brief presentation, the proceedings were often downright dull until nearly the end of the day. Robert Venturi was perhaps the most disappointing

[9]Ibid., 181.

speaker. One naturally expected something quite engaging from the author of *Complexity and Contradiction in Architecture,* that self-described "gentle manifesto" that has often been credited with inaugurating the turn to postmodernist architecture. But in the event, he did little more than offer a few reminiscences on the deplorable state of architectural education in the 1940s, when the modernism of Gropius was regnant, and laud Princeton for its consistently "nondoctrinaire" approach to education.

Venturi's presentation was succeeded by a roundtable discussion moderated by the art historian Irving Lavin. Rather like Dean Maxwell, Professor Lavin turned out to be one of those liberal academics who treat every new intellectual fashion as an expression of the beneficent spirit of pluralism. Accordingly, and again rather like Dean Maxwell, Professor Lavin appeared to be in favor of everything and against nothing—except, of course, any position that presumed to question the cogency or desirability of those new intellectual fashions, for such questioning betrayed a lamentable lack of the pluralistic spirit. Thus he admitted that the architecture critic Ada Louise Huxtable fell from grace in his eyes when she dared to criticize postmodernism. In Professor Lavin's view, postmodernism is an attempt to reconstruct "the ancient legacy of culture"—a bizarre thought, it is true, because postmodernism is no more concerned with the "ancient legacy of culture" than is *Vogue* magazine. But it was no more bizarre than his later suggestion that one of the truly nifty things about deconstruction was that it might provide a common ground between modernism and postmodernism or that it had something to do with "man's eternal search for a noble ideal of harmony, balance, and perfection, or to his equally eternal struggle with irrationality, instability, and chaos." In other words, for Professor Lavin, deconstruction was hardly to be distinguished from classic humanism.

Dean Maxwell brought the session to an end with another roundtable discussion. He began by professing his pluralistic credentials: "I disagree with everybody who has a final answer," he assured us, "and I agree with everybody . . . who believes that constant change is the order of the day." But Eisenman was having none of this wishy-washy, Heraclitean liberalism. He rose from his place in the audience to expound a bit about deconstruction, the end of Western metaphysics, and to announce that "we are all a bunch of old fogeys holding onto a teetering system." "The only truth today is that we are found with the loss of truth," he told us darkly, as if such secondhand Nietzschean sentiments were a startling revelation—or, indeed, as if they were apodictically true.

Despite Eisenman's plea that we study things "not as truth but as some sort of knowledge that can be opened up and studied," Colquhoun's insistence that "education is always a matter of inculcating a certain ideology," and so on, it was often easy to forget that this symposium was supposed to deal with the subject of architectural education. It was with considerable interest, then, that one heard a woman from the audience ask the distinguished members of the panel to compare the requirements for architectural education today with the requirements for a degree in engineering, music, and mathematics. It was, I thought, an unusually intelligent question. A full answer would have had to say something about those aspects of architecture that are akin to art and craft as well as those that are straightforwardly matters of calculation and engineering. A full answer, indeed, would have said a good deal about the hybrid nature of architecture, its functional *and* its aesthetic claims, its sometimes uneasy place between engineering and art. But the question was not deemed serious by Maxwell and company. After a brief embarrassed silence, there were a few half-hearted attempts to dismiss the question with ridicule or patronizing obfuscation. Perhaps this means that Dean Maxwell disagrees not only with "everybody who has a final answer," but even those who ask questions that might admit of such answers. It's a wonderful philosophy for an academic dean.

IV • BUILDING CASTLES IN THE AIR

Many of the themes that were bandied about at Princeton that day were also on display at a debate on the subject of postmodernist classicism versus narrative and deconstruction in architecture which was sponsored by the graduate program in architecture and design criticism at the Parsons School of Design in New York City in the winter of 1988. Moderated by Douglas Davis, the architectural critic for *Newsweek,* the debate was between Charles Jencks, an architect and architectural critic, and James Wines, an architect and director of the graduate program in architecture and design criticism at Parsons.

Jencks is best known for his tireless proselytizing on behalf of post-modernism; it was he, in fact, who gave the term currency in the first edition of his book *The Language of Post-Modern Architecture.* Wines, who first made his reputation as a sculptor in the sixties, is the founder of SITE, an architectural and environmental art group formed in 1970 "for the purpose of exploring new ways to bring a heightened level of communication and psychological content to buildings, interiors, and public spaces."[10] He has emerged in recent years as one of the leading practitioners of deconstructivist architecture or, as he prefers to denominate it, *de-architecture.*

Jencks spoke first and presented himself as the champion of "postmodern classicism," a phenomenon that he described as the third stage of postmodernism. The first stage of postmodernism, according to his scheme, occurred in the 1960s and was essentially a reaction against the strictures of modernism. The second stage, which the 1970s ushered in, was a period of "pluralism and eclecticism." Now, according to Jencks, mature postmodernism in painting and sculpture but especially in architecture "has adopted a classical language." In vocabulary somewhat reminiscent of Peter Eisenman (although it is likely that the influence went the other way), Jencks described the modern secular world as shot through with a "nostalgia for the center." In his view—and here he takes a very different position from Eisenman—architecture should seek to recover the center for a decentered world. His prescription for this task is the frankly symbolic architecture of postmodern classicism.

This is not to say that postmodern classicism recovers any *actual* center, any binding social, religious, or philosophical order. Rather, in a fashion reminiscent of Hesse's *Glass Bead Game,* it merely *plays* with the classic symbols of past systems to recapture the *aura* or illusion of belonging to a greater whole. Jencks enumerated various characteristics of postmodern classicism—its supposition that "disharmony is harmony," for example, or the large role that wit and humor play in its concoctions—but his main point, a point that is illustrated in lavish detail in his new book on the subject,[11] was that the deliber-

[10]James Wines, *De-architecture* (New York: Rizzoli, 1988), 108, 110.

[11]Charles Jencks, *Towards a Symbolic Architecture: The Thematic House* (New York: Rizzoli, 1988).

ately historicizing symbolism employed by postmodern classicism can provide a quasi-spiritual answer to secular man's real spiritual longings for order and meaning. While he distinguishes postmodern classicism from the "decorated sheds" of Robert Venturi—the symbolic ornamentation he has in mind is not just "stuck on" as it is in Venturi's buildings, he tells us—at bottom they amount to two versions of the same thing. Both advocate arbitrarily applied ornamentation, but for Jencks the arbitrariness is half-concealed under the cloak of an elaborate symbol system and edifying rhetoric.

Wines began his presentation by noting that he and Jencks share a concern with the "communicative or public nature of architecture," but that they differed on the "sources" of communication. In many respects, Wines's position is substantively closer to Eisenman's than to Jencks's. Although not nearly as adept at manipulating language to provide camouflage as is Eisenman, he nevertheless shares many of his basic suppositions about the situation of architecture in the contemporary world. For example, he concurs with Eisenman that postmodernism's return to classic iconography is reactionary and to be avoided. He also indulges in a similar prepackaged apocalyptic vision: "We now live in a time of universal melancholy and troubled dreams, a time of introspection and foreboding choices,"[12] he wrote in his recent book and credo, *De-architecture.* For Wines, too, it would seem that the chief task of architecture today is to dislocate and discommode. As he explained in his book, "de-architecture is a way of dissecting, shattering, dissolving, inverting, and transforming certain fixed prejudices about buildings, in the interests of discovering revelations among the fragments."[13] And both Wines and Eisenman—like so many others these days—pretend that *asserting* something about the aim or meaning of a building is tantamount to *accomplishing* it. But in art, as in life, there is often a great gap between between assertion and accomplishment. A poorly designed dining room may be meant to challenge the conventional "metaphysic of dining," but is really only a poorly designed dining room; a dilapidated-looking building may be meant to challenge our consumeristic prejudices, but is really just another ugly building.

[12]Wines, *De-architecture,* 165.

[13]Ibid., 133.

Yet Wines differs from Eisenman in his continued adherence to the idea of architecture as an art. "De-architecture's basic premise," he wrote, "is that art, not design, is the supreme mission of a building, and that the creative process must be revised to reflect this objective."[14] In fact, looking through his book and considering the work of SITE, it soon becomes clear that although Wines has given up the title of sculptor, his ambition has remained essentially sculptural: SITE's installations are basically large environmental sculptures, some of which happen to be habitable.

Probably SITE's best-known architectural work to date are the eight showrooms designed for Best Products Company. Under the patronage of Sydney and Frances Lewis, prominent collectors of contemporary art and owners of Best Products, SITE has designed facades incorporating the principles of de-architecture. The "Indeterminate Facade" (1975) showroom in Houston, for example, "appears to be arrested somewhere between construction and demolition"[15] with its pile of brick punched from the top of the building and cascading down onto the entrance canopy. A more radical, and as yet unbuilt, project is the "Highrise of Homes." In Wines's words, this "visionary and traditional"[16] idea provides "a matrix of housing choices" for city dwellers. Consisting of a large U-shaped steel and concrete grid eight to fifteen stories tall, the Highrise of Homes is meant to provide modules in which individuals could build single-family houses in the style of their choice—modern, colonial, Tudor, Greek revival, you name it. The houses on each level, clustered into "villagelike compounds," would have access to a central elevator and core mechanical services. "The Highrise of Homes," Wines wrote, "is based on the premise that people will benefit from the personal affirmation and territorial definition associated with the detached house, even if it is in the compressed environment of a multistory building." In reality, of course, the Highrise of Homes would be a grotesque architectural nightmare, as patronizing to its intended clients as it is stylistically meretricious.

There is a great deal more that one might say about Wines's

[14]Ibid., 118.

[15]Ibid., 145.

[16]Ibid., 163.

theories and the work of SITE, but here I will only pause to consider his contention that "rarely have contemporary buildings come close to the kind of sociological and psychological content expressed in, say, a Beckett play, a Magritte painting, or a Chaplin film."[17] What do Wines's examples tell us about his conception of architecture? Is the sort of "sociological and psychological content" to which he alludes something we would wish to find embodied in our buildings? Think of it: an office building that reminded one of *Waiting for Godot* or *Endgame,* a home as unsettling as a Magritte painting, a factory as zany as a film by Charlie Chaplin. Does it sound like a wonderful idea? Note that Wines suggested that this paucity of "sociological and psychological content" is a particular problem for contemporary buildings. Are we then to assume that older buildings possess a greater measure of such content? Chartres Cathedral is one of Wines's favorite architectural monuments from the past; he discusses it at length as an model of "narrative" architecture. Does Chartres, then, "come close to the kind of sociological and psychological content expressed in, say, a Beckett play, a Magritte painting, or a Chaplin film"?

In the end, Wines emerges as a kind of anemic, half-hearted imitation of someone like Eisenman; he mimics a good deal of radical rhetoric, but his emphasis on communication binds him to a rather traditional humanistic sentiment. And although SITE's projects are among the most arrogant and high-handed I have seen in recent years, they do not really express the kind of fundamental challenge to traditional architecture practice that Eisenman, for example, advocates. Quite different is the position preached by Jencks. For where Wines and Eisenman are nihilists in the apocalyptic mode, Jencks is a happy nihilist. Like his colleagues—at least, like Eisenman—he assumes that the modern secular world has lost any compelling foundation for shared social meaning; but unlike them, he has no scruples about fabricating a false foundation out of promiscuous fragments gathered from the past. Jencks's basic message seems to be: If we cannot overcome the modern world, at least we can forget it.

The saccharine, archaizing spirit at work in Jencks's latest version of postmodernism is on full view in his new book, *Towards a Symbolic Architecture: The Thematic House.* Beginning with a chapter called "Fa-

[17]Ibid., 14.

bles for our Time," Jencks advocates "the conscious reassertion of the symbolic programme, the idea that every client and architect should make up an iconographic contract as explicit as their economic one," as "first steps in a new tradition, or perhaps the revival of an old one."[18] Not surprisingly, words such as *fable* and *parable* are featured in his exposition, and he sprinkles his text with lots of fake Latin names, capitalized abstract nouns, and deliberately archaic drawings with legends such as "meaning triumphs over time."

After some general considerations about the troubled place of architecture in a secular world, Jencks reviews three of his own architectural projects, including one that incorporates the texts of Milton's poems *L'Allegro* and *Il Penseroso* as mood setters and thematic pointers for a house and garden in California. ("Hence loathed Melancholy," indeed!) But the bulk of the book is devoted to an examination of "The Thematic House," Jencks's extraordinary renovation of an 1840s London townhouse for himself and his family. Beginning with the front door, which sports cleverly stylized initials of each of the family members, the whole house is an elaborate confection of symbolic motifs. The main downstairs rooms are each associated with one or another of the seasons and are decorated accordingly: spring, summer, Indian summer, autumn, and winter; winter boasts a fireplace designed by Michael Graves. Inside the front door, there is a mirrored room that Jencks dubs the Cosmic Oval, in which the two main themes of the house—cosmic time and cultural time—are given preliminary expression in a mural showing, in Jencks's words, the "evolution of the galaxies after the Big Bang."[19] There is also a portrait frieze painted by William Stok depicting a dozen cultural "paragons," including the Emperor Hadrian, and Thomas Jefferson conversing with Hannah Arendt. In the bathroom on the ground floor—the Cosmic Loo, in Jencks's terminology—we have a complicated paint scheme with "light greys below, bright multi-colors in the middle and infinite cosmic gloom above, as in Westminster Cathedral."[20]

Then there is the central staircase, the Solar Stair, whose spiral

[18]Jencks, *Towards a Symbolic Architecture,* 9.

[19]Ibid., 90.

[20]Ibid.

is meant to recall "spiral galaxies, DNA, cyclical motion," according to Jencks. It is also an abstract representation of the solar year: cast in concrete, its fifty-two steps, each of which is inscribed with seven grooves, make a grand total of 365 "days." *The Black Hole,* a mosaic by Eduardo Paolozzi at the bottom of the stairs, is meant to symbolize cosmic gloom or something, and on and on it goes, every room in the house weighted down with its load of symbols and inscriptions.

As Jencks himself has pointed out, there has always been a large element of camp in postmodernist architecture. But with his Thematic House and theory of symbolic architecture, Jencks has gone beyond camp and pushed postmodernism firmly in the direction of kitsch. The difference is that where the camp sensibility retains sufficient self-consciousness to play with the sentimentalized products of bad taste, the kitsch sensibility *surrenders* to them and to the sentimentalized version of reality they promise. Hitherto, postmodernist architecture was funny on purpose; with his Thematic House, Jencks is only unintentionally so. Although Jencks occasionally warns the reader about the dangers of aestheticism in the course of his book, his entire presentation is little more than a recipe for an exquisitely aestheticized—and exquisitely expensive—brand of kitsch.

V • PHILIP JOHNSON'S REVENGE

Between the ironic skepticism of Eisenman and the cloying sentimentalizations of Jencks there is not much to choose. It is difficult to say which impulse, if either, will assume dominance in architecture. Because sentimentality exercises a seemingly inextinguishable appeal, one might think of betting on Jencks. But as has often been pointed out, ours is an ironic age, and the appeal of the radical skepticism preached by Eisenman and others should not be underestimated. The Museum of Modern Art, at any rate, would seem to be backing the latter movement. Its exhibition "Deconstructivist Architecture" included projects by Eisenman, Gehry, and five other architects whose work self-consciously explores architectural disharmony and fragmentariness. Hailed as the successor to Johnson's path-breaking exhibition of modernist architecture in 1932—long before Johnson had given up modernism to become the chief impresario of postmodernist chic—it was easily the most talked about architectural event of 1988.

"Deconstructivist Architecture" featured ten recent projects by seven architects. Some of the projects have been built, some are still under construction, and some are . . . well, let's call them unbuilt if not unbuildable speculative exercises. Two of the architects included in the exhibition, Eisenman and Gehry, are senior practitioners with international reputations; the other five—Rem Koolhaas from Holland, Zaha M. Hadid from Iraq, Daniel Libeskind from Poland, Bernard Tschumi from Switzerland (now the dean of the Columbia School of Architecture), and the firm of Coop Himmelblau from Vienna—are younger practioners whose stars are rising.

What brings these very different architects together is not any shared style or beliefs about the tasks of architecture. One would be hard pressed, for example, to find instances of contemporary architecture more disparate in style, character, and intention than Gehry's renovation of a suburban house in Santa Monica (completed in three stages, from 1978 to 1988) and the massive high-rise apartment *cum* community center and observation tower built by Koolhaas in Rotterdam in 1982. No, deconstructivism is not in this sense a school or movement so much as an *attitude.* As Johnson acknowledged, in the brief preface he contributed to the catalog, deconstructivist architecture, lacking the encompassing vision and "messianic fervor" of modernism, "is not a new style." And far from suggesting the rise of a new school of architecture, he wrote, the exhibition was simply an attempt to bring together the recent work of a few important architects "that [show] a similar approach with very similar forms as an outcome."[21]

The forms in question are said to derive mostly from the art and architecture of Russian constructivism and suprematism that flourished in the late 'teens and early twenties, notably the abstract paintings of Kaismir Malevich and the sculpture and architecture of Vladimir Tatlin, Aleksandr Rodchenko, and others. As it happens, the connection between constructivism and the works on view in the exhibition is sometimes quite tenuous. Often, one suspects, it depends on nothing more than fortuitous formal similarities—where, indeed, there is even *that* connection. Nevertheless, a great deal had been

[21]Philip Johnson and Mark Wigley, *Deconstructivist Architecture* (New York: The Museum of Modern Art, 1988), 7. The reader may also wish to consult *Deconstruction in Architecture,* a special issue of *Architectural Design,* vol. 58, 3/4 (1988) and *What is Deconstruction?* by Christopher Norris and Andrew Benjamin (London: St. Martin's Press, 1988).

made of the influence of the Russian avant-garde on the distinctive forms and aesthetic goals of deconstructivism; we saw this already in *October,* and it reappeared here both in the exhibition itself (which attempted to reinforce the connection by beginning with a smorgasbord of constructivist paintings and sculpture drawn from the museum's collections) and in the catalog essay.

Yet even more revealing than this alleged precursor is Johnson's observation about the difference between the spirit of modernism and the spirit of deconstructivism. "The contrast is," he wrote, appropriating a striking phrase from a younger colleague, "between perfection and violated perfection." Please note the choice of words: the perfection he has in mind is not missed or unattained or half-realized, but *violated.* The lurid overtones of violence and corruption are intentional; they are, in fact, central to the ethos of deconstructive architecture.

This becomes painfully clear when we turn to the catalog essay and commentaries on individual projects, which were written by Mark Wigley, a lecturer at Princeton University and associate curator of the exhibition. *Disturb, torture, interrogate, contaminate, infect:* these are the words he favors to explain and to *praise* deconstructivist architecture. In the projects on view in this exhibition, he tells us proudly, the "dream of pure form has been disturbed. Form has become contaminated. The dream has become a kind of nightmare."[22]

What makes these projects "deconstructive," according to Wigley, is their ability "to disturb our thinking about form," in particular, their ability to disturb or undermine our taken-for-granted suppositions about the values of traditional architectural order and unity. "Architecture is a conservative discipline," he noted sadly near the beginning of his essay: stability, regularity, order, intelligibility, commodiousness—these are prime virtues for traditional architecture. Deconstructivism changes all that by the simple expedient of disparaging traditional architectural values and championing their opposites. Nor should we think that critics have a monopoly on the deconstructivist gambit. We have already considered some samples of Mr. Eisenman's meditations on architecture. Here is Bernard Tschumi, dean of the School of Architecture at Columbia University:

[22]Ibid., 7.

> It might be worthwhile . . . to abandon any notion of post-modern architecture in favor of a post-humanist architecture, one that would stress not only the dispersion of the subject and the force of social regulation, but also the effect of such decentering on the entire notion of a unified, coherent architectural form.[23]

Wigley denied that deconstructive architecture derives from "the mode of contemporary philosophy known as 'deconstruction,' " but this is obviously disingenuous. His own arguments, and those of the architects he discusses, are nothing but a congeries of deconstructionist clichés, beginning with the familiar contentions that everything is a kind of text to be deciphered and that the ostensible meaning of every text contains the seeds of its own destruction.

Then, too, the rhetorical *style* of Wigley's presentation closely mimics the provocative antics of literary deconstruction. "It is," he mused, "as if some kind of parasite has infected the form and distorted it from inside." Hence the projects on view are said to "reopen the wound" that Russian constructivism had inflicted on the tradition but that had healed during the reign of modernism. We also learn that "perfection is secretly monstrous. Tortured from within, the seemingly perfect form confesses its crime, its imperfection." In one particularly bizarre passage, Wigley combines this talk of torture and interrogation with psychoanalysis to produce an image that borders on the surreal: "The deconstructivist puts the pure forms of the architectural tradition on the couch and identifies the symptoms of a repressed impurity. The impurity is drawn to the surface by a combination of gentle coaxing and violent torture: the form is interrogated."[24] And on and on. To read Wigley, one would think that architecture was primarily a form of pathology.

The basic idea behind this overcharged verbiage is that deconstructivist architecture undermines modernist architectural theory and practice and does so not by offering an alternative but by making overt and by exaggerating certain tensions that are said to lurk unrecognized in the tradition of modernism. It is in this sense that it can be said to violate perfection, subverting it by exposing its inherent (albeit unacknowledged) corruption and contamination, locating "the inher-

[23]Quoted in Norris and Benjamin, *What is Deconstruction?,* 40.

[24]Johnson and Wigley, *Deconstructivist Architecture,* 10–20.

ent dilemmas within buildings." Writing about The Peak, Zaha Hadid's 1982 Hong Kong resort, for example, Wigley observed that "the club is stretched between the emptiness of the void and the density of the underground solids, domains normally excluded from modern architecture but found within it by pushing modernism to its limits, forcing it apart. In this way, the pleasure palace, the hedonist resort, is located in the twisted center of modern purity."[25]

Of course, what deconstructive architecture offers is not so much a critique as a caricature of modernism. For one thing, while it is certainly true that a good deal of modernist architecture strove for an abstract formal perfection, its emphasis on form was anchored by its concern with function. Form, as the slogan goes, was intended to follow function. Moreover, as Wigley noted, what is really at issue is not modernism's pretension to formal perfection but its support of established culture. "What is being disturbed" by deconstructivist architecture, he wrote, "is a set of deeply entrenched cultural assumptions which underlie a certain view of architecture, assumptions about order, harmony, stability, and unity." That is to say, what is being "disturbed" is a commitment to the established conventions of Western society and culture, including an allegiance to values such as order, harmony, stability, and unity. And this brings us to the deeper—or we should say, the repressed?—reason that so much is made of the Russian avant-garde by Johnson, Wigley, and company. As we saw in the discussion of the *October* syndrome, the Russian avant-garde offers one of the most dramatic instances of the conflation of art and radical politics in recent history, an instance that commends itself as a model for the revolutionary, subversive rhetoric of deconstructive architecture.[26]

But is it anything more than rhetoric? Discussing Daniel Libeskind's 1987 City Edge project in Berlin, Wigley asserted that by being angled up off the ground, the structure—a mammoth elevated bar—"subverts the logic of the wall." "By dismembering the wall," he continued, "traditional thinking about structure is also broken down."[27] Something there is, clearly, that doesn't love a wall, and its

[25]Ibid., 68.

[26]Ibid., 19–20.

[27]Ibid., 34.

name is deconstruction. It is worth pausing to consider these wholly typical statements from Wigley. In what sense is traditional thinking about structure "broken down" by the eccentricities of this project? How is the "logic of the wall" "subverted"? (What indeed is the logic of a wall?) Is such talk anything more than sophistic blather? Wigley, like so many of his deconstructionist confreres, pretends that simply *asserting* something makes it so, as if a couple of quirky, asymmetrical buildings and a dose of obscure theorizing really undermined anything except the credibility of their proponents. In *The Critique of Judgment,* Kant rightly observed that "the main concern" of architecture is "a certain *use* of the artistic object."[28] For deconstructivism, on the contrary, the main concern of architecture would seem to be to provide an occasion for rhetorical excess.

We thus come to one of the great ironies of deconstructivist theory: although it makes a tremendous show of exposing the obsession with purity and perfection that were ingredients in some forms of modernism, it is itself an architecture that happens mostly in the head, not on the ground. In this respect, too, it resembles deconstructionist literary theory, which in its flights of theory loses sight of anything so mundane as the meaning or quality of the text it is supposedly examining. Similarly, deconstructivist architecture presupposes an exceedingly intellectualized view of architecture, and it is precisely its airy intellectualizing that licenses its more outlandish claims. Untethered by anything so pedestrian as everyday experience, the champions of deconstructive architecture can pretend that architecture is really about "interrogating form," subverting "the logic of the wall," etc., not about building appropriate, serviceable, perhaps even beautiful buildings.

This inveterate intellectualism also helps explain deconstructivism's blindness to its own banality. Wigley wrote that deconstructivist architecture "produces a feeling of unease, of disquiet, because it challenges the sense of stable, coherent identity that we associate with pure form." He presented this as if it were some stunningly novel discovery. But the only thing novel about it is the idea that producing the feeling of unease and disquiet should be the aim of architecture.

[28]Immanuel Kant, *Critique of Judgment,* trans. Werner S. Pluhar (Indianapolis: Hackett, 1987), 191.

In Geoffrey Scott's classic monograph *The Architecture of Humanism,* for example, the possibility that there might be buildings that "suggest the idea of instability, the idea of collapse, the idea of restriction, and so forth" is readily admitted. And Scott cheerfully proceeds to note that, confronted with such buildings, "every spectator will judge [them] ugly, and experience a certain discomfort from their presence."[29] But he assumed, simple soul that he was, that experiences of ugliness and discomfort were compelling arguments *against* a building, that no one would willingly choose to design or inhabit a building that inspired such feelings. The deconstructivists teach otherwise. Discomfort and ugliness are their acknowledged stock in trade—except that they speak not of ugliness but of torturing form and so on.

The hard truth is that "Deconstructivist Architecture" was approximately ninety-nine parts hype and one part achievement. It is doubtful whether any of the projects included in the Museum of Modern Art exhibition measure up to the subversive ideal identified as the goal of deconstructivism, much as some of them—one thinks especially of Eisenman's contribution—tried. Furthermore, whatever architectural interest the projects on view in that exhibition may claim was completely overshadowed by the lucubrations of Wigley—pedantry set in motion, abetted, and applauded by Philip Johnson. Indeed, a desire for truth in advertising makes one wish that this exhibition had been titled "Philip Johnson's Revenge," for that is what deconstructivist architecture is finally about. Revenge for what? Above all, perhaps, for being taken seriously. "What good does it do you to believe in good things?" Johnson said in an interview in 1965 with that other apostle of cultural fashion, Susan Sontag. "It's feudal and futile. I think it much better to be nihilistic and forget all that."[30]

One has long understood that Johnson, the doyen of postmodernist camp, has delighted in foisting off on a credulous public ever more outrageous architectural pranks. He is now aided in this cynical game by the rebarbative academic theories and vocabulary that have been corrupting literary studies for years, as well as by a squadron of academic minions from Graves and Eisenman to Wigley and numer-

[29]Geoffrey Scott, *The Architecture of Humanism: A Study in the History of Taste* (New York: W. W. Norton, 1974), 157–158.

[30]Quoted in Charles Jencks, *Modern Movements in Architecture* (New York: Doubleday, 1973), 209.

ous other academic apologists. Johnson's distinctively postmodernist work—beginning with a skyscraper adorned with a Chippendale top and proceeding to the pretentious, deliberately convoluted projects and theories that he gave his blessing to in this exhibition—constitutes a perfectly logical devolution. When put in the context of Johnson's origins as a disciple of Mies van der Rohe and champion of high modernism, the chronicle assumes the proportions of a farce. In the context of our present examination of the state of the humanities, the spectacle of Johnson's career and the influential role he has played in fostering the subversion of architecture and architectural education by the new academic establishment appear as particularly grotesque and cynical examples of the deformation of contemporary academic culture.

CHAPTER 6

THE NEW SOPHISTRY

"You see before you," [Morris Zapp] began, "a man who once believed in the possibility of interpretation. That is, I thought that the goal of reading was to establish the meaning of texts."

—*DAVID LODGE,*
Small World

What I say is that "just" or "right" means nothing but what is to the interest of the stronger party.

—*THRASYMACHUS,*
in Plato's Republic

I • THE ACADEMY CLOSES RANKS

One of the chief complaints heard from those beleaguered by the attacks on the academy launched by Allan Bloom, William Bennett, Lynne V. Cheney, and others is that such critics have given a distorted picture of what is going on. Instead of pondering the admittedly "challenging" (a favorite code word for "impenetrable") work of contemporary scholars, such conservative critics are said to have focused on provocative course titles or radical-sounding statements taken out of context or a few political incidents on campuses twenty years ago. They have thus, the story goes, given the public—and other potential sources of financial support and succor—the unfortunate impression that the academy today has largely given up its traditional educational aims and has, at the deepest level, become radicalized. This, for example, was one of Barbara Herrnstein Smith's recurrent points in her 1988 presidential address to the Modern Language Association. Deploring the ridicule that has been heaped on the academy in recent years for its pursuit of obscurity, she assured her flock that the "scholarly significance of a piece of published research is not self-evident from its title" and suggested that journalists be "specifically recruited and trained" under the aegis of the MLA to encourage them to provide a more accurate, i.e., a more flattering, picture of the profession than has been evident in the press lately.[1] As we have seen, a similar concern informs *Speaking for the Humanities,* the polemical brochure issued by the American Council of Learned Societies in 1989, which declares that "precisely those things now identified as failings in the humanities actually indicate enlivening transformations."[2]

Anyone acquainted with current academic culture knows that all this is blather. One need hardly believe that the title of a course or conference paper reveals everything about its contents to recognize that it is perfectly legitimate to ridicule ridiculous titles—of which, as we have seen, there is a seemingly inexhaustible supply. Nevertheless, Professor Smith has a point, and in the interests of thoroughness it is worth taking the time to consider in some detail at least one example of high-level writing in the humanities these days. As many of the comments and proclamations from the academic conferences we have examined suggest, it would not be at all difficult to find influential professors whose scholarly work and pedagogical aims are blatantly political. Nor would it be difficult to produce countless examples of well-regarded work in the humanities that is needlessly obscure, hopelessly trivial, or frankly at odds with the traditional purposes of humanistic study. Finding academic scholars whose work in the humanities is at once intelligible, intellectually sophisticated, *and* regarded by the profession as being at the forefront of its discipline is a more demanding task.

Among the handful of candidates that suggest themselves, perhaps none is a more articulate representative of one aspect of the radical ethos prevailing in the humanities today than literary critic and polemicist Stanley Fish. Indeed, at a time when the assault on the humanities by deconstruction and other French imports shows signs of giving way to ever more knowing, overtly political forms of rebuke such as the New Historicism and Cultural Studies, few figures offer

[1]Barbara Herrnstein Smith, "Limelight: Reflections on a Public Year," *Publications of the Modern Language Association of America* 104, no. 3 (May 1989): 290, 292.

[2]Levine et al., *Speaking for the Humanities,* 3.

a more canny version of the academy's revolt against its traditional goals than Professor Fish. Not that he is a newcomer to the academic scene. His early book *Surprised by Sin: The Reader in Paradise Lost* helped to inaugurate the so-called reader response school of literary theory—according to which the meaning of a literary work inheres not in the text but in the interpretive acts of its readers—and instantly established its young author's reputation as a powerful and ingenious critical intelligence.

Professor Fish's later works include a book on the religious poet George Herbert and a study of seventeenth-century literature. But his next professional *tour de force* came in 1980 when he published *Is There a Text in this Class? The Authority of Interpretive Communities.* This influential collection of essays from the 1970s, most of which are exercises in literary theory as distinct from literary criticism, consolidated and extended his reputation as a formidable academic critic. It continued in an increasingly radical key his project of "dislodging [the text] as the privileged container of meaning"[3] and, not quite incidentally, it presented to the reading public the figure of an able and fiercely contentious rhetorician whose name has ever since been at the forefront of academic literary controversy.

Having received his Ph.D. from Yale in 1962, Professor Fish taught for several years at the University of California at Berkeley and then at Johns Hopkins University before going to Duke University in 1985. Today, as we are reminded on the colophon page of his lengthy new collection of essays, *Doing What Comes Naturally: Change, Rhetoric, and the Practice of Theory in Literary and Legal Studies,*[4] he is simultaneously "Arts and Sciences Professor of English, Professor of Law, and Chair of the Department of English at Duke University." This impressive triple-barreled title not only suggests the heights to which Professor Fish's academic career has risen, it also neatly summarizes his professional accomplishments. The dual appointment to a university chair in English and a professorship in law acknowledges Professor Fish's success in his diverse intellectual endeavors. For although he began his career as a scholar of seven-

[3]Stanley Fish, *Is There a Text in this Class? The Authority of Interpretive Communities* (Cambridge: Harvard University Press, 1980), 3.

[4]Stanley Fish, *Doing What Comes Naturally: Change, Rhetoric, and the Practice of Theory in Literary and Legal Studies* (Durham: Duke University Press, 1989).

teenth-century English literature, he now devotes much of his attention to the law, teaching courses in the Duke Law School and publishing about as often in university law reviews as in literary journals.

It must also be understood that his position as chairman of the Duke English department is no merely honorific administrative post. More than any other individual, Professor Fish must be credited—if *credited* is the correct term—with fashioning the contemporary Duke English department. It was largely through his initiatives (backed, as *The Chronicle of Higher Education* reported, by generous amounts of money from the university, which had "targeted" the English department for "development"[5]) that Duke has been transformed in just a few years from a genteel academic conclave into a bastion of every "advanced" and radical trend currently besetting the humanities. Along with providing lavish new offices for the chairman and a select group of professors, the English department in short order acquired a number of professors well known for their antipathy to traditional humanistic study.

In a series of much-publicized and unusually high-paying appointments, the university hired several high-profile "critical theorists," including Barbara Herrnstein Smith, Frank Lentricchia (who an official university publication described as "the 'Dirty Harry' of Critical Theory"[6]), Annabel Patterson and her husband, Lee Patterson, and Professor Fish's wife, the champion of New Historicism, Jane Tompkins. The university also acquired younger aspirants such as the radical feminist Eve Kosofsky Sedgwick, which brings us back to the subject of course titles. According to the English department's description of courses, Professor Sedgwick's 1989 graduate course "Gender, Sexuality, and Power in Victorian Fiction" focused on, among other things, "female and male homosocial, homosexual, homophobic, and cross-gender relations." Nor, apparently, is this sort of thing out of the ordinary for Professor Sedgwick. The program for the 1989 meeting of the Modern Language Association informs us that she is scheduled to lead a special session titled "The Muse of

[5]Scott Heller, "A Constellation of Recently Hired Professors Illuminates the English Department at Duke," *The Chronicle of Higher Education,* 27 May 1987, 12.

[6]*Duke,* May–June 1988, 2.

Masturbation." In addition to Professor Sedgwick's contribution, "Jane Austen and the Masturbating Girl," there are papers on "Clitoral Imagery and Masturbation in Emily Dickinson," and "Desublimating the Male Sublime: Autoerotics, Anal Erotics, and Corporeal Violence in Melville and William Burroughs," this last named by yet another Duke professor.[7] Such titles do not tell us everything about the class and presentations in question, perhaps, but they do give us some clue about what to expect. In any event, together with the much-celebrated Marxist critic Fredric Jameson, who (among his other titles) is chairman of Duke's Graduate Program in Literature, this cadre of chic theorists and literary activists has made Duke one of the most influential antitraditionalist forces in contemporary academic literary studies.

It is another measure of the extent to which Professor Fish has insinuated himself into the imagination of his discipline that he should have served as the model (or so it is widely rumored) for the character Morris Zapp in *Small World,* an hilariously scathing send-up of the high-powered, jet-setting "Lit. Crit." world by the English novelist and literature professor David Lodge. Whether or not Lodge really had Professor Fish in mind when he created Morris Zapp, anyone familiar with Professor Fish's work can easily imagine him defending as his own the quotation from *Small World* that stands at the head of this chapter. (He would endorse Thrasymachus's words, too, as we shall see.) And given Professor Fish's long-standing interest in the subject of professionalism, one can also imagine him responding as did Morris Zapp when, after delivering a paper titled "Textuality as Striptease," he is asked by an exasperated colleague, "Then what in God's name *is* the point of it all?" "The point [of literary interpretation], of course," replied Zapp coolly, "is to uphold the institution of academic literary studies. We maintain our position in society by publicly performing a certain ritual, just like any other group of workers in the realm of discourse—lawyers, politicians, journalists."[8]

[7] *Publications of the Modern Language Association* 104, no. 6, (Nov. 1989): 1028.

[8] David Lodge, *Small World* (New York: Macmillan, 1984), 28.

II • LEARNING TO PLAY THE GAME

Indeed, the issue of professionalism—what an earlier generation might have called gamesmanship—goes a long way toward helping one understand the course of Professor Fish's stunning academic career. Rather like the ambitious Zapp, he is wont to insist that teaching and writing about literature is a profession like any other, concerned more with self-perpetuation and self-aggrandizement than with the disinterested pursuit of knowledge. In fact, Professor Fish—again like Morris Zapp as well as so many real-life academics today—denies that the traditional scholarly ideal of disinterestedness is even possible, let alone desirable. He repeatedly warns his colleagues against the snares of "antiprofessionalism," which he defines as "any attitude that enforces a distinction between professional labors on the one hand and the identification and promotion of what is true or valuable on the other."[9] Such attitudes might be useful as an occasional corrective, Professor Fish admits; in one place he even refers paradoxically to such antiprofessionalism as the "conscience" of the profession. But at bottom, he argues that the attempt to distinguish between mere professional activity and, for example, the disinterested pursuit of truth is a mistake that encourages precisely the kind of false idealism that leads one to ask embarrassing questions such as "What is the point of studying literature?"

In accordance with his own precepts, Professor Fish has been nothing if not professional. One important expression of his professionalism has been his knack of keeping his criticism one short, provocative, step ahead of the criticism practiced by the majority of his colleagues. Looking back over the development of his career, one sees that he early on perfected what Jean Cocteau described as the art of knowing just how far to go in going too far. Thus in *Surprised by Sin,* written at time when the New Criticism, although waning, was still regnant in the academy, Professor Fish made the daring suggestion that the key to the meaning of *Paradise Lost* lay not in Milton's complex text but in the reader's own struggle with that complexity. We are told that, because Milton wanted the experience of struggling with the poem's syntax to mimic the experience of struggling with and facing

[9]Fish, *Doing What Comes Naturally,* 215.

up to one's own sinfulness, he wrote in a convoluted style that deliberately confused and stymied his readers. Professor Fish suggests that it is only when the reader sees through his confusion, usually at the end of a sentence when he at last comes to the verb, that Milton's intended pattern of moral education—"mistake, correction, instruction"—is fulfilled.[10] In this sense, Professor Fish argues, *Paradise Lost* continually traces "the reader's humiliation and his education."[11]

Of course, it does seem odd that, if this really were Milton's intention, no one had noticed it before Stanley Fish. One would have thought such a lofty moral design would have been more accessible to ordinary mortal scrutiny. But even odder is the caliber of the reader of Milton that Professor Fish assumes. While Professor Fish pursued his case with considerable erudition, ingenuity, and even brilliance, the reader he posits is a model of obtuseness. He never wises up to Milton's supposed intentions and is certainly too shallow a fellow to appreciate the argument of *Surprised by Sin.* As the critic Frederick Crews has observed, Professor Fish's reader is a straw man, "a dunce—a Charlie Brown who, having had the syntactic football yanked away a hundred times, would keep right on charging it in perfect innocence, never learning to suspend judgment until he arrived at the poet's verb."[12]

Professor Fish has long since abandoned the reader response suppositions he argued for in *Surprised by Sin.* But he has continued in his role of intellectual provocateur, sprinkling his work with arguments and asides that seem designed as much to taunt his readers as to enlighten them. Why else would he have blithely described his style of criticism as a "superior fiction," whose very status as fiction relieves him "of the obligation to be right . . . and demands only that [he] be interesting"?[13] Again, it must be noted that Professor Fish later repudiated this Wildean assertion from the mid-1970s, calling it "the most unfortunate sentence I ever wrote."[14] (His readers may wish to propose alternative candidates for that honor.) Yet it is difficult to know quite what to make of his retractions. There are so many of them. The

[10]Stanley Fish, *Surprised by Sin: The Reader in Paradise Lost* (Berkeley: University of California Press, 1967), 42.

[11]Ibid., ix.

[12]Crews, *Skeptical Engagements,* 124.

[13]Fish, *Is There a Text in This Class?,* 180.

[14]Ibid., 174.

truth is that Professor Fish has made a speciality of repudiating in one season the provocative statements that had earlier gained him the notice—if often the irritated notice—of his peers. The detailed introduction to *Is There a Text in This Class?,* for example, traces the development of the notion of "interpretive communities" and is a veritable inventory of his own discarded positions, each abandoned for one slightly more extreme or, to use a word he favors in this book and elsewhere, "subversive."

Professor Fish's habit of denying the positions he had once forcefully insisted on might simply be evidence of an unusual openness to criticism and willingness to change his mind when confronted with superior arguments. But a suspicious observer might wonder whether the driving force of his intellectual life was not truth but the desire for a certain notoriety. The question is whether blustering pronouncements like the one quoted above are products of momentary exaggeration—incautiously penned in the heat of debate, perhaps—or whether they are the result of deliberate calculation and a striving for effect.

III • THE NEW COMMON SENSE

Professor Fish's latest collection of essays effectively answers that and a good many other questions one might have about the nature and lasting value of the work of this influential critic and academic entrepreneur. Part of a new series from Duke anomalously called "Post-Contemporary Interventions,"* the volume contains twenty-two essays, all but three of which have appeared previously in one form or another. After a long introduction setting forth the author's current credo, the book is divided into four sections: "Meaning and Constraint," "Professionalism," "Consequences," and "Rhetoric." The essays thus range freely over Professor Fish's standard repertoire. And

*This series, incidentally, is edited by the indefatigable Professor Fish and his colleague Fredric Jameson. One may safely hazard that the nonsensical phrase *postcontemporary* was the result of a search for something even more up to date, more fashionable, than *postmodern*—that ubiquitous but nonetheless catachrestic term that, as Professor Fish observes of those old workhorses *structuralist, poststructuralist,* and their cognates, has had something of a period flavor for some time now. The addition of the word *interventions* is obviously meant to impart an aura of decisive activism: as if the series comprised not mere books but political acts. An outsider cannot, of course, be certain about the genesis of the title, but in Professor Fish's defense it must be said that this aggressively barbarous phrase has all the earmarks of being Professor Jameson's brainchild.

as with everything Professor Fish writes, the pieces collected there are clearly written and display considerable wit and learning. Unlike many of his colleagues, at Duke and elsewhere, Professor Fish not only does his homework but also values clarity of expression. It is noteworthy, though, that none of the essays in the bulky volume concerns itself explicitly with a literary text considered as *literature.* About as close as we get to literature is an essay called "Transmuting the Lump," which deals with the changing critical fortunes of books XI and XII of *Paradise Lost.* But even here, the poem is adduced solely in order to illustrate the politics of literary taste in contemporary English studies. (Appropriately, the essay appears in the section titled "Professionalism.")

True, literary texts are often *mentioned* in *Doing What Comes Naturally.* But—and here, alas, he resembles many of his colleagues in English and comparative literature throughout the country—Professor Fish seems to have given up literary criticism to play at being a philosopher. Accordingly, several essays deal with what for lack of a better term one may call the philosophy of language. Some of these advance Professor Fish's views on rhetoric, about which more below. ("Rhetorical," he correctly noted, is "a master-word" in these essays.[15]) Others explicate and criticize rival theories of language and meaning. Typical of the latter is a lengthy piece that compares the work of the doyen of French deconstruction, Jacques Derrida, and the British ordinary language philosopher J. L. Austin. One would hardly have thought this a subject to inspire humor, but who can resist an incredulous smile when Professor Fish confides that "Derrida is very much a philosopher of common sense," that "one might even say, with the proper qualifications, that he is a philosopher of ordinary language"?[16] To appreciate the extent to which Derrida is a philosopher of "common sense" and "ordinary language," consider this passage, of about average clarity, from the main article by Derrida on which Professor Fish bases his claim:

> A written sign is proffered in the absence of the receiver. How to style this absence? One could say that at the moment when I am

[15]Fish, *Doing What Comes Naturally,* 25.

[16]Ibid., 57.

> writing, the receiver may be absent from my field of present perception. But is not this absence merely a distant presence, one which is delayed or which, in one form or another, is idealized in its representation? This does not seem to be the case, or at least this distance, divergence, delay, this deferral must be capable of being carried to a certain absoluteness of absence if the structure of writing, assuming that writing exists, is to constitute itself. It is at that point that the *différance* as writing could no longer (be) an (ontological) modification of presence.[17]

Common sense? Ordinary language? I guess they really do talk differrent down there in Durham, North Carolina.

Doing What Comes Naturally also contains a half dozen pieces on the law, including three much-discussed attacks on the work of the legal theorist Ronald Dworkin ("Working on the Chain Gang," "Wrong Again," "Still Wrong after All These Years") as well as, under the rubric "Professionalism," a well-known essay titled "No Bias, No Merit." In that essay, Professor Fish argues against the policy many academic journals follow of accepting articles for publication only after they have been submitted to a blind peer review. Now there are plenty of reasons to be wary of this policy; often it seems blind in more than the desired sense of "impartial." But how many sought-after academics would admit that they are against it because it prevents them from cashing in on their reputations? "I am against blind submission," Professor Fish proclaims with characteristic bravura, "because the fact that my name is attached to an article greatly increases its chances of getting accepted. . . . I have paid my dues and earned the benefit of the doubt I now enjoy and don't see why others shouldn't labor in the vineyards as I did."[18]

It is important to note that Professor Fish's case against the policy of blind submission goes well beyond this expression of blatant self-interest. In fact, at the center of his animus toward blind submission is a contention that, in one way or another, surfaces in nearly every article in *Doing What Comes Naturally.* Professor Fish duly acknowledges that the intention behind the policy is to minimize bias and provide the proverbial level playing field for the hordes of academics

[17]Jacques Derrida, "Signature Event Context," in *Limited Inc,* trans. Samuel Weber and Jeffrey Mehlman (Evanston: Northwestern University Press, 1988), 7.

[18]Fish, *Doing What Comes Naturally,* 175.

hungry for publications to add to their résumés. But he rejects the idea that bias is a problem; more specifically, he rejects the idea that, given the limitations of human knowledge, the notion of bias is even *intelligible.* "Bias," he writes, "is just another word for seeing from a particular perspective as opposed to seeing from no perspective at all, and since seeing from no perspective at all is not a possibility, bias is a condition of consciousness and therefore of action."[19]

When he is not being deliberately provocative, Professor Fish has a tendency to present the obvious as if it were a stunning discovery. In one of his new book's key essays, "Critical Self-Consciousness, Or Can We Know What We're Doing?" he explains how it is that even our best efforts to be impartial turn out to be biased. "We say to ourselves," he writes, " 'with respect to this matter I am going to put aside my interests, preferences, and biases; and consider the evidence and alternatives in an impartial manner.' " In his view, what this resolution overlooks is "the extent to which the specification of what is and is not an 'impartial manner' is itself an 'interested' act, that is, an act performed within a set of assumptions" about what will count as evidence. Hence, he concludes, it is an ineluctably "partial" view of the world.[20] Rightly understood, this would seem to be an unexceptionable point. For what does it portend except that our ideas have a history, that they arise in particular circumstances and are the products of diverse situations? Does any of this dilute the ideal of impartiality?

The answer is no, but for Professor Fish, the insight that we are not gods, endowed with perfect knowledge, seems to have come as a shocking revelation. It leads him to one of his chief polemical points—a point made repeatedly in that volume, namely, that we are imprisoned by our interpretive schemes and hence any attempt to achieve critical distance on those schemes is doomed to failure. Although Professor Fish presents this idea as a hard-won discovery, in one version or another it has been gospel in the literary academy for several years. Whether one turns to Jacques Derrida with his insistence that "there is nothing outside the text" or to Professor Fish's colleague Fredric Jameson who speaks of "the prison house of language," the notion that (to adapt yet another popular formulation) the

[19]Ibid., 176.

[20]Ibid., 439.

limits of language exhaustively define the limits of the world is an unquestioned assumption in the allegedly all-questioning precincts of literary academia.

There was a time, however, when the academy was not so besotted with language. Traditionally, reflection was seen as a means of achieving critical distance on what Professor Fish calls our interpretive schemes. Reflecting on our point of view, it was held, we could in some sense transcend that point of view, appreciate its limitations, and entertain alternatives. But for Professor Fish, this sense of transcendence is largely an illusion. It could be achieved, he tells us, only "if the moment of self-reflection is in no way dependent on that from which it is to set us free," i.e., our "deeply assumed norms and standards." "Reflection," he concluded, "is just a fancy name for persuasion."[21] But why should we insist that reflection, in order to be effective, in order to be liberating, must be utterly free from the "norms and standards" out of which it arises? Does not the simple fact of our being able to entertain points of view very different from our own show that we can meaningfully transcend our taken-for-granted interpretive schemes?

Like many of his colleagues who are impatient with "authoritarian" concepts such as objectivity and disinterestedness, Professor Fish tends to prosecute his antitraditional brief by caricaturing the opposition. As we have seen in the case of Professor Hartman's reconstruction of Paul de Man, one basic tactic is to postulate a kind of super-Cartesian whose view of what counts as knowledge is so stringent that it is inevitably defeated and whose defeat is then chalked up as a victory for the champions of deconstruction, interpretive communities, critical theory, etc. Faithful to this tradition, at least, Professor Fish assures us that for anyone who believes in objectivity,

> the trick then is to think of sentences that would be heard the same way by all competent speakers no matter what their educational experience, or class membership, or partisan affiliation, or special knowledge, sentences which, invariant across contexts, could form the basis of an acontextual and formal description of the language and its rules.[22]

[21]Ibid., 448.

[22]Ibid., 320.

But who believes such sentences exist, outside the precincts of pure mathematics? And who believes that we need such a rigorous view of language to make sense of, say, impartial judgment? Just as Professor Fish's reader of *Paradise Lost* was rather a dim chap whose primary virtue was to bring glory to the reader response view of literary criticism, so those who dispute his skeptical notion of interpretive authority are held to be benighted souls who have never suspected that human knowledge is a fallible thing.

IV • DON'T WORRY, BE HAPPY

One of Professor Fish's neatest rhetorical gambits is to assure us that his radical view of meaning and interpretation is benign. Are you worried about making decisions on the basis of merit, not prejudice? Don't worry: because all judgments are prejudiced, decisions that claim to be based on merit are just as prejudiced as any others, only they are less self-consciousness, because they fail to recognize their own prejudices. Are you concerned about preserving the ideal of disinterested scholarship? Forget about it: "disinterestedness" is a chimera; and what is impossible or illusory can't very well be preserved. Professor Fish's favorite method of introducing such charming sophisms is by bluntly denying the obvious. "There is no such thing as . . ."—you name it: truth, merit, justice, facts. For example,

> there is no such thing as literal meaning . . .
>
> there can be no such thing as theory . . .
>
> there is no such thing as intrinsic merit . . .
>
> Indeed, there is no such thing as a "mere" preference in the sense that makes it a threat to communal norms, for anything that could be experienced as a preference will derive from the norms inherent in some community."[23]

Let us allow the first three of these pronouncements to stand as what they primarily are: verbal provocations, without (since we have just been assured that there are no such things) literal meaning or intrinsic merit. But do let us pause to consider some of the implica-

[23] Ibid., 4, 14, 164, 11.

tions of Professor Fish's dismissal of anything so scandalous as "mere" preference and his assurance that nothing "that could be experienced as a preference" can be "a threat to communal norms." First, note that he is not just making the unarguable point that our desires and preferences have a social component, that what we want is to some extent the product of the community we happen to find ourselves in. On the contrary, he believes that socialization (to borrow a phrase from the philosopher Richard Rorty) goes all the way down. Like Rorty, Professor Fish maintains that there are no independent criteria to which we might appeal to justify, or to condemn, our beliefs or actions. Indeed, he is fond of declaring that phrases such as "independent criteria" and "disinterested judgment" are self-contradictory.

Yet, as is often the case in these essays, part of Professor Fish's purpose in denying the obvious is to sweeten his message, to reassure us that his view of language and meaning entails no important loss. If there are no such things as intrinsic merit or disinterested judgment to begin with then we need hardly worry about their corruption or loss. Of course, most of us have been taught the opposite. We believe, for example, that there *is* a difference between action based on "mere preference" and action based on principle, between acting in a way that is self-interested and acting for the sake of something greater than self-interest. We believe that there is such a thing as unprincipled behavior, based on "mere preference," and that such behavior can be dangerous. Professor Fish is in effect telling us that we are being too fastidious. Because, in his view, every decision and every action is inexpungably colored by undeclared interests, the effort to distinguish between preference and principle is otiose. Moreover, because all values, preferences, facts, desires, and principles are themselves products of some "interpretive community," " 'mere' preference" cannot be a "threat to communal norms." Professor Fish's slogan for this happy state of affairs is that "all preferences are principled."[24]

But think about it. In the spring of 1989, a gang of adolescent boys raped and brutally beat a woman in Central Park, leaving her for dead. The extreme youth of the attackers and the ghastly savageness of their crime ensured that the case made national headlines. When asked why he had repeatedly beat the helpless woman about the head

[24]Ibid., 11.

with a metal pipe, one of the boys is reported to have replied, "Because it was fun." In other words, there was no particular reason. It was a whim. He just felt like doing it. Not to worry, though; Professor Fish has informed us that because preferences always "derive from the norms inherent in some community," they cannot be a "threat to communal norms." On what grounds, then, do we condemn this act? Is our condemnation merely the expression of prejudice—the expression, that is to say, of unacknowledged values inculcated by our "interpretive community"? Would we want to allow that another point of view, one that sanctioned rape and brutality, might be equally legitimate and morally compelling because it, too, derived from norms inherent in some interpretive community? Is Hitler to be exonerated because, after all, his preferences derived from the norms that won out in *his* interpretive community?

V • PULLING THE RUG OUT FROM UNDER YOURSELF

Looming behind all Professor Fish's startling denials and rhetorical antics is a single large claim about the nature of truth. In brief, there isn't any. That is to say, there isn't any if one insists that judgments of truth require independent criteria, that there must be external checks or constraints on meaning and interpretation. In Professor Fish's terms, this insistence is formalist or foundationalist. He defines *foundationalism* as "any attempt to ground inquiry and communication in something more firm and stable than mere belief or unexamined practice." It follows that we are guilty of foundationalist thinking if we believe there are criteria or "constraints" on judgment independent of our particular situation.[25]

Although it is castigated under a variety of names—objectivism, formalism, hierarchical thinking, even, for shorthand, truth—we have seen that what Professor Fish calls foundationalism has emerged as a prime whipping boy for many contemporary academic humanists. It is indeed one of the favored academic terms of contempt for the late 1980s. We are thus treated to the darkly comic spectacle (to employ Harold Rosenberg's memorable phrase) of this herd of independent

[25]Ibid., 342.

minds, safely tenured within its ivy-covered walls, assuring each other in paper after paper, conference after conference, book after book that everything is a text, that reality is only a "construction," that truth is merely a sociological convention.

Of course, the campaign against foundationalism comes in varying degrees of sophistication. Many literary academics simply parrot a set of impressive-sounding phrases culled from the writings of fashionable stars such as Derrida, Foucault, Jameson, and the like. In these cases, one is dealing not so much with an argument as an *attitude,* a posture of skepticism that is often adopted more from intellectual laziness and fear of being unstylish than from conviction. As usual, Professor Fish presents a more complicated case. Like many of his academic colleagues, he repeatedly assures us that "there are no higher or more general constraints, only constraints that are *different,* constraints built into practices other than the one whose reform is now being contemplated."[26] But it turns out that Professor Fish is not your garden variety relativist; he is a relativist of a more sophisticated stripe. He recognizes that to make sense of judgment at all one has to appeal to something like criteria. It's just that he doesn't believe that criteria ever possess the independence traditionally imputed to them. Hence he insists there are "no constraints that are more than the content of a practice from which they are indistinguishable"; "Whatever is invoked as a constraint on interpretation will turn out upon further examination to have been the product of interpretation."[27] Hence, too, the frankly political aspect of his view of meaning: "It is first and last," he wrote in his introductory chapter, "a question of *power* in relation to the putting of *constraints.*"[28]

This set of ideas has been dawning on Professor Fish for years, and has now assumed the proportions of an *idée fixe.* It is indeed the lodestar around which all his critical work currently circles. As he notes in the preface to *Doing What Comes Naturally,* the essays therein collected, although ostensibly on diverse topics, are really "the same." All develop or defend or explain this one idea about the nature of truth and meaning. Not surprisingly, Professor Fish's preferred term

[26]Ibid., 13.

[27]Ibid., 512.

[28]Ibid., 5.

for his outlook is "antifoundationalism." He himself, he assures us, is a "card-carrying anti-foundationalist,"[29] and he thinks we should be, too. Not that he wants for company. While he is more rigorous in his exposition than most of his literary colleagues, Professor Fish is hardly alone in his antifoundationalist sympathies. As we have seen again and again, although it travels under a variety of aliases, the antifoundationalist creed has installed itself as the reigning ideology of American higher education in the humanities. Indeed, examples of well-known literary academics dissenting from the antifoundationalist ethos are much harder to come by than those who champion it. Typical of the majority voice is the proclamation by Professor Fish's colleague Barbara Herrnstein Smith in her new book, *Contingencies of Value,* of a "radically contingent . . . conceptualization and discourse of 'reality,' 'validity,' 'justification,' 'reason,' 'truth,' 'facts,' and so forth."[30]* Or consider, as another example, Richard Rorty's endorsement of a "postmetaphysical" and "postreligious" culture in which "the sermon and treatise" are being replaced by "the novel, the movie, and the TV program" as the "principle vehicles of moral change and progress."[31]

In this context, it may be worth noting that one of the things Professor Fish is proudest of is the unusually wide range of his enemies. He is fond of reminding one that he is attacked as often by the Left as by the Right. The academic Left is unhappy with him because he is impatient with their claims for the practical consequences of "theory"—what he aptly calls "theory talk" or "theory hope." In accordance with the principle of knowing how far to go in going too far, Professor Fish outflanks most of his radical brethren, claiming that they aren't quite radical enough. They may have plowed through

[29]Ibid., 347.

[30]Barbara Herrnstein Smith, *Contingencies of Value: Alternative Perspectives for Critical Theory* (Cambridge, MA: Harvard University Press, 1989), 156.

*Again, it is worth calling attention to the use of scare quotes. Obviously, Professor Smith wishes to cast doubt on such conceptual dinosaurs as reality, validity, justification, reason, truth, facts, "and so forth." But it is useful to ask what reality, validity, truth, "and so forth" would be left in her own "discourse" once *"the realist/objectivist sense"* (as she contemptuously puts it) of these ideas is jettisoned. Readers interested in experiencing current academic prose at its most self-important and intellectually pretentious may wish to wade through a few of the essays collected in *Contingencies of Value.*

[31]Richard Rorty, *Contingency, Irony, and Solidarity* (Cambridge: Cambridge University Press, 1989), xiii–xvi.

volumes of Derrida and Althusser and Habermas, to say nothing of Hegel, Marx, Nietzsche, and Heidegger; they may rail against the logocentric hegemony of an elitist patriarchal faith in objectivity and science—but what good does it do them? In the midst of their orgies of disillusionment and skepticism, there is one belief they never abandon: the belief in theory itself, the belief that in some important sense theory *matters.* That is to say, they always assume that their current pet theory provides them with a critical purchase on language or the world that is somehow truer, better, more accurate than that enjoyed by their neighbor. Accordingly, Professor Fish charges that even antifoundationalist theory (and is there any other kind in the academy?) is covertly, yes, *foundationalist.* And that, clearly, is not a charge calculated to win one friends in the humanities departments of our universities.

The academic Right, on the other hand, is unhappy with Professor Fish primarily because he is a relativist who believes that "political justifications are the only kind there are"[32] and because he consequently denies that traditional ideals such as truth or justice—to say nothing of our old friends intrinsic merit, disinterestedness, and objectivity—have any meaning except as rhetorical gestures. Yet it would be a grave error to suppose that Professor Fish plies a middle road between the intellectual Left and the Right. Both the Right and the Left have misunderstood him, he complains, but it is clear that he regards some misunderstandings as more equal than others. He criticizes the naïveté of his leftist colleagues and attracts their ire (a certain species of feminist seems to be especially exercised by his writings). But as a "card-carrying antifoundationalist" his political sympathies—and remember, for Professor Fish there are no other kind—are all with them.

If this were not already clear enough from his antifoundationalist ideas about meaning, truth, and interpretation, it becomes pellucidly clear whenever he steps out of his preferred role as radical epistemological proselytizer and discusses concrete issues of policy. Consider, for example, the very different ways he characterizes two articles by fellow academics in "Profession Despise Thyself: Fear and Self-Loathing in Literary Studies." The primary occasion for this lecture on the

[32]Fish, *Doing What Comes Naturally,* 340.

virtues of professionalism was a 1982 article by the eminent Harvard professor Walter Jackson Bate decrying the new faddishness and politicization that was erupting in English departments around the country. Naturally, Professor Fish has little patience with Bate's criticism. But it is instructive to compare his attack on Bate's piece with his treatment of another attack on the academy that appeared in 1982: this one by Columbia University's redoubtable PLO sympathizer and professor of comparative literature, Edward Said. No one acquainted with the work of Bate and Said will be surprised to learn that where Bate criticized the profession for abandoning standards, Said criticized it for being overly narrow and insufficiently political. After spending several pages excoriating Bate for his small-mindedness, Professor Fish then turns, reluctantly, to criticize Said. Said must be criticized because he thinks something is wrong with the profession of English being professional. But Professor Fish is careful to describe Said's piece as "infinitely more attractive" than Bate's, claiming that it is "everything that Bate's is not: generous, learned, humane, compassionate, responsible."[33] Again, anyone familiar with the work of these authors will recognize that this characterization is preposterous. Clearly, though, one tangible advantage of Professor Fish's policy of doing what comes naturally is that it relieves him of the chore of even attempting to be evenhanded.

VI • THE NEW SOPHISTRY

The development of Professor Fish's antifoundationalist campaign also explains a good deal about the direction his own work has taken. It explains, for example, why he has increasingly abandoned literary criticism for the study of rhetoric. Already in *Is There a Text in This Class?,* he concludes that

> the business of criticism was not (as I had previously thought) to determine the correct way of reading but to determine from which of a number of possible perspectives reading will proceed. . . . The business of criticism in other words is not to decide between interpretations by subjecting them to the test of disinterested evidence but to establish by political and persuasive means (they are the same thing) the set of interpretive assumptions from the vantage of which

[33]Ibid., 212.

> the evidence (and the facts and the intentions and everything else) will hereafter be specifiable.[34]

Given this interest in the art of persuasion—that is to say in rhetoric—it is no wonder that Professor Fish should have increasingly turned away from literature toward legal texts to provide fodder for his theories. At least since Plato, as the *Phaedrus* reminds us, rhetoric has been understood as having to do principally with "lawsuits . . . and of course public harangues also."

In broad outline, Professor Fish's position is nothing new. Similar presuppositions about language can be found in certain strains of American pragmatism as well as in Ludwig Wittgenstein's late philosophy of language, especially in his theory of language games. And, as Professor Fish proudly acknowledges, the spirit and intellectual pedigree of his antifoundationalist views hark back to the sophists of Plato's time. Like them, Professor Fish argues that "man is the measure of all things," that justice "means nothing but what is to the interest of the stronger party," etc. Here is Professor Fish's own version of Thrasymachus's claim: "Does might make right? In a sense the answer I must give is yes, since in the absence of a perspective independent of interpretation some interpretive perspective will always rule by virtue of having won out over its competitors."[35] In other words, whatever interpretive scheme happens to have "won out" is not only victorious but is therefore *right.*

It is hardly surprising that Professor Fish has attracted many disciples in the academy. Yet for all its professional cachet and shock value, his position is far from convincing. For one thing, as with the sophists before him, there is an insurmountable contradiction at the heart of the Fish course on meaning. It is this: he cannot claim truth for his own theory without at the same time denying the antifoundationalist principles on which it is based. He rightly points out that the various aspects of his antifoundationalist creed are closely connected, noting that the "first step down the anti-formalist road," the denial of literal meaning, "contains all the others."[36] But then how are we to understand that denial? Is it . . . *true?* Or is it merely an interpretive

[34]Fish, *Is There a Text in This Class?,* 16.

[35]Fish, *Doing What Comes Naturally,* 10.

[36]Ibid., 25.

gesture? As with every thoroughgoing relativist since Protagoras, Professor Fish faces the problem of not being able to assert his position without self-contradiction. He hastily assures us that this is an objection that is "easily gotten around." But is his response convincing? Does it help to say, as he does, that, yes, there is a foundation for his relativistic position, but it is only "rhetorical," based on evidence that is "cultural and contextual"?[37] Waffles, anyone?

Like the relativistic theories of his colleagues, Professor Fish's antifoundationalist view of language and interpretation is most grievously deficient when it comes to science and the idea of objective truth. The insistence that all our notions of truth are products of particular interpretative communities does not go very far in accounting for the cogency of scientific discourse, nor, in fact, for the everyday notion of empirical truth. It is difficult, for example, to see how the truth of the assertion "The sun is shining" is culturally contingent or relative to the presuppositions of the interpretive community one happens to inhabit.

It must also be said that, pace Professor Fish, science offers us not just "another" perspective on the world but, in a way that can be precisely specified, a higher, more precise, more objective perspective than that provided by ordinary language. This is not to deny that the view of the world furnished by scientific rationalism is deeply reductive; indeed, it is reductive *in principle,* excluding as far as possible any reference to the fluctuating, uncertain realm of values and sense perception. Nor is it to deny that the concept of objectivity itself is the product of a particular culture and assumptions about the nature of truth. Of course it is. But the fact that all our concepts and theories have a history does not by itself gainsay their truth or validity. Nor does the fact that the idea of objectivity happened to arise out of a particular interpretive community mean that its application is limited to that community. The truth of Euclidean geometry is hardly limited to the Greeks, nor the truth of algebra to the Arabs. Moreover, the very power that science has given us to predict, manipulate, and control reality shows that its truths, although reductive, are genuinely universal.

Like virtually every other English professor eager to debunk the

[37]Ibid., 29.

authority of science and objectivity, Professor Fish quotes abundantly from Thomas Kuhn's *The Structure of Scientific Revolutions,* somehow under the impression that this much misused book abets the project of collapsing science into a form of literary chitchat. But for all his talk of "paradigm change" and recognition that science, too, inevitably works with theories that themselves unfold in particular cultural circumstances, Kuhn is not the freewheeling relativist that professors of English have attempted to turn him into. To be sure, he insists that scientific theories are shaped by the shared values of the communities out of which they arise, but he also is careful to insist that "later scientific theories are better than earlier ones for solving puzzles in the often quite different environments to which they are applied. This is not a relativist's position, and it displays the sense in which I am a convinced believer in scientific progress."[38] Whatever one thinks of Kuhn's overall theory of scientific truth, one can see that these are not statements calculated to console the antifoundationalist faithful. The simple fact of scientific progress—relying as it does on there being some descriptions of phenomena that are demonstrably more objective than others—effectively undercuts the antifoundationalist ambition to disenfranchise the notion of truth and transform facts into a form of exotic political capital generated by "interpretive communities."

It is important to stress that the implications of Professor Fish's antifoundationalist fantasies are not confined to abstract matters of epistemology. As he acknowledges early on in *Doing What Comes Naturally,* the effects of the antiformalist, antifoundationalist creed he champions are "almost boundless." We have seen, however, that notwithstanding this admission he is also everywhere at pains to assure his readers that "when you get to the end of the anti-formalist road nothing will have changed except the answers you might give to some traditional questions in philosophy and literary theory."[39] "The dangers of excessive interpretive freedom, of 'masked power,' of random or irresponsible activity," he wrote, "are *unrealizable,* because the conditions that would make them the basis of a reasonable fear—the

[38]Thomas S. Kuhn, *The Structure of Scientific Revolutions,* 2nd ed. (Chicago: University of Chicago Press, 1970), 206.

[39]Fish, *Doing What Comes Naturally,* 26.

condition of free subjectivity, of 'naturally' indeterminate texts, or unprincipled authority—could never obtain."[40] Once again, we find there is nothing to worry about: "nihilism is impossible" and of course "it is unnecessary to combat something that is not possible."[41]

But in fact there is a great deal to worry about. For not only is the antifoundationalist creed wrong, it is—as Professor Fish himself has been eager to declare—subversive. Not least, it is subversive of the intellectual foundation of liberal democratic society. Indeed, Professor Fish blithely notes that the entire tenor of antifoundationalism is subversive of "a general assumption of liberal thought," namely, the ideal of disinterested knowledge.[42] For if one can no longer cogently distinguish between impartial judgment and *parti pris* lobbying, between dispassionate description and partisan propaganda, one can no longer make sense of the moral and intellectual ideals on which our society is based.

And this brings us back to that master-word of Professor Fish's new book: *rhetoric.* What we see at work throughout is a deliberate attempt to supplant reason by rhetoric, truth by persuasion, using the simple device of denying that there is any essential distinction to be made between them. This would be troubling enough if it were confined to literary texts; extended to legal texts and basic political concepts such as justice, it is nothing short of disastrous.

There was a time when one studied rhetoric to equip oneself to employ its resources effectively for the sake of truth and justice and to inoculate oneself against rhetoric's seductive charms. For Professor Fish, however, rhetoric is all there is. This has always been the contention of professional rhetoricians, from the time of sophists such as Thrasymachus, Callicles, and Protagoras, down to contemporary sophists such as Rorty, Fish, and their many disciples. Plato rightly condemned rhetoric as a "shadow play of words" that was concerned with semblance, not reality. Does it help to be told that Plato's qualms were groundless because there is no such thing as reality or facts or literal meaning or truth? (Given the large material triumphs of Professor Fish and Company at Duke, one cannot help recalling that Plato

[40]Ibid., 138.

[41]Ibid., 139.

[42]Ibid., 348.

also remarked the astounding amounts of money that sophists make.)

Considered as a representative instance of what contemporary academic culture holds up as exemplary work in the humanities, Professor Fish's writings are more reasoned but no less radical than most. By the time he published *Is There a Text in This Class?* in 1980, he was already far down the antiformalist, antifoundationalist road. Like most errors, this one did not improve with time. Regarding his new book with its updated litanies, one can hardly do better than to quote one of Professor Fish's own condemnations: Still wrong after all these years.

More generally, however, his recent work illustrates the extent to which academic literary studies have abandoned the most elementary distinctions of taste, judgment, and value. It is one of the clearest symptoms of the decadence besetting the academy that the ideals that once informed the humanities have been corrupted, willfully misunderstood, or simply ignored by the new sophistries that have triumphed on our campuses. We know something is gravely amiss when teachers of the humanities confess—or, as is more often the case, when they boast—that they are no longer able to distinguish between truth and falsity. We know something is wrong when scholars assure us—and their pupils—that there is no essential difference between the disinterested pursuit of knowledge and partisan proselytizing, or when academic literary critics abandon the effort to identify and elucidate works of lasting achievement as a reactionary enterprise unworthy of their calling. And indeed, the most troubling development of all is that such contentions are no longer the exceptional pronouncements of a radical elite, but have increasingly become the conventional wisdom in humanities departments of our major colleges and universities.

CHAPTER 7

THE REAL CRISIS IN THE HUMANITIES

Live with your century, but do not be its creature; render to your contemporaries what they need, not what they praise.

—FRIEDRICH SCHILLER,
Letters On the Aesthetic Education of Man

I • THE NEW ESTABLISHMENT

The overheated rhetoric and pose of beleaguered defiance that one regularly encounters in the academy may suggest that those railing against, say, European dominance or "white, male, WASP hegemony" (to recall Cornel West's memorable phrase) are isolated figures on the margins of academic power. Unfortunately, the opposite is the case. Far from being the work of a besieged minority, these voices represent the new academic establishment of tenured radicals. Often they are among the most highly paid professors—those for whose services our leading universities bid against each other in little-publicized auctions. Nor is the influence of these professors confined to the present moment. At many prestigious institutions, they are precisely the people helping to shape the future by making faculty appointments, overseeing promotions, and devising the educational program in the humanities—efforts at self-propagation that virtually ensure their continued dominance for another generation.

The truth is that when the children of the sixties received their professorships and deanships they did not abandon the dream of radical cultural transformation; they set out to implement it. Now, instead of disrupting classes, they are teaching them; instead of attempting to destroy our educational institutions physically, they are subverting them from within. Thus it is that what were once the political and educational ambitions of academic renegades appear as ideals on the agenda of the powers that be. Efforts to dismantle the traditional curriculum and institutionalize radical feminism, to ban politically unacceptable speech and propagate the tenets of deconstruction and similar exercises in cynical obscurantism: Directives encouraging these and other radical developments now typically issue from the dean's office or Faculty Senate, not from students marching in the streets.

It would be difficult to imagine a more revealing illustration of the new academic establishment at work than that offered by Williams College at its two-day fall convocation ceremonies in September 1989. The festivities at the venerable liberal arts college in Williamstown, Massachusetts, were held not only to mark the beginning of the term and confer various academic prizes and honors but also to inaugurate the new Center for the Humanities and Social Sciences at Williams. The highlight of the event was an evening panel discussion devoted to the question "Crisis in the Humanities?" Members of the panel included Houston A. Baker, Jr., whom we met in Chapter One; the renowned Jacques Derrida; Werner Gundersheimer, a specialist in Renaissance European history who was recently appointed director of the Folger Shakespeare Library in Washington, D.C.; Gertrude Himmelfarb, professor emeritus of history at the Graduate Center of the City University of New York; and E. D. Hirsch, Jr., of *Cultural Literacy* fame, who is also a professor of English at the University of Virginia. These five—who were awarded honorary degrees at the convocation ceremonies the following day—were joined by two members of the Williams faculty: Mark C. Taylor, professor of religion and director of the Williams Center for the Humanities and Social Sciences, who acted as moderator for the panel, and Lynda Bundtzen, professor of English and chair of Williams's Women's Studies Program.

What made this event noteworthy was not its novelty; similar panels have been convened at major universities for years now. Nor was the opening of a new center for the humanities and social sciences much news; there are already some 300 such institutions at colleges and universities across the country. If Williams has only now acquired a humanities center, it is because only recently has the interdisciplinary humanities center entrenched itself securely enough in the academic mainstream to be an attractive ornament for a small, mainstream liberal arts college. No, the inauguration of a humanities center and a debate over the state of the humanities at Williams College are important not so much for their own sake as for what they tell us about the progress that academic radicalism has made in transforming itself into the new academic establishment.

Nearly a thousand people, most of them students, crowded into Williams's elegant Chapin Hall to listen to the panel debate. Professor Taylor introduced the discussion by recalling the question mark that formed part of the title: Yes, he said, we've all heard a great deal about the humanities lately, but is there really a crisis? And if so, what is it? Professor Taylor made it clear that he doubted that the popular perception that the humanities are in trouble was at all accurate. But he had no doubt about where to place the blame for that mistaken perception. In his view, the widespread sense that the humanities are in a state of crisis has largely "grown out of an extraordinary attack on recent tendencies in humanistic studies that had been carried out during the Reagan years and is continuing in the Bush administration."*

Whether Professor Taylor actually believed that the Reagan and Bush administrations themselves had undertaken or otherwise abetted this alleged attack, or whether he thought they merely provided a climate conducive to attacking the humanities, was never made terribly clear. What was clear, however, was his deep antipathy to the voices that "are calling us back to what they regard as the traditional values of the Western humanistic tradition." Professor Taylor did not mention any names, but it was not long before the specters of William Bennett, Allan Bloom, and Lynne Cheney loomed large and threatening in the wings. For Professor Taylor, if there is a crisis in the humanities today, it has arisen not from in the way the humanities are in fact pursued at our colleges and universities—where, we were given to understand, things couldn't be better—but precisely from efforts by people such as Bloom, Bennett, and Cheney to resuscitate those "traditional values of the Western humanistic tradition."

*Unless otherwise noted, quotations in this chapter are taken from the presentations delivered at this conference.

Professor Taylor's main supporting text was *Speaking for the Humanities*—a document written, he assured his attentive audience, by a group of "the nation's leading humanists." Alluding to and quoting copiously from this report from the American Council of Learned Societies, Professor Taylor's remarks also conveyed a good deal of its spirit of arrogant and politically tinged condescension. Following the report, for example, he maintained that the people of the United States have always exhibited a marked anti-intellectual bias—hence, you see, it is not surprising that many people are uneasy with recent developments in the academy—and then proceeded to point out that the humanities are "inextricably bound up with philosophical and political traditions that many in today's world find problematic."

Professor Taylor passed on quickly to other matters; but let's pause for a moment to consider this last suggestion. What does it mean that a professor of religion and director of a center for the study of the humanities and social sciences should think that the humanities are inextricably linked to traditions that "many" find "problematic"? Which philosophical and political traditions, exactly, does he have in mind? Just who are the "many" taking issue with these traditions? And what does the euphemistic "problematic" imply? Again, Professor Taylor did not offer specifics. But his invocation of the legacy of Greece and Rome as the ultimate source of the humanistic tradition made it clear that he meant the philosophical and political traditions of the West—traditions that, in philosophy, developed the ideals of truth, objectivity, and disinterestedness, and that, in politics, are responsible for the rise of liberal democratic society. The "many" who dispute this legacy are of course Professor Taylor and his colleagues—that is, precisely those academics charged with teaching and preserving the humanities and the traditions on which they are based.

What Professor Taylor was saying, then, is very close to the message of *Speaking for the Humanities.* It goes something like this: Recent attacks on the humanities have been misplaced. Indeed, the humanities today are thriving, but there remains the unfortunate detail that the philosophical and political ideas that have traditionally supported the humanities are essentially racist, sexist, and elitist—and so they must be scrapped for a more enlightened set of ideas. The institutional corollary to all this was unexpressed but also fairly obvious: More "research" is needed to discern and foster such enlightened alternatives, so please, all you anti-intellectual, unenlightened people who continue to labor under the prejudices of an outmoded tradition, please keep sending your children to college to be disabused of such prejudices and keep supporting us posthumanist humanists with grants from the National Endowment for the Humanities and other government institutions. Given such an understanding of the humanities, it was little wonder that Professor Taylor should conclude his remarks with another echo of the ACLS report, reminding his audience that he considers the "stakes" in the controversy over the humanities to be primarily "social and political." Who could doubt it?

Instead of offering prepared remarks on the large issues that Professor Taylor had broached in his introduction, members of the panel were asked to respond individually to questions that had been previously formulated by individuals from the Williams community and that Professor Taylor addressed to each of them in turn. Some of the questions, and certainly some of the responses, tended to wander off the announced topic of the evening's discussion; but, taken together, some half dozen of the exchanges bring us up to date on many of the chief issues that define the controversy over the humanities today.

The first question, addressed to Professor Bundtzen, returns us to the issue of the canon: How should it be defined and what is its importance for contemporary debate? Professor Bundtzen began conventionally enough by alluding to Matthew Arnold: he had been invoked by the authors of *Speaking for the Humanities,* she noted, and indeed the traditional idea of the canon could be summed up in Arnoldian terms as "masterpieces, the great works, those works deemed as of lasting value and significance, important for critics to return to again and again." In this context she mentioned Samuel Johnson's notion that great works are those that continue to be read for a hundred years. But it soon became clear that Professor Bundtzen had little patience with this whole idea of the canon, at least as it has been traditionally defined. For who occupies its ranks? People such as Chaucer and Shakespeare and Milton—those whom Professor Bundtzen repeatedly and contemptuously referred to as "the big guys" and "the big names"—the likes of Picasso, Matisse, and Rembrandt in painting, and Nietzsche and Kant in philosophy. "It's like having a big list of names," Professor Bundtzen complained, working up to her main point. "The names, I hope you all noticed, are . . . *men.* They're white men; they're Western European. . . . [The canon is] the list of the white men who have created Western culture." One wasn't sure which she thought was worse, the creators or their creation. Professor Bundtzen went on to support the "feminist contention" that "surely there must be some women somewhere who did something that might be deemed of interpretive significance."

Having already encountered many variants of this position, we know that Professor Bundtzen's complaint is so predictable as to approach the status of a cliché. But she did not limit herself to lamenting the exclusion of women writers from the canon. Echoing academic feminists such as Elaine Showalter, she also made a more radical point. "There is a way in which there is a canonization of unique genius," she told us "and genius as it's attached to the male imagination: *their* problems, *their* desires, what *they* love and *they* think is important, and *their* narratives and *their* stories, *their* events, *their* history, the way in which they paint their often female subjects." In other words, it's not only the predominance of men in the canon that Professor Bundtzen objected to, but also *the very criteria for inclusion* in the canon: the whole idea of unique genius, for example, seemed specifically male to her, as did the problems, desires, stories, and so on that were expressed in works created by men. The possibility that there might be something *human* in these aspirations and achievements, something that transcended the contingency of gender, was rejected out of hand.

Professor Bundtzen's comments were nothing more than a commonplace expression of commonplace feminist sentiments; but of course they are so disturbing precisely *because* they have become commonplace. It is an important measure of the triumph of radical feminism in the academy that ideas that were considered an extreme idiosyncrasy only a few years ago are these days taken for granted and repeated as gospel by professors everywhere. Thus even at an elite liberal arts college such as Williams, once considered an epitome of the small but rigorous traditional college, we find faculty propagating the notion that the "value" placed on "unique genius" in our culture is somehow distinctively "male" and therefore subject to feminist dismantling.

Later in the evening, when the discussion returned to the question of the canon, Professor Bundtzen provided additional evidence of how deeply she has absorbed the conventional feminist ideology. Elaborating on her point about the essentially masculine nature of traditional aesthetic, intellectual, and spiritual criteria, she spoke of a countercanon of women authors and questioned the high esteem that has been accorded to certain sorts of creative endeavor while being withheld from others. "When the Western male tradition was canonized," she informed us,

> certain values about individual genius were canonized, and mastery, and transcendence; and in other words the canonization of women authors [might be read] as a countercanonization of different values. . . . [It would be] an enrichment of the canon overall to have a discordant woman's voice saying "I'm not creating this poem for eternity," "I don't want to celebrate transcendent truth, I want to celebrate the little things in women's lives, . . . the small nurturing things that women do."

In the feminist reconstruction of the canon that Professor Bundtzen envisioned, then, allegedly male values such as individual genius, transcendence, mastery, and truth must be put aside to make room for allegedly female values and the "discordant woman's voice" undertaking to champion "the small nurturing things women do." Concrete examples are always useful in these situations, but about as far as Professor Bundtzen went was to wonder "What did Dorothy *feel* like when she found herself at Tintern Abbey and what was her brother William doing with her?"

II • ARE YOU NOW OR HAVE YOU EVER BEEN CONSERVATIVE?

We shall return to Professor Bundtzen and her discordant woman's voice. But first, to get a fuller sense of the issues that were raised at Williams, let us consider the responses some of the other panelists gave to the questions that were addressed to them. The first question that was put to Professor Hirsch concerned the relationship between his book *Cultural Literacy* and Allan Bloom's *The Closing of the American Mind.* Professor Hirsch's work on cultural literacy had been widely associated with the spirit of *The Closing of the American Mind;* how, if at all, would he distinguish his position from Bloom's? And what does the enthusiastic public response to their books tell us about the educated public's attitude toward the educational mission of our colleges today?

These questions were, so to speak, tailor-made for Professor Hirsch. Ever since the raging success of *Cultural Literacy* brought him not only fame but also the uncomfortable label "conservative," he has taken every opportunity to shake off the label and attempt to ingratiate himself with the academic Left. It was hardly surprising, then, that he should have responded gratefully that, "thank heavens," the question of his relation to Allan Bloom had finally become "obsolete." Although his name unfortunately had been linked with Bloom's when their books were first published, people now understood that they were up to fundamentally different things. Bloom really was a conservative critic of new trends in the academy, whereas Professor Hirsch now declared that the new trends were, in his opinion, splendid; he just wanted more people to be able to participate in them, and so wanted young students to know enough to squeeze into college. The names that are now, and more appropriately, paired as being antagonistic to recent changes in the humanities, Professor Hirsch explained, are those of Allan Bloom and William Bennett—who, he told an amused audience, are known in some quarters as "the killer *B*s." Moreover, he continued, "I presume that, on the simplest level, Bloom votes or least talks to Republicans and emotionally that has not been my own history." This, too, greatly entertained the audience—although Professor Himmelfarb had the bad taste to point out later that, in fact, Professor Bloom is a Democrat and talked to whichever groups invited him.

Professor Hirsch then went on to suggest that, while Allan Bloom's book was an embittered response to the student unrest of the late sixties, his own work grew out of his study of reading and writing. *Cultural Literacy,* he said, was aimed primarily at disadvantaged children and sought to make the elementary point that some degree of shared knowledge was essential to academic success. What that shared knowledge should be, Professor Hirsch insisted, was another question entirely: He himself would certainly not wish to make invidious distinctions among various curricula. The important thing was not *what* was taught but only that it be shared. Continuing his effort at self-exoneration, he claimed to be "appalled" that his book had been read as a conservative tract. It was his "misfortune," he said, to enter the debate about education at a time when any effort at reform would be looked on with suspicion because it would seem conservative. What he really wanted, Professor Hirsch confided in his closing piety, was to give everybody an opportunity to go to college—an opportunity that did not now exist in American society.

Because questions are often more revealing than the answers they elicit, we may quote the next question, which was addressed to Professor Derrida, as much for what it tells us about the person who framed it as for the answer it received. "To what extent does the very notion of crisis," Professor Taylor read aloud, "serve to reaffirm the institutional structures it apparently threatens, and, for those of us who feel that the humanities are hardly threatened enough, how optimistic should we be about the possibility of establishing a discourse which moves beyond the agonistic, and apparently endlessly recuperable, language of 'crisis?' " This is a classic so-called Derridean question; whoever wrote it—and one cannot help suspecting Professor Taylor himself—is obviously well steeped in deconstructivist argot. Not only does it begin with a facile inversion of common sense (the prospect of a crisis "reaffirming" what it seems to threaten) and express a marked current of subversion ("those of us who feel the humanities are hardly threatened enough"), but it also uses an appropriately forbidding jargon ("discourse," "agonistic," and "endlessly recuperable") and, above all, it is everywhere at pains to place the emphasis on language, not on the reality language describes.

Not to be outdone at his own game, however, Professor Derrida's response was itself a consummate exhibition of deconstructivist gamesmanship. Instead of addressing himself to the question, he began by posing questions of his own. He asked Professor Bundtzen whether she thought it was possible to stop the process of canonization once it had started. He himself, he said, did not believe that it could be stopped, for every attempt to do so would simply lead to an alternative process of canonization, producing a countercanon such as the one Professor Bundtzen and so many others had proposed. One might wish to change what was canonized, dropping, for example, the notion of the masterpiece. But this would not bring the process of canonization itself to a halt, merely channel it into a different route.

Before proceeding with Professor Derrida's response, it is worth pausing to note how far we have come from the notion of an academic canon with this talk of canonization. Whatever the ecclesiastical roots of the term *canon,* the process by which specific works are included in the literary canon is radically different from the process whereby an individual is "canonized" as a saint by the Roman Catholic Church. Yet *canonization* has become a vogue word in the academy. No doubt this is partly because, poaching on the aura of religious canonization, it suggests something supernatural, authoritarian, even—for many secular observers—inherently fraudulent. But it is always useful to track such misuses of language, and one cannot help pointing out that Professor Derrida's suggestion about "dropping" the notion of the masterpiece from discussions of the literary canon would be more or less like dropping the notion of "saint" from canonization in the religious sense; in other words, it would make a travesty of the whole idea, a literary canon without masterpieces being like a religious canon without saints. Professor Derrida is hardly one to be detained by such details, however, and he went quickly on to ask Professor Hirsch what his—Professor Hirsch's—earlier theories of interpretation revealed about his relation to Allan Bloom, and whether there was any essential connection between his current proposals for establishing cultural literacy and his theories of interpretation.

These were particularly naughty questions to put to E. D. Hirsch. Before Professor Hirsch burst on the scene as the apostle of cultural literacy, he had acquired a certain reputation in the world of literary criticism as the author of *Validity in Interpretation.* This book was a polemic against "radical historicism" and theories of linguistic indeterminacy—then still mostly of German, not French, extraction—as well as a plea for the idea that texts possess a literal meaning that provides a criterion for valid interpretation. "There is clearly a sense in which we can neither evaluate a text nor determine what it means 'to us, today' until we have correctly apprehended what it means," he wrote in one characteristic passage.[1] Not that *Validity in Interpretation* won a particularly enthusiastic following: Proponents of literary hermeneutics and, later, deconstruction dismissed it as hopelessly reac-

[1]E. D. Hirsch, Jr., *Validity in Interpretation* (New Haven: Yale University Press, 1967), viii, 209.

tionary, while many of those who might have been sympathetically inclined toward the book's overall spirit regarded it as simpleminded. It became widely known, then, not so much because it was influential but because it was among the most clearly written expositions of the minority view in the academy that there might be such a thing as literal meaning or, indeed, validity in interpretation. One tended to see it cited mostly as a straw man, a cardinal example of an overly literal approach to literary theory. For someone as desperate as Professor Hirsch to disencumber himself from the label conservative, it must have been galling to be reminded of his former sins—especially by Derrida, an enormously celebrated writer whose entire *oeuvre* stands in the most glaring contradiction to Professor Hirsch's own earlier ideas. Poor Professor Hirsch declared that people had once again been wrong to see him as conservative, and then favored us with a little self-exposition according to which the argument of *Validity in Interpretation* was scarcely to be distinguished from the kind of relativism espoused by Stanley Fish.

For his own part, Professor Derrida then launched into a typical deconstructive gambit. We should not worry about the humanities being in a state of crisis, he said, because it is in the nature of the academy to be always in crisis. Noting that the etymology of "crisis" suggests choice or decision, he assured us that "the rhetoric of crisis" is "fundamentally optimistic" because it looks forward to a solution, a choice, a decision. In fact, the problem today is that the academy is no longer in crisis and hence "there is no choice, no decision to be made." But while Professor Derrida is obviously expert at the interpretive shenanigans that make things seem the opposite of the way they really are, his subsequent comments showed that—about certain subjects anyway—he is as interested as the next person in preserving the ordinary meanings of words. For he admitted that even if there is, alas, no crisis in the humanities today, there are some serious problems. One of the most important, he said, comes from outside the academy and concerns money. A great deal of money is being given to the sciences, while the humanities, having to make do with far more meager amounts, are in danger of being "marginalized." At least when it came to talking about money, Professor Derrida abandoned his customary intellectual high jinks and was perfectly straightforward. There was no attempt to make a lack of money seem like an abundance, or to show that the "margins" of this kind of "discourse" were really the center.

He was not quite so straightforward about what he identified as an "internal" problem that the humanities face today—namely, the problem of conservatives who want to preserve the traditional canon and fundamental values of the humanities. Recognizing the threat that these conservatives pose to the agenda of the new academic establishment, Professor Derrida resorted to paradox: The desire to preserve the traditional role of the humanities, he said, threatens to destroy the humanities "from within." Indeed, according to Professor Derrida, the real way to save the humanities is to shoulder the "dangerous responsibility" of subjecting them to radical criticism, "to transform the canon, to enlarge the field." But lest it seem that he wanted simply to . . . well, to deconstruct the humanities, which after all would risk further marginalizing the humanities from sources of financial support, he hastened to assure us that "we all share the same respect for Shakespeare, for Milton, for others."

But do we? Does Professor Bundtzen, for example? Wasn't Professor Derrida ignoring the fact that on many American campuses, and indeed in many cases largely under the influence of his writings, *respect* is about the last word one would choose to describe the prevailing attitude toward Shakespeare, Milton, or—to employ a phrase one sees a lot these days—other "Dead, White, European Males" (DWEMs for short)? In fact, he wants to have it both ways, to indulge in an all-out critical assault on the traditional idea of the humanities and everything they stand for and yet, when the occasion calls for it, to be able to mouth a few pious phrases about respect for Shakespeare, Milton, and those unnamed others.

III • WHO NEEDS TRANSCENDENT TRUTHS?

Such questions returned with renewed force when the next panelist, the historian Gertrude Himmelfarb, took the floor. Before answering the first question that was addressed to her, however, she made a few observations about the proceedings thus far. It was unfortunate, Professor Himmelfarb said, that the word *conservative* should have been introduced so blithely into the discussion as a term of censure. For by intimating at the outset that *conservative* means "bad," an overtly politicized framework for the entire discussion had been established. Professor Himmelfarb acknowledged that most of the panelists would insist that anyone wanting to preserve the traditional canon was already pursuing a political agenda of his own. But it would be far more productive, she continued, if questions about politics came in at the end of the discussion rather than at the beginning. Professor Himmelfarb also noted that she had many friends who, although they were very much on the Left politically, considered themselves "conservative" in cultural and educational matters. Consequently, she suggested, a more neutral word such as *traditional* or *conventional* would be preferable to *conservative* as a descriptive term.

Professor Himmelfarb went on to remind the audience that the moderator, Professor Taylor, had opened the discussion in a highly charged political manner by accusing the Reagan and Bush administrations of mounting "an extraordinary attack on recent tendencies in humanistic studies." What could this mean, she wondered? After all, the very center of humanistic study whose inauguration they were gathered together to celebrate was being supported by a large grant from the National Endowment for the Humanities under the Bush administration. Is that the sort of "extraordinary attack" Professor Taylor had in mind?

And in response to Professor Derrida's call for more rigorous questioning in the humanities, Professor Himmelfarb noted that questions were being asked on more than one side of the issue. Professor Derrida claimed to champion the questioning of authority, the legitimacy of tradition, and the nature and composition of the humanities. But were not others—including Allan Bloom, William Bennett, and Lynne Cheney—also asking hard questions about the humanities? Were they not questioning the authority of the dominant voices in the academy, the legitimacy of the attempt to delegitimate the tradition, the right of entrenched powers to determine the nature and composition of the curriculum on purely political grounds? Of course they were. Why then, she asked, should such questions be dismissed at the outset as an "attack" on the humanities? Are not critics such as Bloom, Bennett, Cheney, and others doing precisely what Professor Derrida and his like-minded colleagues would have their own students do: scrutinizing the unacknowledged assumptions of "contemporary modes of discourse"?

Professor Himmelfarb then turned to the question that had been addressed to her: How would she distinguish between traditional intellectual and political history on the one hand, and the new social history that has taken the academy by storm on the other. She explained that the rise of social history, which concentrates on the texture of everyday life and the mundane activities of ordinary people, has tended to undermine the practice of traditional history, which was essentially "elite history," concerned with what she called high politics and great ideas. Indeed, she said, traditional intellectual and political history was precisely the history that had been enacted mostly by those Professor Bundtzen contemptuously referred to as "the big guys": great statesmen and military leaders in politics, great thinkers and artists in intellectual and cultural matters.

Speaking of "the big guys," Professor Himmelfarb asked Professor Bundtzen whether she was not worried that her proposals might foster a new stereotype of women, one that might be "limiting, restrictive, even possibly demeaning"? For why shouldn't women as well as men be concerned with large questions? "What about the woman who does want to celebrate transcendence and uniqueness and genius and large things," Professor Himmelfarb asked, "and doesn't want to be confined to 'a nurturing role.' Is she to be illegitimized as a woman?"

This question elicited a great round of applause from the audience but considerable confusion from the podium. An obviously stunned Professor Bundtzen replied that what she had said did not preclude the possibility of genius, although she did admit that she was "very reluctant" to use the phrase "transcendent truths"—after all, why should transcendent truths be "better or of greater value to us than the kind of truths we need to live our lives, which are not usually terribly transcendent from moment to moment or hour to hour?" One might wish to inquire a little more deeply into Professor Bundtzen's understanding of transcendent truths. Why did the word "transcendent" inspire so automatic a rejection? What kind of truths, exactly, did she believe we needed to live our lives? This was not the occasion to ponder such details. Instead, in case there were any doubt about the matter, Professor Bundtzen declared that she would characterize herself as a feminist critic. As such, she did not want to leave us with the impression that she would confine women to "the small things," as she put it earlier. In fact, she particularly admired women authors who regularly challenged male authors on their own terms, "who discover that beneath the guise of this extraordinary genius and potency and all the terms that are traditionally associated with male genius, there are vulnerabilities and weaknesses and ways in which to create a dialogue with that male tradition."

Professor Bundtzen then responded to Professor Himmelfarb's criticism of the way politics had intruded into the discussion. The problem is, she said, that if as an educator in the humanities you read that you should be "teaching transcendent truths" and you have difficulty with the very notion of transcendent truth then you feel under attack, especially if the definition of the humanities as having to do with transcendent truths is also tied to purse strings. What if, she asked, the Humanities Center at Williams decided that this year "we're not going to deal with transcendence, we're not going to deal with truths this year, we're going to deal with . . . I don't know, I can imagine another agenda which would not be outside the realm of humane studies." In that case, the Humanities Center would no doubt find that their requests for money from the government would be denied—and that, she concluded, she would regard as a "truly political" act.

It must be said that Professor Himmelfarb responded with great restraint. Did their application to the National Endowment, she wondered, say something to the effect that "this year we plan to deal with transcendent truths"? Did it not rather represent quite faithfully the program they have in fact been carrying out? One might ask, in addition, what the alternative to dealing "with truths" might be: dealing with untruths, perhaps? Is this an alternative within the realm of "humane studies" we would want humanities centers to pursue with public funds? Is it not ironical that this so-called center for the study of the humanities should in fact be dedicated to an attack on the idea of "the center" in just about every sense of the word? Professor Bundtzen did not exactly reply to Professor Himmelfarb's question, although—no doubt searching for a safe way to reintroduce a note of political virtue into the discussion—she did offer the stunning non sequitur that "I do think a lot of people feel threatened by the Helms amendment recently."

What a gift to the cultural Left the proposed Helms amendment has been! Formulated in the wake of the controversy over federal funding for Robert Mapplethorpe's photographs of homosexual sadomasochistic acts, the proposed amendment would have imposed a ban on giving federal money to art that is construed as offensive to a wide range of groups. It had already been soundly defeated by the time Professor Bundtzen spoke out against it, but that didn't seem to matter. To declare oneself against the amendment was still to show that one was on the side of virtue. Indeed, Professor Bundtzen's comment showed that the Helms amendment, even though it never had a prayer of being passed in its original form, has continued to provide a wonderfully convenient icon for politically correct academics, artists, and other cultural figures to attack: where else these days can one bask in the aura of outraged virtue by risking so little?

IV • A LESSON IN REPRESENTATIVE DEMOCRACY

The discussion at Williams that evening proceeded with many other memorable insights. Professor Baker, for example, won a round of applause for noting that the phrase *shared values* reminded him of the black sharecropper who was always being exploited. Werner Gundersheimer assured us that the "contestations" in the humanities today over the canon, appropriate forms of language, and so on really derived from the "extreme vitality and diversity" the humanities now enjoy, not a crisis. And Derrida replied to the charge that deconstruction was fundamentally ahistorical by asserting that, on the contrary, deconstruction offers "the most historical approach" to history, and that, in fact, the techniques of deconstruction provided the best way to preserve the intellectual vitality of the university.

But the evening's single most dramatic moment came when Professor Baker decided to weigh in against Professor Himmelfarb. If he was short on coherence and consecutive reasoning, he nonetheless succeeded in making himself abundantly clear. He was troubled, he told the Williams audience, by the ease with which Professor Himmelfarb had seemed to score points against Professor Bundtzen using "what I call the Strom Thurmond strategy." He went on to explain what he meant with an anecdote. Once, after having heard Martin Luther King's famous "I Have a Dream" speech, Professor Baker turned on his television only to find Senator Thurmond exclaiming that "Negroes here have more refrigerators, more shoes, more appliances, than colored people anywhere in the world. Why are they out here marching? I just do not understand it." According to Professor Baker, Professor Himmelfarb's observation that the Williams Center for the Humanities and Social Sciences was supported by a grant from the National Endowment for the Humanities betrayed a similarly patronizing attitude, which he summed up as follows: "We've given you, even you . . . a grant, so how can we conservatives be politically motivated?"

Professor Baker then wandered on to consider Professor Himmelfarb's remark that she had many friends who were politically liberal but who were conservative on cultural and educational issues. These were the sort of people, Professor Baker said contemptuously, "who speak Marxist and send their kids to elite prep schools." Such people might talk a good line, he explained, but when it came time "for Buffy or Cokie" to go to school, it was off to some elite institution such as Choate for them. Of course, the idea that Professor Himmelfarb, the very embodiment of the modern Jewish intellectual, had such vacuous WASP caricatures in mind when she spoke of her liberal friends who happened to be cultural conservatives is almost as amusing as it is absurd. She later responded with some pique that she knew no one who answered to Professor Baker's description of Buffy or Cokie.

By now Professor Baker was really warmed up. He more or less abandoned the attempt to frame an argument, letting himself be carried along by a gush of increasingly strident rhetoric. There were several notable elements in the oratorical collage he constructed. First, we were informed that "the fact is, the institutional site of authority is constituted by the National Endowment for the Humanities and the National Endowment for the Arts." As we have seen, *authority* is always a term of reproach in the academy these days, as is *institutional.* So identifying the Endowments as the "site of institutional authority" is to suggest something particularly malevolent. Exactly what it portended was not clear, except that the phrase provided a kind of transition to Professor Baker's observation that "it is a fact that the people who run these institutions are not elected by voters in this room. President Reagan doesn't call you up and say, 'Hey, Houston, what do you think?' "

Professor Baker next told us that he saw no evidence that people such as William Bennett, Allan Bloom, and Professor Himmelfarb had "immersed themselves in the very topics of inquiry that constitute our consensus" and charged that such people dismissed out of hand recent curricular innovations "precisely on the basis of gender, class, race, and sex." Professor Baker also opined (no doubt correctly) that Allan Bloom would not have much to tell us about the work of Frederick Douglass and other nineteenth-century American Black writers or the about the marvels of contemporary lesbian plays—although why a specialist in Plato and Rousseau, such as Professor Bloom, should have much to tell us about these subjects was not made clear.

We were now approaching Professor Baker's peroration. "Mr. Helms and that amendment have to do entirely with the institutional framework that I have discussed," he said, referring again (one conjectures) to the National Endowments as the "site of institutional authority." He then went on to issue a warning about those who criticize the dismantling of the traditional curriculum. "They are dangerous to all of us" and even, he said, to democracy. Why are those who criticize the politicization of the humanities dangerous? Professor Baker offered a few reasons, not all of which were intelligible. One reason I did hear is that such people are dangerous "because they are conservative." Moreover, he charged, alluding to Professor Himmelfarb's description of traditional historiography, while this conservative view of education pretends to strive to be objective and to respect the facts, it really "assigns the values and makes the facts correspond to them," in other words, although Professor Baker didn't put it so bluntly, it lies. He then squeezed in a few words about racial stereotypes and concluded in ringing tones by saying that while it may be too early to know whether all the new movements sweeping our campuses are right, we know "indisputably that what we have seen in the past is wrong." This remarkable performance was met by wild applause.

What can we make of Professor Baker's denunciation? Consider only his observation that officials administering the National Endowments were not elected by the "voters in this room." It may be that Professor Baker is unacquainted with the idea of representative democracy. It's possible, too, that he has something to learn about the character of the American electorate. Does Professor Baker believe that the voters at large in this country favor spending their tax dollars to support university humanities programs that have frankly devoted themselves to a radical political agenda? Perhaps he believes that most voters wake up thinking, "I wish the government would give more money to professors who spend their time criticizing the site of institutional authority in this country and teaching my children about lesbian plays." Or maybe, because he, too, mentioned the Helms amendment, he is convinced that most voters want more federal money spent on exhibitions of photographs of sexual degradation and coercion? The fact is, it is impossible to know just *what* Professor Baker thinks about these or the other matters he touched on. We can be pretty sure, though, that he is blissfully unaware of how privileged and protected a position he and his colleagues occupy in society, thanks precisely to their being insulated by the authority and largesse of the institutions they excoriate.

IV • THE COLLAPSE OF THE CENTER

No doubt sensing that he had let himself get carried away, Professor Baker later apologized to Professor Himmelfarb for comparing her to Strom Thurmond. He found nothing else in his declamation to retract, however, and as the audience filed out of Chapin Hall a little later that evening, his denunciations seemed to continue to echo. Professor Taylor had concluded by reassuring us yet again that even if there is a crisis in the humanities, it is "a sign of vitality rather than demise." Judging from snatches of conversation overheard after the discussion let out, the students were not so sure. Sentiment seemed to be running largely in favor of Professor Himmelfarb, not only with respect to the violence of Professor Baker's rhetoric but also with respect to the issues of feminism and the practice of history. Indeed, the proceedings at Williams that weekend reminded one that at many campuses today the political relation between undergraduates and the faculty has shifted in important ways since the late sixties and seventies. Increasingly, what one sees is not a radical student body importuning a recalcitrant faculty and administration for greater "diversity," relaxing of standards, and so forth, but a more traditionalist student body resisting the exhortations of a markedly more radical faculty. Often, the resistance expresses itself as simple indifference to the humanities: if studying the humanities has come to be an exercise in intellectual obscurantism and political sloganeering, well, there are other subjects worth pursuing. Is it any wonder that humanities enrollments have fallen off so precipitously in recent years?

The proceedings at Williams also reminded one of the extent to which the centrist position among our academic faculties has collapsed into a species of accommodating leftism. There was, first, the continuing spectacle of Professor Hirsch busily disassociating himself from charges of conservatism and traditionalism. But an even more egregious example of this surrender to the Left was Werner Gundersheimer's convocation speech the following day. Although obviously meant to represent a "moderate" position midway between, say, Professors Himmelfarb and Baker, this historian and director of the Folger Shakespeare Library—a man whose very position would seem to require him to act as a guardian of one of the greatest writers in the literary canon—in effect showed to what extent academic moderates have capitulated to the radical extreme. His speech, titled " 'Our Battles join'd': The Struggle for the American Mind," had two chief messages: (1) new trends in the humanities, from deconstruction and feminism to radical curricular revision, are only so many signs of vibrancy and health, and (2) the real danger to the humanities comes from those who wish to preserve the traditional curriculum and the values it embodies.

Professor Gundersheimer's address was full of the requisite clichés and slogans: the humanities today had been "enriched" by "diversity" and "innovation," they had "moved with the times . . . by accepting new subjects and approaches into their curricula, and so on." He did speak with some nostalgia about the English professor of old whose task was to master the literature in his field and then teach and write about it "in plain, accessible English that any educated person could understand and appreciate." No doubt that was precisely the ideal once held up to and perhaps even espoused by Professor Gundersheimer himself. He admitted that it had long since been abandoned by fashionable academics, yet went on to assure us that, because "change is the only constant within existing academic disciplines," its loss was not a tragedy but an exciting new challenge.

At the center of Professor Gundersheimer's speech to the dutifully assembled Williams community was a solemn warning about the dangers of attempts to reinstate a more traditional view of the humanities and what he called "the genteel ideal of plain talk in support of timeless verities." Predictably, Allan Bloom came in for particular censure because of his allegedly "simplistic attacks on colleges and universities." Yet Professor Gundersheimer was careful to assert that the problem went beyond Bloom and his followers. "Many distinguished scholars," he said, "see the flux of scholarship as a threat to the very substance of received doctrines, or what they are likely to call 'the truth.' " (One wondered what Professor Gundersheimer would be likely to call it.)

As a recent example of this "revolt against complexity," he quoted a book review that had appeared in *The Wall Street Journal.* The review was written by Edward Shils, the eminent sociologist and professor at the University of Chicago, and concerned *The Culture We Deserve,* a collection of essays on culture and the academy by the historian Jacques Barzun. One of Professor Barzun's chief complaints in that book is that, in the name of specialization, much academic discourse in the humanities has mired itself in a jargon that is both trivial and unintelligible. Professor Shils seconded this criticism and took it a step further. He castigated "the destructiveness of deconstruction," a movement of thought he aptly described as "that most chic of French academic exports, which preaches a nihilistic skepticism of language and that has now gained an almost unchallenged empire in American universities."[2] Professor Shils went on to note that the collaboration of deconstruction and other instances of academic "theory" with "a smattering of Marxism and political antinomianism" had "ravaged" the study of the humanities.

Professor Gundersheimer was quick to ridicule Professor Shils's description of the state of the humanities. He began by telling us that it was little more than an example of "the discourse of alienation" and "the old 'evil empire' gambit." (One can be sure that the damning allusion to President Reagan was not lost on the audience.) He then proceeded with a few words about his own view of matters in the academy. Portraying himself as the embodiment of moderation, Professor Gundersheimer proposed the adoption of common sense as an

[2]Edward Shils, "The Sad State of Humanities in America," *The Wall Street Journal,* July 3, 1989.

effective antidote to extremists on both sides of the debate over the humanities. That might seem a worthy proposal—common sense being in notably short supply in the humanities these days. But lest anyone think he was suggesting something reactionary, Professor Gundersheimer explained that "I am of course prepared to believe that one person's common sense is another person's nonsense." In other words, he supports a wonderful version of common sense—what we might perhaps call a "deconstructed" version—that is common only to the individual who happens to hold it.

This custodian of the legacy of Shakespeare scarcely even mentioned Shakespeare's name. Instead of worrying about literature, he favored us with a few axioms that he claimed to find useful when thinking about the mission of the humanities. For example, he informed us that the humanities do not thrive on sameness, but on "difference and conflict"; similarly, we discovered that "complexity in the world of ideas isn't scary. It's fun." "What *is* scary," Professor Gundersheimer pursued, "is reductionism. . . . Hitler knew exactly what art was. So does Jesse Helms." (You see how useful Senator Helms has proved to be.) And it's the same way, apparently, with those who claim to know the "original intent of the framers of the Constitution"—that is to say, those who, like Judge Robert Bork, have fallen afoul of the Left. Professor Gundersheimer concluded by assuring us that although he was all in favor of conflict, he did think it would be "regrettable if the great issues that now divide us—the sanctity of the so-called canon; the referentiality of language; the legitimacy of new methods and subjects of inquiry—were to lessen the claims of humanists and social scientists to serious public attention."

The contrast between the message of Professor Gundersheimer's speech and the setting could hardly have been starker. Here we had the most traditional of academic ceremonies, replete with academic regalia and communal singing of "My Country, 'Tis of Thee," providing the setting for a speech whose essential point was that the humanities can cut themselves off from both their foundation and their ideals and still be said to be thriving. What else are we to make of the evocation of a common sense that has a constituency of one? Or the contemptuous reference to "the sanctity of the so-called canon"? Or the suggestion that "the referentiality of language" is something the humanities today could just as well do without? Or the idea that "new methods"—meaning deconstruction and its progeny—and new "subjects of inquiry"—meaning everything from pulp novels to rock videos—are fit subjects for humanistic inquiry? Indeed, what else are we to make of the sum of Williams College's inquiry into the question "Crisis in the Humanities?"

Professor Gundersheimer insists that it would be regrettable were public interest in the humanities to falter. But why shouldn't it falter? Would it be surprising if the public spurned the claims of these new-style "humanists" and social scientists to "serious public attention"—to say nothing of serious public funding—when those claims are often expressly at odds with the public interest in preserving and transmitting our intellectual and cultural heritage? Imagine: A New Historicist analysis of convocation ceremonies at small New England colleges "proving" that they were instruments of cultural repression, or a deconstructionist reading of "My Country, 'Tis of Thee" showing that it was really a subversive or coercive text. Such exercises are legion in the academy; are they worth "serious public attention"?

The point is not that Professor Gundersheimer is an especially important or radical figure on the academic scene; he is neither. Nor is his message at all out of the ordinary. Again, this is precisely the problem: that even an ordinary, self-proclaimed moderate should as a matter of course abandon moderation and adopt "moving with the times" as a criterion of critical judgment. In his famous *Letters on the Aesthetic Education of Man* (1795), the German poet-philosopher Friedrich Schiller exhorted his readers to give their contemporaries what they need, not what they praise. It is good advice, as timely today as it was at the end of the eighteenth century. Yet to be effective, Schiller's admonition requires not only insight but also the courage to dissent from the entrenched pieties of one's time. Professor Gundersheimer's performance was one of many recent events reminding us that our colleges and universities have entered a new era of intellectual conformity in which such dissent is all but excluded from serious consideration. This alone shows that—notwithstanding the equivocations of Professors Taylor, Gundersheimer, and company—the humanities are indeed in a state of crisis today. One measure of the severity of that crisis is the extent to which a genuinely moderate center has collapsed in the face of ideological pressure from the Left. In this respect, the events at Williams in September 1989 are a depressing token of the situation of the humanities in the academy. What we have witnessed is nothing less than the occupation of the center by a new academic establishment, the establishment of tenured radicals.

EPILOGUE

I

When *Tenured Radicals* was published in April 1990, many critics—including some who were generally sympathetic to the book's chief arguments—wondered whether recent developments in the academy were really quite as bad as I claimed. Surely, the argument went, professors of literature who specialize in the rock videos of Madonna are exceedingly rare; there can't be many professors who devote their scholarly energies to showing that *Paradise Lost* is a sexist document or that *The Tempest* is an exposé of Western imperialism; are there more than a handful who maintain that there are no compelling reasons for judging *Middlemarch* to be a greater artistic achievement than the cartoons of Bugs Bunny? And how many professors, really, would dismiss the traditional notion of literary quality and the ideal of disinterested scholarship as oppressive legacies of white patriarchal culture? Surely such professors are a tiny minority, freak or comical exceptions in an otherwise blandly moderate intellectual universe.

It would be consoling to think so. Unfortunately, subsequent developments in the academy have shown that if *Tenured Radicals* erred in its indictment, it erred on the side of understatement. It is not just that the peddlers of such politicized nonsense are in many cases among the most celebrated academics in the country: senior professors safely ensconced at Yale and Stanford, at Princeton and Harvard, Duke, the University of California, and other premier institutions, where they chair departments, sit on promotion and tenure committees, and busy themselves developing and implementing radical curricular changes for their own and other institutions. That was already clear in the late 1980s. Nor is it simply that, unlike most of their moderate colleagues, such tenured radicals tend to be indefatigable proselytizers, bent on winning converts in their war against the traditional moral and intellectual values of liberal education. Troubling though that be, it, too, has been obvious for some time. Nor, finally, is it news that even the most bizarre writings and proclamations coming out of the academy, instead of being regarded as exotic or repellent curiosities, are often instrumental in setting the terms of debate both in the classroom and within the profession as a whole. No one familiar with the kind of thing that passes for scholarship today will be surprised to discover—to take just one example—that the presentation of a paper called "Jane Austen and the Masturbating Girl" at the 1989 annual meeting of the Modern Language Association was matched by a paper at the 1990 meeting on "The Lesbian Phallus: Or, Does Heterosexuality Exist?"[1] (One might have thought that the evidence for the existence of heterosexuality was well established, but evidence does not necessarily count for much among our new academic elite.)

All this is wearisomely familiar. What is new is the extent to which the constellation of radical trends that dominate the teaching of the humanities at many of our best institutions has found common cause in the rise of a new political ideology: the ideology of multiculturalism. Notwithstanding the emancipationist rhetoric that accompanies the term, "multiculturalism" as used in the academy today is not about recognizing genuine cultural diversity or encouraging pluralism. It is about undermining the priority of Western liberal values in our educational system and in society at large. In this sense, multiculturalism provides a convenient umbrella for the smorgasbord of radical ideologies regnant in the academy. The one thing your literary deconstructionist, your Lacanian feminist, your post-structuralist Marxist, your new historicist, and your devotee of what goes under the name of "cultural studies" can agree on is that the Western humanistic tradition is a repository of ideas that are naïve, repressive, or both.

[1]This is the title of a paper in a session on "Lesbianism, Heterosexuality, and Feminist Theory." The other papers listed for this session—which by the way is not at all uncharacteristic of the offerings the MLA has seen fit to make available to its members—are "Mapping the Frontier of the Black Hole: Toward a Black Feminist Theory" and "Perverse Desire, the Lure of the Mannish Lesbian." *Publications of the Modern Language Association of America,* vol. 105, no. 6 (November 1990), 1248.

At the center of the multicultural imperative is the assumption that all cultural life is to be explained in political terms, preeminently in terms of gender, race, class, and ethnic origin. In other words, categories of thought that have their home in the social sciences are imported into the arts and humanities and granted the status of golden explanatory keys. In good Marxist fashion, culture is denied autonomy and is reduced to being a coefficient of something else: class relations, sexual oppression, racial exploitation, etc. Questions of artistic quality are systematically replaced with tests for political relevance, even as the whole realm of aesthetic experience is "demythologized" as an insidious bourgeois fiction designed to consolidate the cultural hegemony of the ruling class. The thought that there might be something uniquely valuable about culture taken on its own terms, that literature, for example, might have its own criteria of achievement and offer its own distinctive satisfactions that are independent of contemporary political battles—none of this seems to matter or indeed to be seriously considered by our multiculturalist radicals.

Some partisans of multiculturalism will claim that in placing issues of gender, class, and race at the center of the humanities they are merely following a time-honored procedure for enriching their discipline by asking novel questions. Just as the New Critics of a previous generation enlivened literary criticism by focusing on verbal complexity, ambiguity, and irony at a time when philology and textual scholarship still ruled literary studies, so what we might call the New New Critics, marching under the banner of multiculturalism, are invigorating the humanities by concentrating on issues of gender, race, and class. The subjects addressed by their criticism may differ markedly from the subjects addressed by criticism of previous generations; the judgments made about what matters in literature and in life may differ radically as well; but that, we are told, is only to be expected; in essentials, such critics are doing what humanists have always done: interpreting texts with the categories that seem most pertinent to contemporary experience.

So goes the argument when the new academic orthodoxy is challenged. But the difference is that whereas the New Critics drew on the essentially literary resources of rhetorical analysis to give us a deeper appreciation of literature, our multiculturalists employ the tools of ethnic and sexual redress in order to transform literature into a species of political propaganda and virtue mongering. Our appreciation of literature is not enhanced; it is cancelled and replaced with something else. We are told that by concentrating on questions of gender, class, and ethnicity, multiculturalism provides new ways of looking at literature; in fact, literature per se never really comes into focus at all. The freedom that belongs to the exercise and experience of art is delivered over to a preordained set of political scenarios. The effect is to impoverish, not to enlarge, our experience. Furthermore, the notion that criticism is a free-floating activity, equally valuable whether applied to comic books or to the poems of Dante, underscores the deep cynicism that characterizes so much academic criticism today. It is as if what is actually said, believed, or advocated in our critical judgments is somehow incidental to the character of the humanistic enterprise—as if the value of a particular interpretation were independent of its truth!

Implicit in the politicizing mandate of multiculturalism is an attack on the idea of a common culture, the idea that, despite our many differences, we hold in common an intellectual, artistic, and moral legacy, descending largely from the Greeks and the Bible, supplemented and modified over the centuries by innumerable contributions from diverse hands and peoples. It is this legacy that has given us our science, our political institutions, and the monuments of artistic and cultural achievement that define us as a civilization. Indeed, it is this legacy, in so far as we live up to it, that preserves us from chaos and barbarism. And it is precisely this legacy that the multiculturalist wishes to dispense with. Either he claims that the Western tradition is merely one heritage among many—and therefore that it deserves no special allegiance inside the classroom or out of it—or he denies the achievements of the West altogether. As a student at Williams College patiently explained to me when I spoke there recently about some of these issues, "You are telling us, Mr. Kimball, that we undergraduates ought to focus our attention on the monuments of Western civilization. But you don't seem to understand that Western civilization is responsible for most of the world's ills."

The sources of the multicultural animus against the West are varied. In its more radical versions, as the historian Diane Ravitch has pointed out in a perceptive essay on the subject, multiculturalism "has its roots in the ideology of ethnic separatism and in the black nationalist movement."[2] In this sense, multiculturalism denies the ideal of the United States as an integrated society in which peoples of different races, creeds, and ethnic backgrounds can live together in a state of social harmony. The multiculturalist replaces the traditional integrationist image of our society with the ethnically and racially divisive image of the United States as a kind of salad or mosaic: a potpourri of essentially unassimilable elements. Despite occasional rhetoric to the contrary, he scorns the motto *e pluribus unum*—out of many heritages, one society—in order to bolster ethnic, racial, or class-oriented fiefdoms. It follows that the multiculturalist will also have little patience with the idea of universal humanity. Corresponding to the attack on the idea of a common culture is a rejection of the idea of a common humanity. The multiculturalist rejects the idea that our identity as human beings transcends our membership in a particular class, race, or gender. On the contrary, for the multiculturalist what is important is not what binds us together but what separates us. And what separates us—be it gender, ethnicity, class, or race—is used as a totem to confer the coveted status of victimhood upon certain approved groups.

In order to appreciate what is at stake in the debate over multiculturalism, consider the phenomenon of Afrocentricity, one of the more extreme but also most influential manifestations of the multicultural ethos. The basic supposition of the movement for Afrocentricity is that Western culture is a bastardization of African, and especially Egyptian, culture, which in a highly innovative piece of ethnography is said to have been predominantly black. Consequently, black Americans—often referred to as "diasporan African people"—are enjoined to discard the "the preponderant Eurocentric myths of universalism, objectivity, and classical traditions" and reclaim their proper intellectual, cultural, and spiritual legacy by returning to African sources.[3] What might be left of culture after dispensing with the "myths" of "universalism, objectivity, and classical traditions"—in other words, with rationality, science, and history—is never really discussed because the truly radical nature of the enterprise is never brought to

[2]"Multiculturalism," *The American Scholar,* vol. 59, no. 3 (Summer 1990), 342.

[3]Molefi Kete Asante, *The Afrocentric Idea* (Philadelphia: Temple University Press, 1987), 9.

light. One hears the call for Afrocentricity on many campuses, but—what is even more disturbing—it has so far been most successful influencing the curriculum in high schools around the country.

The journalist Andrew Sullivan provided a kind of introduction to the subject in his account of the Second Annual Conference on the Infusion of African and African-American Content in the High School Curriculum that was held early in November 1990 in Atlanta.[4] As Sullivan points out, the impetus for the conference was the Afrocentric aim to rid black education of "white influences" and "to transform the high school curriculum by giving it an exclusively Afrocentric base." A fantasy? In Portland, Oregon, a version of the Afrocentric curriculum informed by a document called the *African-American Baseline Essays* has already been adopted.[5] Similar documents are planned for other "geocultural" groups. The Portland curriculum, which has come to serve as a national model for curricular transformation, is being adopted at schools in Pittsburgh, Indianapolis, Atlanta, and Washington, D.C. In New York, a recent task force presided over by Thomas Sobol, State Education Commissioner, recommended sweeping changes in the teaching of history in New York schools in order to accommodate ethnic pressure groups and to root out what Commissioner Sobol called the "hidden assumptions of white supremacy" in the textbooks currently used.[6] And what is taught? Like much about Afrocentricity, it is beyond satire and would indeed be funny if it were not in earnest. In the *African-American Baseline Essays* students learn about the great "African-Jewish" scientist and philosopher Maimonides. Old Testament history is conveniently rewritten to portray the ancient Hebrews as guests, not slaves, of the Egyptian pharaohs. It is suggested that the "so-called Pythagorean theorem" was discovered—like just about everything else—by the ancient Egyptians. There is even a section on ancient "Egyptian Metallurgy and Electrical Engineering." Sullivan reports that ninth graders are to immerse themselves in the study of Egyptian hieroglyphics, cleansing rituals, and numerology. Students are taught that Greek philosophy was pla-

[4]Andrew Sullivan, "Racism 101," *The New Republic,* November 26, 1990, 18–21.

[5]Michael D. Harris, et al., *African-American Baseline Essays* (Portland: Portland Public Schools, 1987; rev. 1990).

[6]Karen Brady, "Principal Presses Indians' Place in Textbooks," *The Buffalo News,* August 21, 1990.

giarized from black African Egypt (Plato and Aristotle, it turns out, are figures of derision for Afrocentrists) and, more generally, that "all Western knowledge is a corruption of Egyptian, i.e., black African thought, and must therefore be junked." One charming participant in the conference explained this point as follows:

> When we adopt other people's theories, we are like Frankenstein doing other people's wills. It's like someone drinking some good stuff, vomiting it, and then we have to catch the vomit and drink it ourselves. . . . The Greeks gave back the vomit of the African way. . . . Don't become the vomit-drinkers!

Leave aside the objection that it was not Victor Frankenstein but his monstrous creation that the speaker has in mind here: who would expect someone who considers the Western European tradition of literature and philosophy to be a kind of vomit to bother to acquaint himself with any of it firsthand? The movement for Afrocentricity reminds one of nothing more than Evelyn Waugh's portrait, in his novel *Scoop,* of the Consul-General from the fictional African country of Ishmaelia haranguing passersby in Hyde Park:

> "Who built the Pyramids?" cried the Ishmaelite orator. "A Negro. Who invented the circulation of the blood? A Negro. Ladies and gentlemen, . . . Who discovered America? . . . As that great Negro Karl Marx has so nobly written . . . Africa for the African worker, Europe for the African worker, Asia, Oceania, America, Arctic and Antarctica for the African worker . . ."[7]

But the terrible truth is that instead of being a novelist's wicked parody of certain fringe elements, the movement for Afrocentricity is a powerful ideology affecting the curricula in high schools and colleges across the country.

There is something grimly ironic about the spectacle of our new multiculturalists using ethnocentricism as a stick with which to beat the West. After all, both the idea and the critique of ethnocentricism are quintessentially Western. There has never in history been a society more open to other cultures than our own; nor has any tradition been

[7]Evelyn Waugh, *Scoop* (Boston: Little, Brown, 1977), 65, 68.

more committed to self-criticism than the Western tradition: the figure of Socrates endlessly inviting self-scrutiny and rational explanation is a definitive image of the Western spirit. Moreover, "Western" science is not exclusively Western: it is science plain and simple—yes, it is universal science—which, though invented and developed in the West, is as true for the inhabitants of the Nile Valley as it is for the denizens of New York. That is why, outside the misty precincts of the humanities departments of Western universities, there is a mad dash to acquire Western science and technology. The deepest foolishness of multiculturalism shows itself in the puerile attacks it mounts on the cogency of scientific rationality, epitomized poignantly by the Afrocentrist who flips on his word processor to write books decrying the parochial nature of Western science and extolling the virtues of the "African way."

II

Despite the racist character of Afrocentricity, it pleases advocates of multiculturalism to present it and other forms of ideological posturing as prime examples of freedom, diversity, and tolerance. In order to understand what our tenured radicals mean when they use such words, let us remind ourselves of the ingenuous student from the University of Pennsylvania who made the mistake of expressing her "deep regard for the individual," only to be reprimanded by a university administrator who responded that the word *individual* "is a 'RED FLAG' phrase today, which is considered by many to be RACIST." As Professor Alan Charles Kors from the University of Pennsylvania has noted, the real lesson to be drawn from this episode—as from the many similar episodes that could be cited—is that the university "is a tolerant and diverse community, and if you do not agree with its particular notions of tolerance and diversity, it will gladly re-educate you."[8]

We were given a good sense of how the virtues of tolerance and pluralism have been faring in the academy when some professors at Duke University decided to establish a chapter of the National Associ-

[8]Alan Charles Kors, "It's Speech, Not Sex, the Dean Bans Now," *Wall Street Journal*, October 12, 1989.

ation of Scholars this fall. The NAS is a group of tradition-minded teachers and scholars whose motto is "For Reasoned Scholarship in a Free Society." Among the faculty who organized the Duke chapter of the NAS was James David Barber, the eminent political scientist whose impeccable liberal credentials include leading a successful fight against establishing the Nixon library at Duke and serving as president of Amnesty International. Nevertheless, as soon as word got out that a chapter of the NAS was being established at Duke, the redoubtable Stanley Fish, chairman of the Duke English department, sent an anguished letter to a student newspaper, *The Chronicle,* in which he warned, among other things, that the NAS is "widely known to be racist, sexist, and homophobic."

Professor Fish was apparently so worried that reasoned scholarship in a free society might come to Duke that he also took it upon himself to write to the provost "advising him," as one commentator observed, "that faculty belonging to the NAS should not be appointed to key committees involving tenure or curriculum decisions."[9] Professor Fish denied proposing this. But he had made the error of sending copies of this missive to a handful of trusted colleagues, one of whom was upset enough at the suggestion that basic civil rights of Duke faculty members should be summarily abridged to suit Professor Fish's politics that he made the contents of the letter public. Hearing of Professor Fish's denial, an editor at *The Chronicle* commented, "It was really strange to hear him say that. We had the letter with his own words asking just that, right in front of us." But then we must remember that Professor Fish proudly identifies himself as a sophist, one who, in the classical formula, "makes the stronger argument appear weaker, the weaker argument appear stronger." Perhaps he should remind himself that what works between the covers of a contemporary text of literary criticism is not always so convincing when exposed to the steady, if pedestrian, light of common sense.

Embarrassing and, indeed, disappointing as Professor Fish's exhibition is—one might have expected a modicum of principled behavior from so gifted a scholar—what is most revealing about this new controversy at Duke is that those organizing support for the NAS are

[9]Dorothy Rabinowitz "Vive the Academic Resistance," *Wall Street Journal,* November 13, 1990. Unless otherwise noted, quotations regarding this controversy are taken from Miss Rabinowitz's article.

not arch conservatives but, by any conventional measurement, liberals. "What's happened to Duke," said one observer, is "the remaking of a mainstream university into a radical one—with terrible consequences—and I speak as a man who campaigned for George McGovern." The episode dramatizes the extent to which the traditional, moderate center of university life has been occupied by the new radicalism. As another scholar—one not, incidentally, affiliated with the NAS—put it: "Today they have something they should call the House *American* Activities Committee because people and ideas that are pro-American or pro-Western are now treated on the campuses as though they were some sort of subversive evil."

Notwithstanding the charges blithely hurled by Professor Fish and his allies against those supporting the NAS—"racist, sexist, and homophobic" for starters—the real battle that is now shaping up is not between radicals and conservatives but between radicals and old-style liberals. Or perhaps one should say that the classical liberal position—which fought for the ideals of quality, disinterested scholarship, and for advancement according to merit, not adherence to a given political line—is now castigated as conservative and reactionary. Professor Fish, for example, has gone to great lengths to demonstrate that "there is no such thing as intrinsic merit," only conventional opinion. The result is that at many institutions any middle ground has been abolished. On the one side we have the remnants of the much besieged liberal tradition attempting to maintain traditional standards of civility and scholarship. On the other side we have the ruling academic clique, the tenor of whose educational philosophy was vividly summed up by Stanley Hauerwas, a well-known professor of theological ethics at Duke. When the controversy over the NAS broke out, Professor Hauerwas disparged the educational goals of the NAS, explaining in a local newspaper that "The canon of great literature was created by high Anglican – – – holes to underwrite their social class."[10] Edifying, is it not, to acquaint oneself with the table talk of our contemporary academic theologians?

[10]Pam Kelley, "For Duke Profs, the Hot Debate Is What to Teach," *Charlotte Observer,* September 28, 1990.

III

Professor Hauerwas's comment reminds us that a major issue in the whole debate over multiculturalism—as indeed in the controversy at Duke over the establishment of the NAS—centers on the question of the proper content of a liberal arts education. For both better and worse, discussion of this question in recent years has crystalized around the word *canon.* On the positive side, putting the traditional literary canon at the center of the debate effectively calls attention to some of the more egregious assaults on the humanities in our colleges and universities. When professors of literature begin teaching Louis L'Amour—to say nothing of the rock videos of Madonna—instead of Henry James, when they begin teaching Frantz Fanon instead of John Locke in their political philosophy classes, something has gone terribly wrong. And it is well to remember that instances of such pedagogical frivolity are now increasingly the rule, not the exception. A major legacy of the 1960s in the academy has been the destruction of intellectual standards. The very idea that some works might be more worth reading than others, together with the ideal of excellence that informs it, is regarded with suspicion as "hierarchical" and "elitist." Nowhere has this been more apparent than in the attack on the canon. Between the introduction of works of popular culture into the humanities curriculum and the unending search for works by authors of the requisite sex, skin color, sexual orientation, or ethnic heritage—between, that is, the trivialization and politicization of the curriculum—the substance of liberal arts education at many institutions has suffered catastrophic damage. Nowadays, many liberal arts majors are being graduated having read little more than a handful of popular novels, a bit of esoteric literary theory, and various works that confirm their chosen ideological prejudices. The great works of the tradition remain, literally, a closed book.

Nevertheless, there are reasons to be uncomfortable about the prominence that the word *canon* has assumed in the debate over the future of the humanities. For one thing, by concentrating on *what* is taught critics have sometimes tended to slight the question of *how* teachers are approaching the material they teach. Few would deny Jane Austen a place in the canon; but "Jane Austen and the Masturbating Girl" is not exactly a candidate for responsible pedagogy. Plato and Aristotle belong in any liberal arts curriculum, but not as examples of how the white race has corrupted the wisdom of black Egypt. No author is immune to the depredations of such ideologically motivated criticism, which is to say that our concern for the integrity of the canon must be a concern for responsible interpretation and teaching as well.

It must also be said that the scramble to draw up approved reading lists has had the unfortunate effect of suggesting to some that those supporting the canon wish to impose a changeless tablet of previously certified texts on unsuspecting students. In fact, no serious commentator believes—or has said—that the canon is a sacrosanct catalogue of works that may never be altered or added to. But this is not to deny that there is a body of works from the Western tradition that should form the core of a liberal arts education, works that embody what Roger Shattuck, one of our leading scholars of modern French literature, has called "accepted versions of greatness," "scales of human eminence, qualities to admire and perhaps to emulate."[11] Of course, the number of works belonging to this core is far larger than the most voracious student could hope to master even if he were granted several lifetimes. In this sense, "being educated" is an ideal any one person can only aspire to. Yet when it comes to the content of a liberal arts education—when it comes, that is, to the works and authors one should study in the four years of one's undergraduate career—decisions have to be made. The criterion is first of all not whether a given work is included on the Received List of Great Books but whether it has proved to be of permanent interest. It happens that some works have demonstrated their insight, beauty, or truth to so many educated people for so long that failing to read them is tantamount to consigning oneself to the ranks of the ill-educated. My own view is that liberal arts education should concentrate as rigorously as possible on works that have proved to be of permanent value; in practice, that means that few if any contemporary works should be part of the undergraduate curriculum. This is not to say that students shouldn't read contemporary fiction and criticism, or that they shouldn't go to the movies, listen to contemporary music, and gener-

[11]Roger Shattuck, *Perplexing Dreams: Is There a Core Tradition in the Humanities?* American Council of Learned Societies Occasional Paper No. 2, 1987, 6.

ally immerse themselves in the life of the moment. In fact, any young person who is intellectually alive and curious will do so as a matter of course. But contemporary culture should not form the basis of a college education. One should look to the past, not to the streets, for the substance of the liberal arts curriculum.

Some critics of *Tenured Radicals* have complained that the book fails to outline alternatives to the morass it describes—where by "alternatives" most seem to mean reading lists. But unless one subscribes to the ethos of multiculturalism, which looks to cultural politics instead of intellectual substance to dictate educational policy, the question of what one should read is not an esoteric matter. Nor is the rationale for a liberal arts education. One reads as much of what has stood the test of time as one can, beginning if possible with the oldest and most influential books of the Western tradition; and one does so because one desires the gifts of a liberal education: knowledge, intellectual freedom, and a cultivated appreciation of the traditions that have been instrumental in forming our culture. If that sounds like a list of clichés, well, it is—just as any true description of what matters in education will be. It is in the nature of generalizations about life's difficult choices to be perfectly obvious, which is perhaps why both are so often confounded by those making a profession of sophistry.

John Searle, a professor of philosophy at the University of California at Berkeley and one of the most thoughtful critics of *Tenured Radicals,* put the conventional rationale for liberal education with consummate simplicity when he observed that

> there is a certain Western intellectual tradition that goes from, say, Socrates to Wittgenstein in philosophy, and from Homer to James Joyce in literature, and it is essential to the liberal education of young men and women in the United States that they should receive some exposure to at least some of the great works in this intellectual tradition; they should, in Matthew Arnold's overquoted words, "know the best that is known and thought in the world." The arguments given for this view—on the rare occasions when it was felt that arguments were even needed—were that knowledge of the tradition was essential to the self-understanding of educated Americans since the country, in an important sense, is the product of that tradition; that many of these works are historically important because of their influences; and that most of them, for example sev-

> eral works by Plato and Shakespeare, are of very high intellectual and artistic quality, to the point of being of universal human interest.[12]

Until recently, as Professor Searle notes, this description would have seemed so obvious as to have been a "platitude"—which in this context we might define as a statement sufficently self-evident that its utterance is superfluous.

It is a measure of how drastically things have changed that in the academy today Professor Searle's vignette would, as he acknowledges, generally be regarded as "wildly reactionary." Indeed, I can think of few major universities that would dare to endorse it, even as an educational platitude. (Seismic shifts in a culture's values show up first in its choice of platitudes.) From Socrates to Wittgenstein? Where are the women, the blacks, the Hispanics, the Asians? Ditto on Homer to Joyce. Furthermore, why should a liberal arts education focus on "the best" that has been thought and said? What about populations and points of view that have been "marginalized"? What about popular culture? What about Madonna? What about the tradition essential to *un*educated Americans? Moreover, who says that America is a product of the white, male, Eurocentric tradition outlined above? What about Native American influences? What about Africa?

And so on. A swamp yawns open before us, ready to devour everything. The best response to all this—and finally the only serious and effective response—is not to enter these murky waters in the first place. As Nietzsche observed, we do not refute a disease. We resist it. And yet there are two issues that must be engaged. The first concerns the often-heard charge of "elitism." The traditional notion of a liberal arts education is unquestionably elitist in the sense that it focuses on the pinnacle of human cultural and intellectual achievement. It must also be admitted that not everyone is either interested in or capable of taking advantage of a liberal arts education conceived in this way. In a deeper sense, however, the whole impulse behind a traditional liberal arts education is radically democratic. For its riches are in principle available to anyone with talent and energy, regardless of class, sex, skin color, ethnic origin, and so on. The real tyranny is to deprive students of the best that has been thought and said in the

[12]John Searle, "The Storm Over the University," *New York Review of Books,* vol. 37, no. 19 (December 6, 1990), 34–42.

name of one or another version of political rectitude.

The second issue that must be engaged concerns the last item in Professor Searle's inventory, the fundamental question of "universal human interest." To speak of universal human interest is to acknowledge faith in a community of human endeavor that transcends the contingencies of race, gender, ethnic heritage, and the like. As the multiculturalists realize, some such faith is central to the tradition of liberal education; this is one reason they are so eager to repudiate that tradition. Many commentators have pointed out that the demography of the United States is changing so rapidly that the non-white populations in this country may outnumber the white by the end of the next century. Already in certain areas more than half the population is non-white. Shouldn't the liberal arts curriculum acknowledge this change by questioning the priority still granted to Western culture and by including more literature by blacks, Hispanics, Asians, etc.? The multiculturalists think so.

Demographics notwithstanding, the truth is that by virtue of its history, its political institutions, its major cultural affiliations, and its dominant language the United States is essentially a Western society. And short of a major cataclysm, it will remain so. As Donald Kagan, dean of Yale College, observed in an address that counts as one of the most hopeful signs from the academy in recent years, the United States does enjoy a common culture,

> itself various, changing, rich with contributions of Americans who come or whose ancestors came from every continent in the world, yet recognizably and unmistakably American. At this moment in history an objective observer would have to say that it derives chiefly from the experience of Western Civilization, and especially from England, whose languages and institutions are the most copious springs from which American culture draws its life. I say this without embarrassment, as an immigrant from a tiny country on the fringe of the West, without any connection to the Anglo-Saxon founders of the United States.[13]

Because the roots of our society are so deeply imbedded in Western culture, being ignorant of that culture means being ignorant of one-

[13]Donald Kagan, "E Pluribus Unum," an address delivered to the freshman class at Yale College in September 1990. The address is reprinted in *Commentary,* vol. 91, no. 1 (January 1991), 47–49.

self. Consequently, as Dean Kagan argues, "It is both right and necessary to place Western Civilization and the culture to which it has given rise at the center of our studies, and we fail to do so at the peril of our students, our country, and of the hopes for a democratic, liberal society emerging throughout the world today."

IV

The emergent democracy to which Dean Kagan refers with justified pride is essentially a Western phenomenon. But next to the triumphs of hope and liberty we have seen in Eastern Europe, the Soviet Union, and elsewhere, we must place the many forboding signs of resurgent nationalism, ethnic separatism, and ancient racial hatreds that have also been a prominent feature of recent history. It wasn't long ago that we were assured that the "end of history" was nigh: that a Western-style liberalism was on the verge of establishing itself the world over and that peace and amity were breaking out everywhere. But instead of that attractive version of the end of history, we are now witnessing what some have called the retribalization of the world: a violent turn against Western liberalism and its tradition of rationality, respect for individual rights, and recognition of a common good that transcends the accidents of ethnic and racial identity. Given this situation, it is all the more imperative that we educate our students in the Western tradition, that we teach them about the virtues of our society and its democratic institutions. Such education is the staunchest bulwark against the forces of disintegration we are facing.

The multiculturalists rant on about the repressive, inequitable nature of U.S. society. It is instructive to note, however, that people all over the world continue to flock here. They do so not because they believe the United States is perfect, but because they believe that the Western democratic institutions that govern this society will allow them greater freedom, economic opportunity, and personal dignity than they are likely to find anywhere else in the world. The multiculturalists notwithstanding, the choice facing us today is not between a "repressive" Western culture and a multicultural paradise, but between culture and barbarism. Civilization is not a gift, it is an achievement—a fragile achievement that needs constantly to be shored up and defended from besiegers inside and out. These are facts that do not easily penetrate the cozy and coddled purlieus of the academy, where hatred of the West and its institutions can be indulged and propagated at no cost. But such facts are part of the permanent challenge that any civilization worth saving must face. This was something that Evelyn Waugh understood with exceptional clarity. "Barbarism," he wrote in a somber moment in 1938,

> is never finally defeated; given propitious circumstances, men and women who seem quite orderly will commit every conceivable atrocity. The danger does not come merely from habitual hooligans; we are all potential recruits for anarchy. Unremitting effort is needed to keep men living together at peace; there is only a margin of energy left over for experiment however beneficent. Once the prisons of the mind have been opened, the orgy is on. There is no more agreeable position than that of dissident from a stable society. Theirs are all the solid advantages of other people's creation and preservation, and all the fun of detecting hypocrisies and inconsistencies. There are times when dissidents are not only enviable but valuable. The work of preserving society is sometimes onerous, sometimes almost effortless. The more elaborate the society, the more vulnerable it is to attack, and the more complete its collapse in case of defeat. At a time like the present it is notably precarious. If it falls we shall see not merely the dissolution of a few joint-stock corporations, but of the spiritual and material achievements of our history.[14]

Tenured Radicals is about the privileged beneficiaries of the spiritual and material achievements of our history who, out of perversity, ignorance, or malice, have chosen to turn their backs on the culture that nourished them and made them what they are. It is about intellectuals who have defiled reason with sophistries, and teachers who have defrauded their students of knowledge. Because of the times we live in and the hard choices we face as a society, it is, above all, a cautionary tale.

RK
December 1990

[14]Quoted from *The Essays, Articles and Reviews of Eveyln Waugh,* edited by Donat Gallagher (Boston: Little, Brown, 1984), 161–162.

SELECTED BIBLIOGRAPHY

Allardyce, Gilbert. "The Rise and Fall of the Western Civilization Course." *American Historical Review* 87 (June 1982): 696–725.

Althusser, Louis. *Lenin and Philosophy and Other Essays.* Translated by Ben Brewster. New York: Monthly Review Press, 1971.

Arendt, Hannah. "The Crisis in Education." *Between Past and Future: Eight Exercises in Political Thought.* New York: Penguin, 1978.

Arendt, Hannah. *The Origins of Totalitarianism.* New York: Harcourt Brace Jovanovich, 1973.

Arnold, Matthew. "The Function of Criticism at the Present Time." *The Portable Matthew Arnold.* Edited by Lionel Trilling. New York: Viking Press, 1972.

Arnold, Matthew. "The Literary Function of Academies." *The Portable Matthew Arnold.* Edited by Lionel Trilling. New York: Viking Press, 1972.

Balch, Stephen H., and Herbert I. London. "The Tenured Left." *Commentary* 83 (October 1986): 41–51.

Barringer, Felicity. "Drives by Campuses to Curb Race Slurs Pose a Speech Issue." *The New York Times* 25 April 1989.

Barzun, Jacques. *The Culture We Deserve.* Middletown: Wesleyan University Press, 1989.

Bennett, William J. *To Reclaim a Legacy: A Report on the Humanities in Higher Education.* Washington, D.C.: National Endowment for the Humanities, 1984.

Berger, Brigitte. "Academic Feminism and the 'Left'." *Academic Questions* 1 (Spring 1988): 6–15.

Berger, Joseph. "U.S. Literature: Canon Under Siege." *The New York Times* 6 January 1988.

Bloom, Allan. *The Closing of the American Mind: How Higher Education Has Failed Democracy and Impoverished the Souls of Today's Students.* New York: Simon and Schuster, 1987.

Bourdieu, Pierre, and Jean-Claude Passeron. *Reproduction in Education and Society.* Translated by Richard Nice. Vol. 5, *Sage Studies in Social and Educational Change.* Silver Spring: Sage Publications, 1977.

Bromwich, David. "The Future of Tradition: Notes on the Crisis of the Humanities." *Dissent* 36 (Fall 1989): 541–557.

Cassirer, Ernst. *The Philosophy of Symbolic Forms.* Vol. 1, *Language.* Translated by Ralph Manheim. New Haven: Yale University Press, 1955.

Cheney, Lynne V. *Humanities in America: A Report to the President, the Congress, and the American People.* Washington, D.C.: The National Endowment for the Humanities, 1988.

Crews, Frederick. *Skeptical Engagements.* New York: Oxford University Press, 1986.

Culler, Jonathan. "It's Time to Set the Record Straight About Paul de Man and His Wartime Articles for a Pro-Fascist Newspaper." *The Chronicle of Higher Education* 13 July 1988.

Daniels, Lee A. "Stanford Alters Western Culture Course." *The New York Times* 2 April 1988.

de Man, Paul. *Allegories of Reading: Figural Language in Rousseau, Nietzsche, Rilke, and Proust.* New Haven: Yale University Press, 1979.

de Man, Paul. *Blindness and Insight: Essays in the Rhetoric of Contemporary Criticism.* New York: Oxford University Press, 1971.

de Man, Paul. *Wartime Journalism, 1939–1943.* Edited by Werner Hamacher, et al. Lincoln: University of Nebraska Press, 1989.

Derrida, Jacques. "Like the Sound of the Sea Deep within a Shell: Paul de Man's War." Translated by Peggy Kamuf. *Critical Inquiry* 14 (Spring 1988): 590–652.

Derrida, Jacques. "Point de la folie—maintenant l'architecture." *Psyche: Inventions de l'autre.* Paris: Galilee, 1987.

Derrida, Jacques. "Signature Event Context." *Limited Inc.* Translated by Samuel Weber and Jeffrey Mehlman. Evanston: Northwestern University Press, 1988.

Detlefsen, Robert R. "White Like Me." *The New Republic* 10 April 1989, 18–21.

Eisenman, Peter. *Houses of Cards.* New York: Oxford University Press, 1988.

Fanon, Frantz. *The Wretched of the Earth.* Translated by Constance Farrington. New York: Grove Press, 1963.

Finn, Chester E., Jr. "The Campus: 'An Island of Repression in a Sea of Freedom.' " *Commentary* 86 (September 1989): 17–23.

Fish, Stanley. *Doing What Comes Naturally: Change, Rhetoric, and the Practice of Theory in Literary and Legal Studies.* Durham: Duke University Press, 1989.

Fish, Stanley. *Is There a Text in this Class? The Authority of Interpretive Communities.* Cambridge: Harvard University Press, 1980.

Fish, Stanley. *Surprised by Sin: The Reader in Paradise Lost.* Berkeley: University of California Press, 1967.

Fox-Genovese, Elizabeth. "Gender, Race, Class, Canon." *Salmagundi* 72 (Fall 1986): 131–143.

Hamacher, Werner, et al., eds. *Responses: On Paul de Man's Wartime Journalism.* Lincoln: University of Nebraska Press, 1989.

Hartman, Geoffrey H. "Blindness and Insight." *The New Republic* 7 March 1988, 26–31.

Hegel, G. W. F. *The Phenomenology of Spirit.* Translated by A. V. Miller. Oxford: Oxford University Press, 1977.

Heller, Scott. "A Constellation of Recently Hired Professors Illuminates the English Department at Duke." *The Chronicle of Higher Education* 27 May 1987, 12.

Heller, Thomas C., et al., eds. *Reconstructing Individualism: Autonomy, Individuality, and the Self in Western Thought.* Stanford: Stanford University Press, 1986.

Hirsch, E. D., Jr. *Cultural Literacy: What Every American Needs to Know.* Boston: Houghton-Mifflin, 1987.

Hirsch, E. D., Jr., Joseph F. Kett, and James Trefil. *The Dictionary of Cultural Literacy: What Every American Needs to Know.* Boston: Houghton-Mifflin, 1989.

Hirsch, E. D., Jr. "On Cultural Literacy: Canon, Class, Curriculum" *Salmagundi* 72 (Fall 1986): 118–124.

Hirsch, E. D., Jr. *Validity in Interpretation.* New Haven: Yale University Press, 1967.

Holt, Elizabeth Gilmore. *A Documentary History of Art: From the Classicists to the Impressionists:* Vol. 3, *Art and Architecture in Nineteenth Century.* New York: Doubleday, 1966.

Hook, Sidney, ed. "Stanford Documents." *Partisan Review* 55 (Fall 1988): 653–674.

Hook, Sidney. "Civilization and its Malcontents." *National Review* 13 October 1989, 30–33.

Husserl, Edmund. "Philosophy and the Crisis of European Man." *Phenomenology and the Crisis of Philosophy.* Translated by Quentin Lauer. New York: Harper & Row, 1965.

Jameson, Fredric. *The Political Unconscious: Narrative as a Socially Symbolic Act.* Ithaca: Cornell University Press, 1981.

Jencks, Charles. *Modern Movements in Architecture.* New York: Doubleday, 1973.

Jencks, Charles. *Towards a Symbolic Architecture: The Thematic House.* New York: Rizzoli, 1988.

Johnson, Philip, and Mark Wigley. *Deconstructivist Architecture.* New York: The Museum of Modern Art, 1988.

Johnson, Richard. "What is Cultural Studies Anyway?" *Social Text: Theory/Culture/Ideology.* 6 (Winter 1986/7): 38–80.

Junkerman, Charles. "Letter to the Editor." *The Wall Street Journal* 6 January 1989.

Kant, Immanuel. *Critique of Judgment.* Translated by Werner S. Pluhar. Indianapolis: Hackett, 1987.

Kaplan, E. Ann. *Rocking Around the Clock: Music Television, Postmodernism, & Consumer Culture.* New York: Methuen, 1987.

Kierkegaard, Søren. *Either/Or.* Vol. 1. Translated by David F. Swenson and Lillian Marvin Swenson. Princeton: Princeton University Press, 1971.

Kierkegaard, Søren. *The Present Age.* Translated by Alexander Dru. New York: Harper & Row, 1962.

Kimball, Roger. "Guns and Other 'Hermeneutical Acts' at Columbia." *The New Criterion* 6 (May 1988): 77–79.

Kors, Alan Charles. "It's Speech, Not Sex, the Dean Bans Now." *The Wall Street Journal* 12 October 1989.

Krauss, Rosalind E. *The Originality of the Avant-Garde and Other Modernist Myths.* Cambridge: M. I. T. Press, 1985.

Kuhn, Thomas. *The Structure of Scientific Revolutions,* 2d ed. Chicago: University of Chicago Press, 1970.

Levine, George, et al. *Speaking for the Humanities.* American Council of Learned Societies Occasional Paper No. 7, 1989.

Lodge, David. *Small World.* New York: Macmillan, 1984.

Malcolm, Janet. "Ingrid Sischy." *The New Yorker* 20 October 1986, 49–89.

Marcuse, Herbert. *Eros and Civilization: A Philosophical Inquiry into Freud.* Boston: Beacon Press, 1966.

Marcuse, Herbert. "Repressive Tolerance." In *A Critique of Pure Tolerance.* Robert Paul Wolff, et al. Boston: Beacon Press, 1969.

Michelson, Annette, et al., ed. *October: The First Decade, 1976–1986.* Cambridge: M. I. T. Press, 1987.

Miller, J. Hillis. "NB" column on Paul de Man, *The Times Literary Supplement* 17 June 1988, 676, 685.

Morse, J. Mitchell. "Some Variations." *Salmagundi* 72 (Fall 1986): 148–163.

Nietzsche, Friedrich. *Beyond Good and Evil.* in *The Basic Writings of Nietzsche.* Translated by Walter Kaufmann. New York: Random House, 1966.

Norris, Christopher. "Paul de Man's Past." *The London Review of Books* 4 February 1988, 7–11.

Norris, Christopher, and Andrew Benjamin. *What is Deconstruction?* London: St. Martin's Press, 1988.

Perloff, Marjorie. "An Intellectual Impasse." *Salmagundi* 72 (Fall 1986): 125–130.

Rorty, Richard. *Contingency, Irony, and Solidarity.* Cambridge: Cambridge University Press, 1989.

Schiller, Friedrich. *On the Aesthetic Education of Man: In a Series of Letters.* Translated by Reginald Snell. New York: Frederick Ungar, 1965.

Scholes, Robert. "Aiming a Canon at the Curriculum." *Salmagundi* 72 (Fall 1986): 101–117.

Scholes, Robert. "Afterword on Canons." *Salmagundi* 72 (Fall 1986): 164–165.

Scott, Geoffrey. *The Architecture of Humanism: A Study in the History of Taste.* New York: W. W. Norton, 1974.

Shils, Edward. "The Sad State of Humanities in America." *The Wall Street Journal* 3 July 1989.

Short, Thomas. " 'Diversity' and 'Breaking the Disciplines': Two New Assaults on the Curriculum." *Academic Questions* 1 (Summer 1988): 6–29.

Sisk, John P. "What Is Necessary." *Salmagundi* 72 (Fall 1986): 144–147.

Smith, Barbara Herrnstein. *Contingencies of Value: Alternative Perspectives for Critical Theory.* Cambridge: Harvard University Press, 1989.

Smith, Barbara Herrnstein. "Limelight: Reflections on a Public Year." *Publications of the Modern Language Association of America* 104 (May 1989): 285–293.

Todorov, Tzvetan. "Crimes Against Humanities." *The New Republic* 3 July 1989, 26–30.

"Undergraduate Courses of Study, Fall and Spring Terms." *Bulletin of Yale University* 54:6, 15 March 1958.

Venturi, Robert. *Complexity and Contradiction in Architecture.* New York: The Museum of Modern Art, 1966.

Venturi, Robert, et al. *Learning From Las Vegas: The Forgotten Symbolism of Architectural Form.* Cambridge: Massachusetts Institute of Technology Press, 1972.

Wasow, Thomas, and Charles Junkerman. "The Process and the Product: The Inside Story on the Western Culture Debate." Letter sent by the Dean and Assistant Dean of Undergraduate Studies to Parents of Stanford University Students. Fall 1988.

West, Cornel, and John Rajchman, eds. *Post-Analytic Philosophy.* New York: Columbia University Press, 1985.

Willey, Basil. *The Seventeenth Century Background: The Thought of the Age in Relation to Religion and Poetry.* London: Chatto & Windus, 1950.

Wines, James. *De-architecture.* New York: Rizzoli, 1988.

"Yale College Programs of Study." *Bulletin of Yale University* 84: 7, 1 August 1988.

INDEX